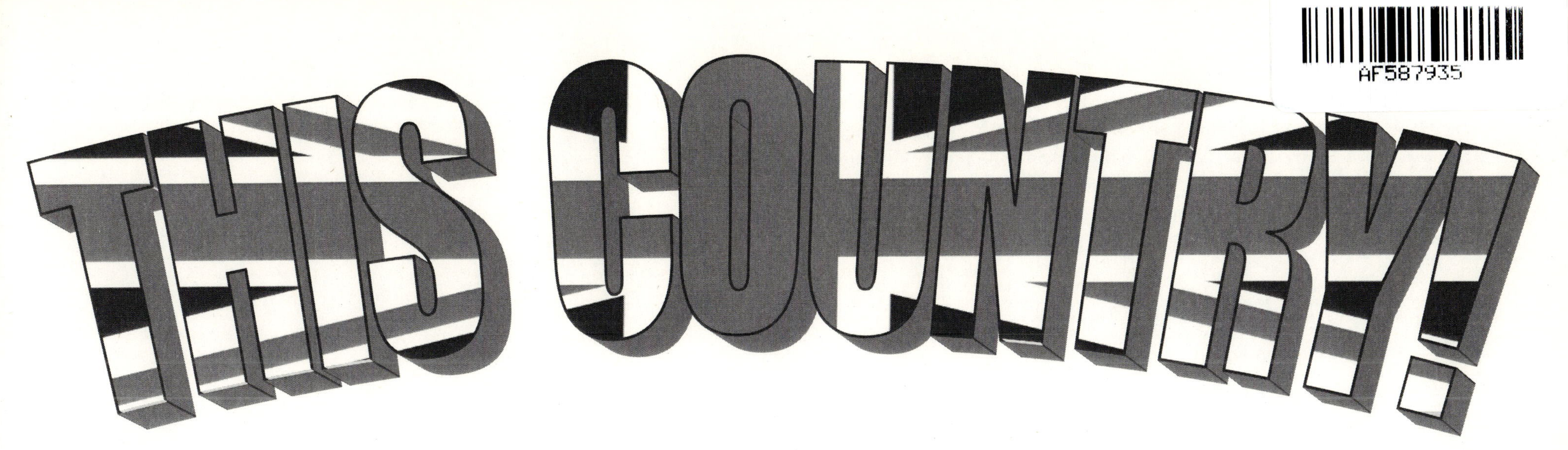

ROB MARTIN

EMPIRE
PUBLICATIONS

First published in 2017

EMPIRE PUBLICATIONS
1 Newton Street, Manchester M1 1HW

ISBN: 978-1-909360-53-2

Printed in Great Britain.

...In this book are 158 illustrations, that have been inspired by the most oddest observations spotted whilst travelling around the UK. This is a book which shows a future of scratch cards, unhealthy cheap pastries, obsessive texting disorders and angry Pensioners raging against the dying of the light.
"Everywhere is the same!" Is a line you hear a lot in the U.K.
It gives away a person that has never travelled a mile beyond the Bowling Green.
Everywhere is NOT the same.
Many thanks to all who inspired and brought this book into the World.
Thank you to the weirdness that is all around.

This book is suitable for vegetarians.

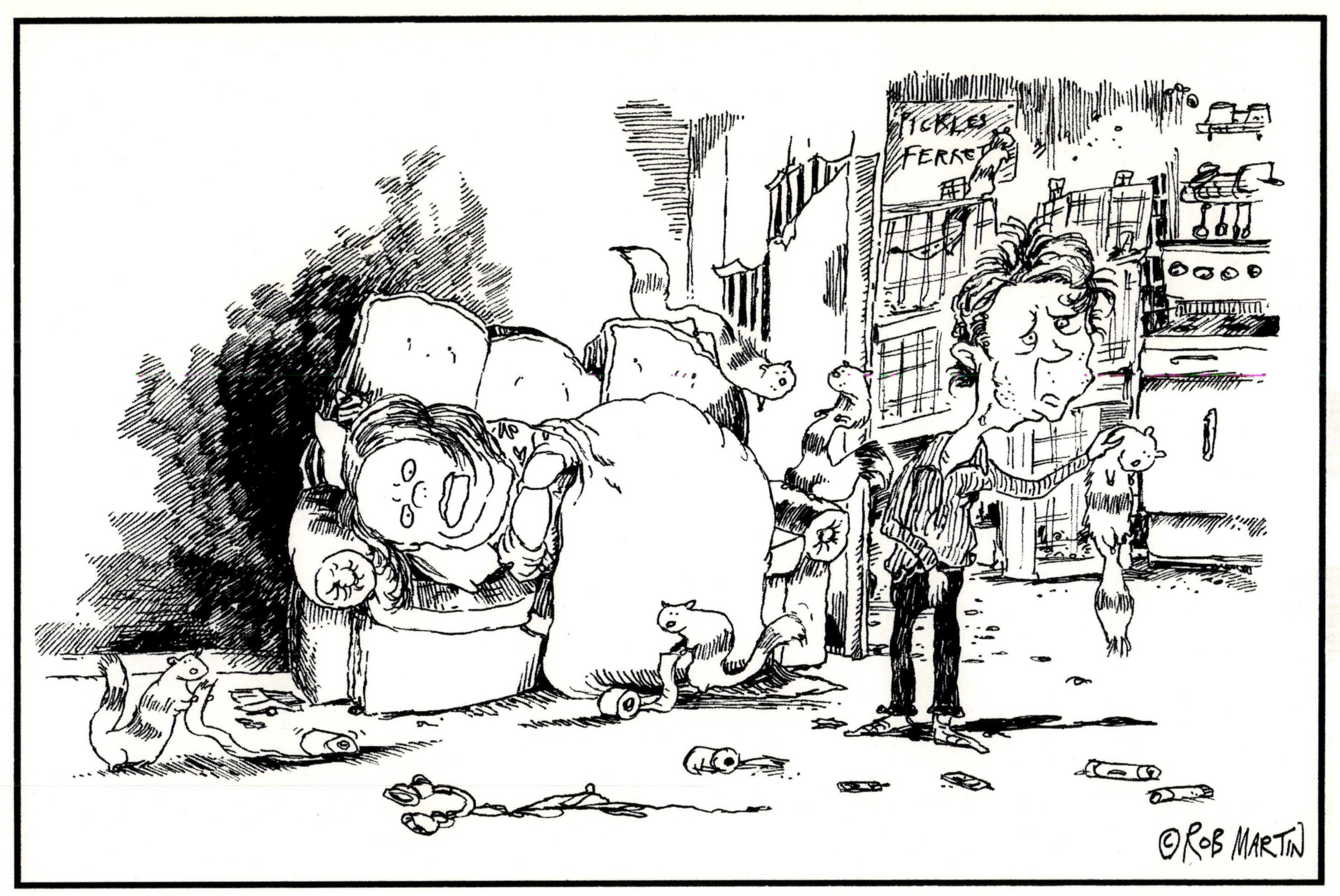

Four years after the marriage and Elvis the Ferret wants out.

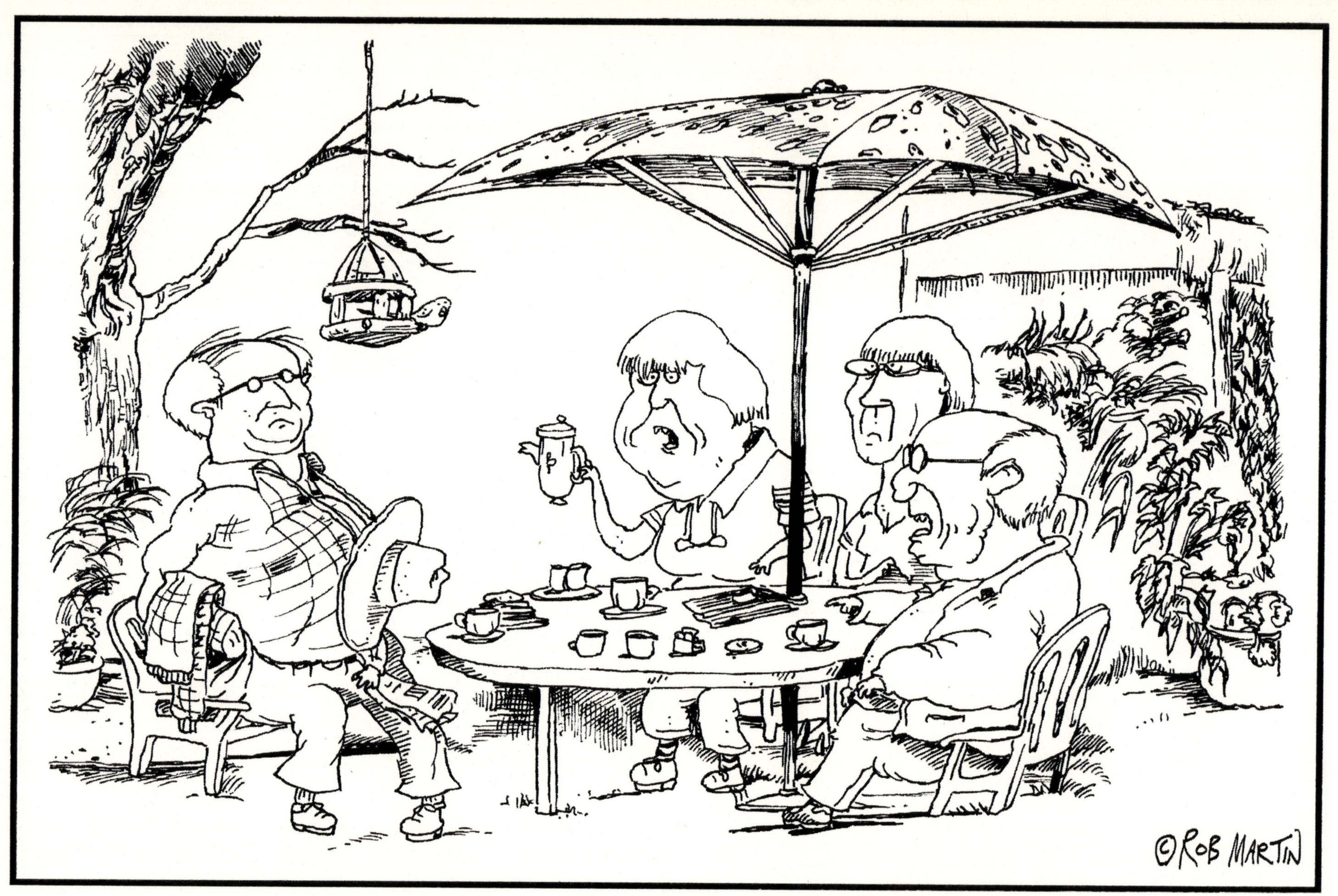

Having afternoon cream tea, sat on plastic pound shop chairs,
in the shade of a bird poo covered umbrella.
"Aren't the riffraff absolutely ghastly!" States Mable.

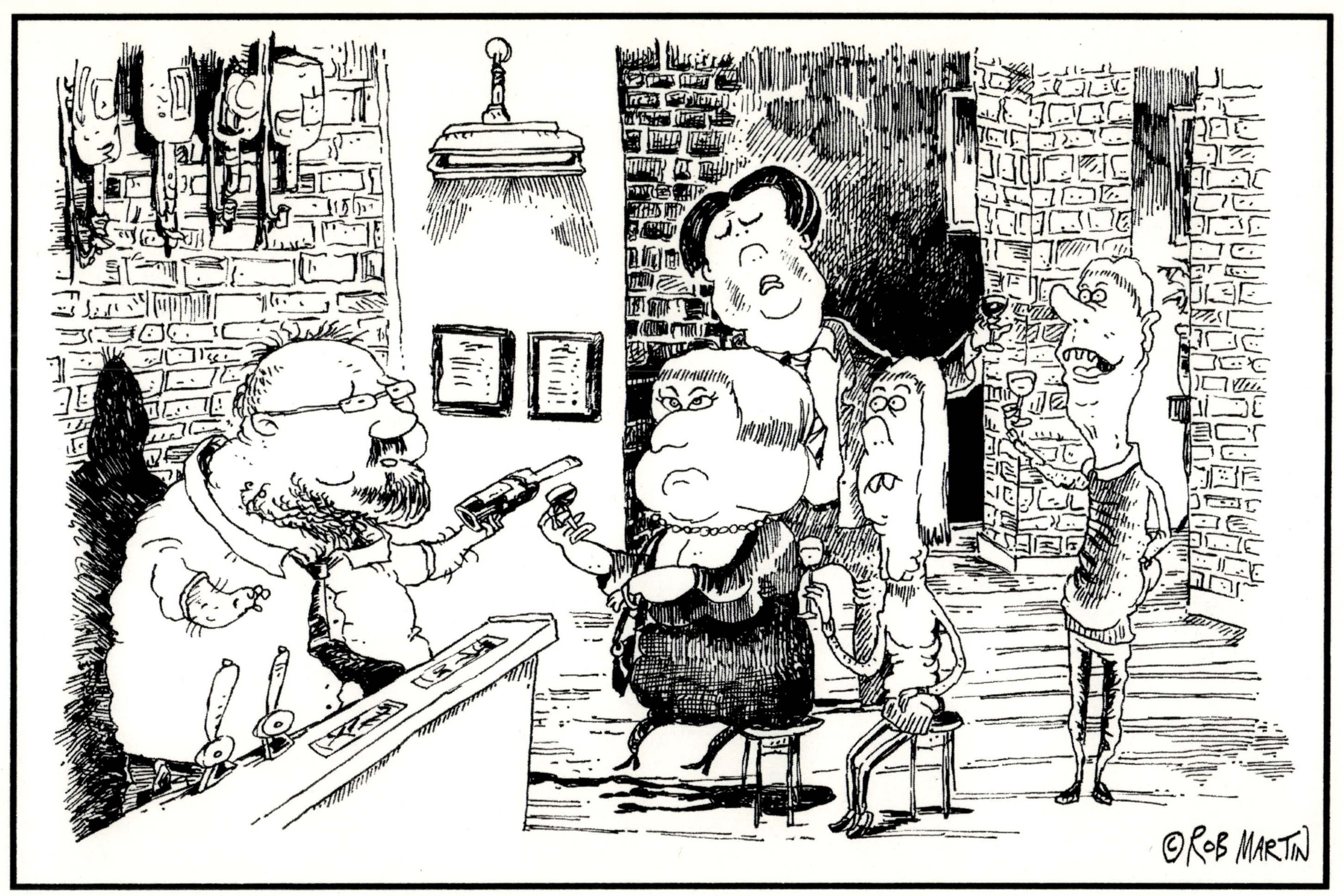

Pretentious snobs drink cheap wine and talk about shopping.

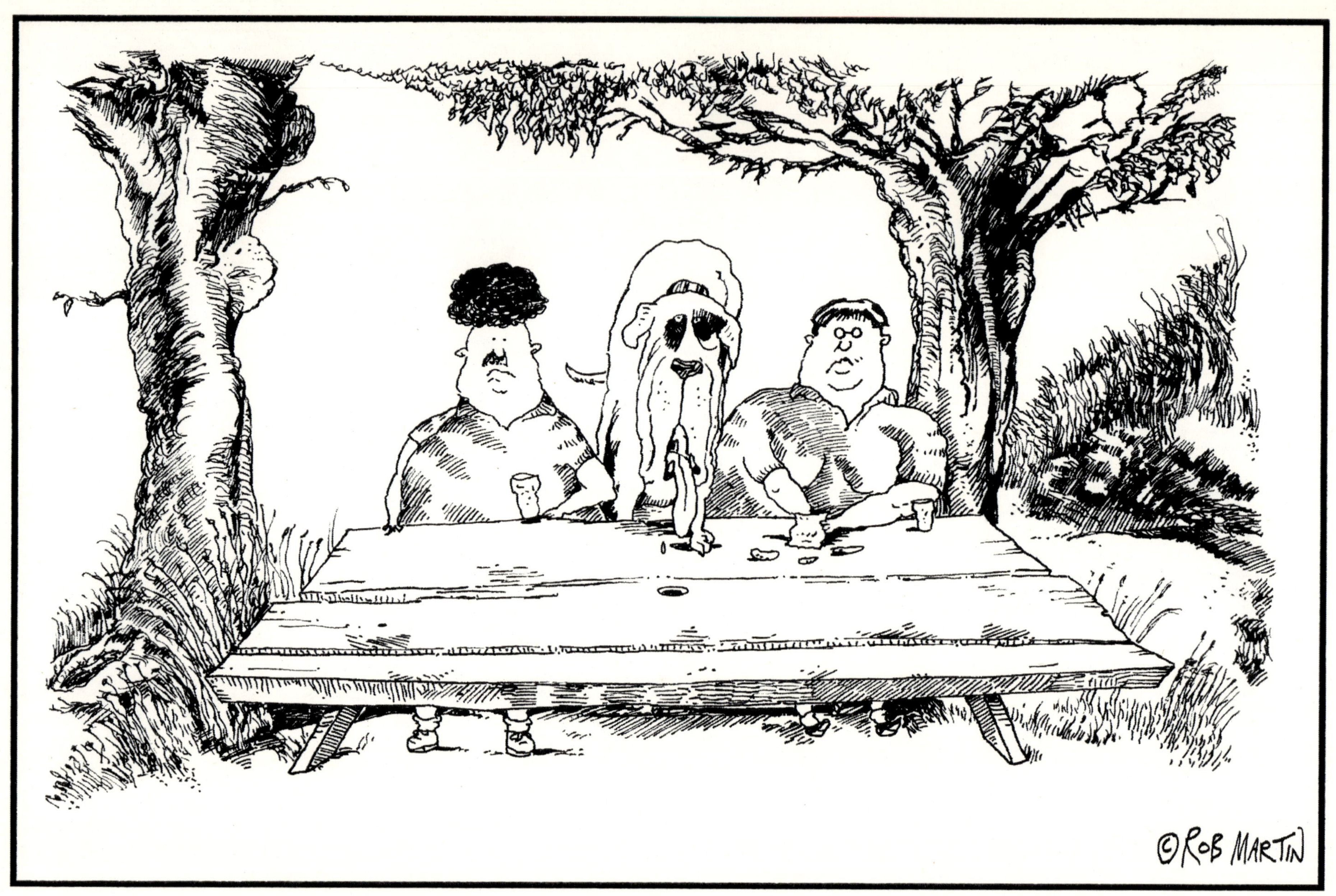

A Dog wants a crisp, crushing any chance James has of putting his arm around Patty.

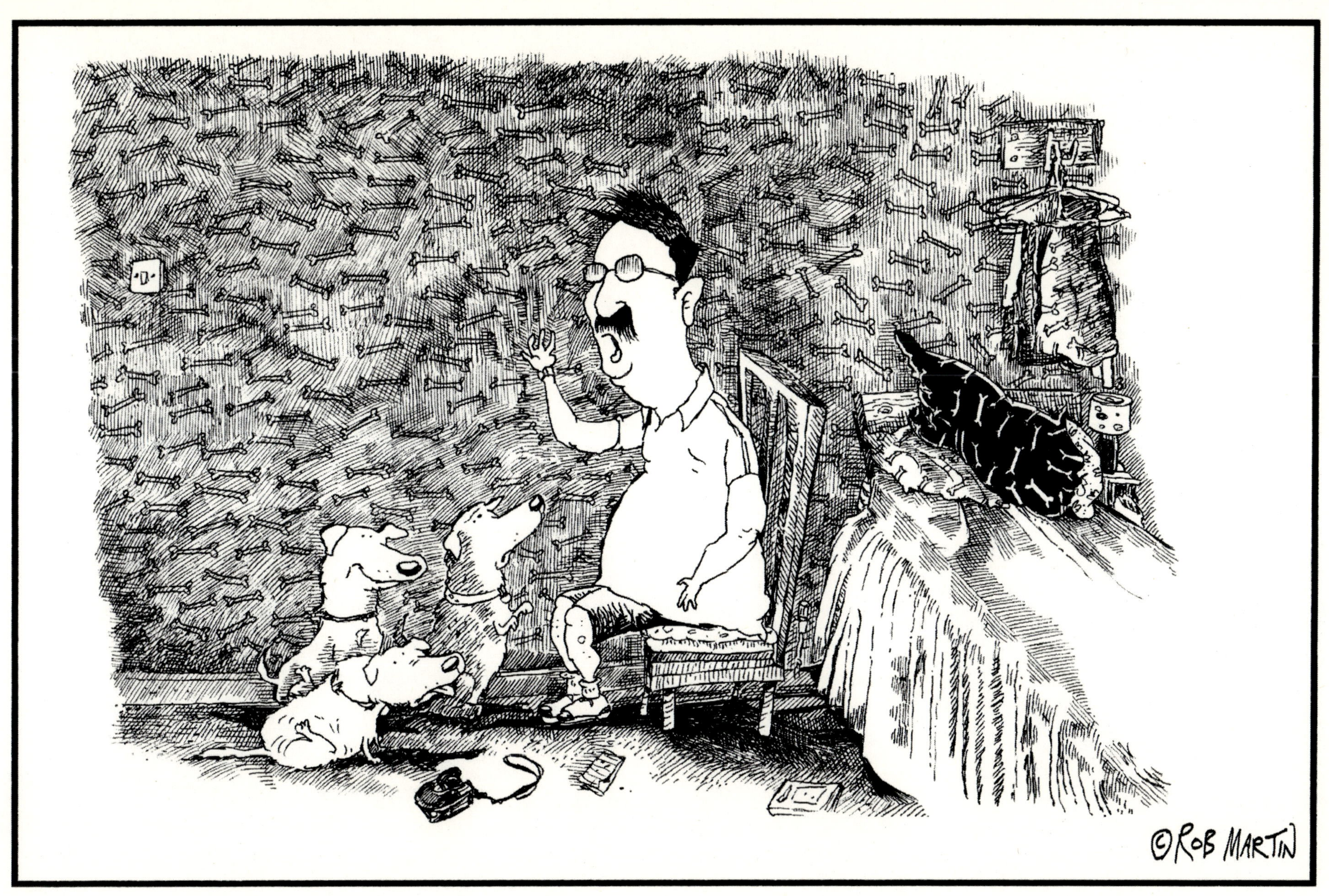

Herman warns Fido, Basil and Poozer about the dangers of Global warming.

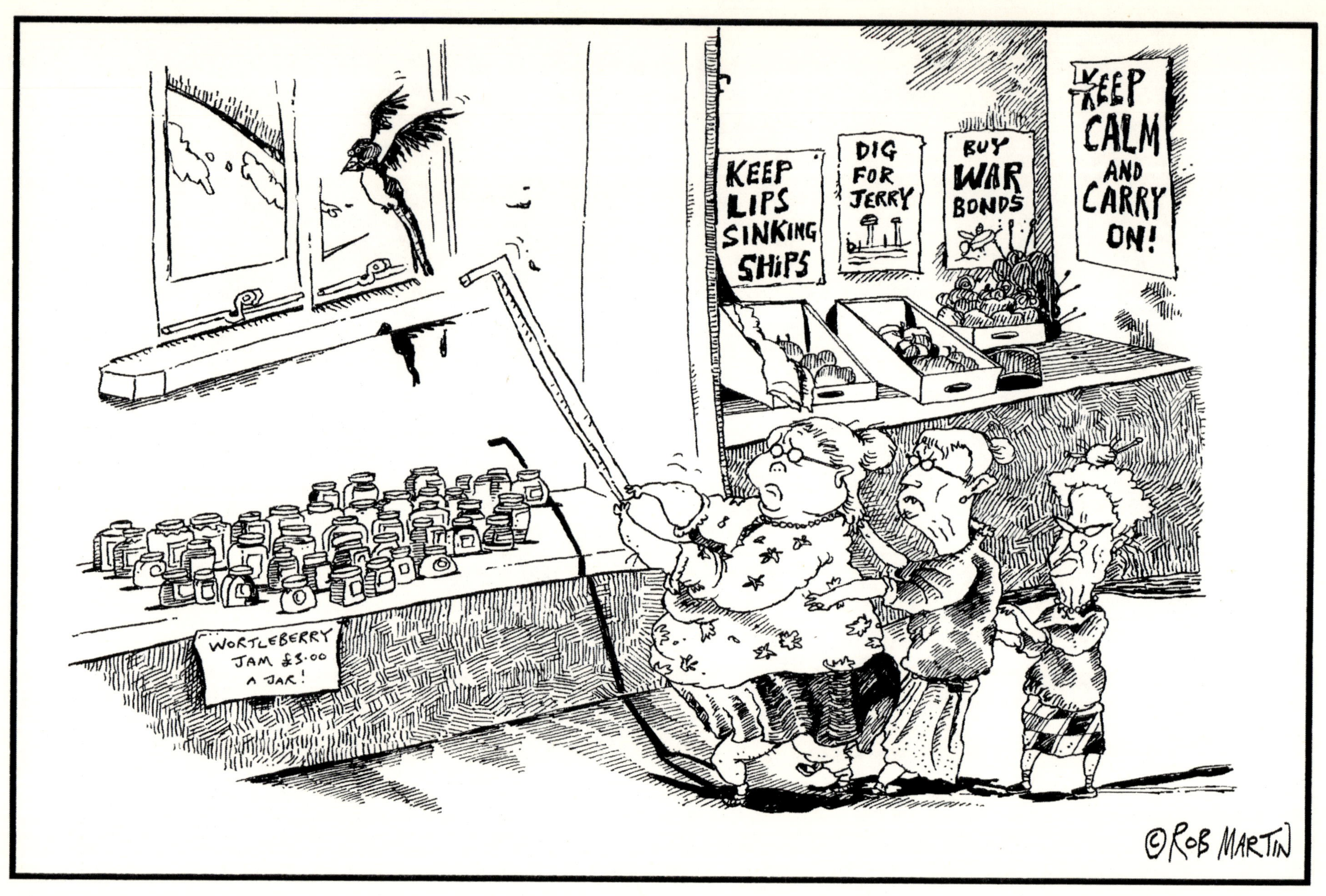

Grannies try to release a puzzled Swallow from the village 'Tourist Centre'.

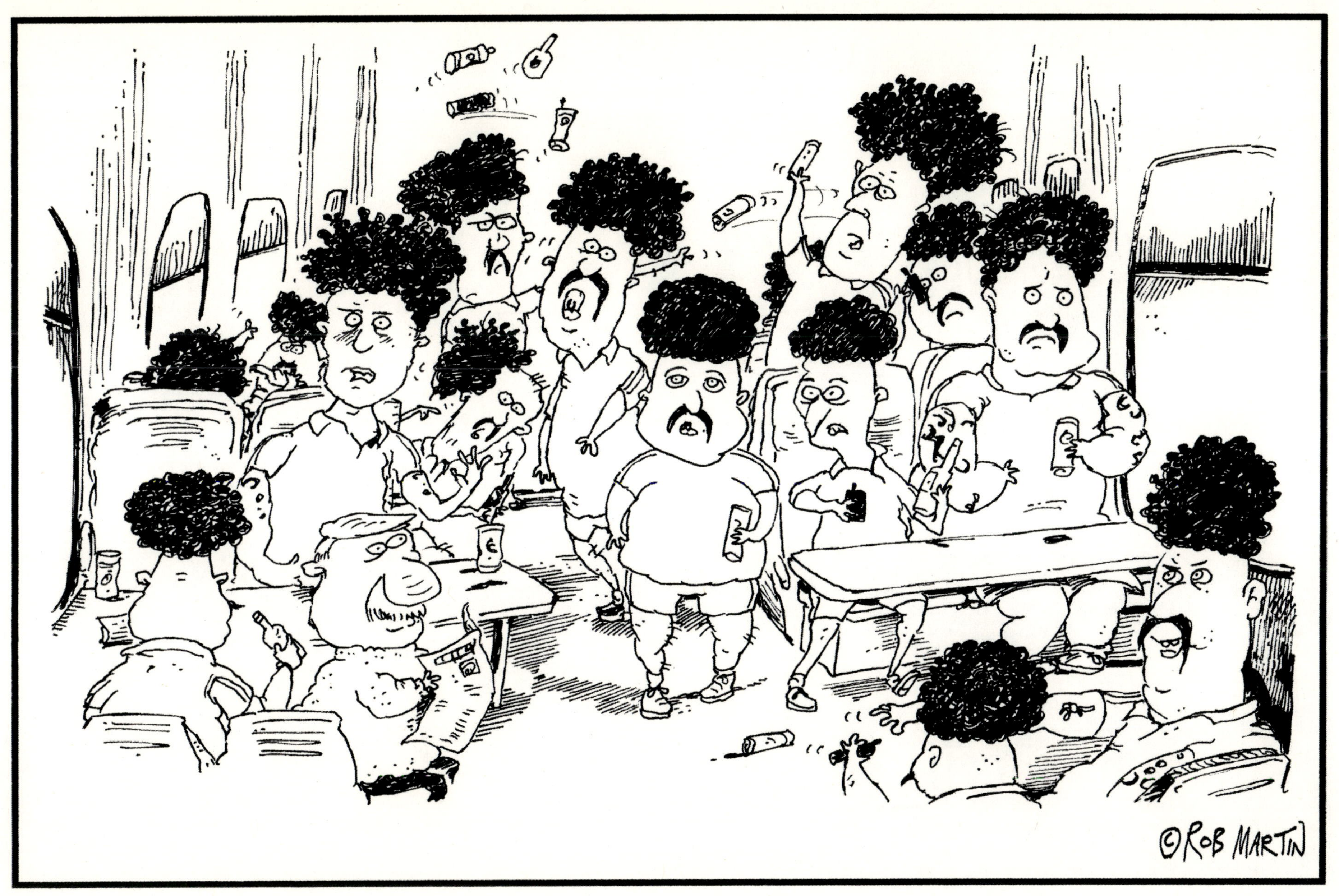

"We're not bullying you! It's just banter mate!"

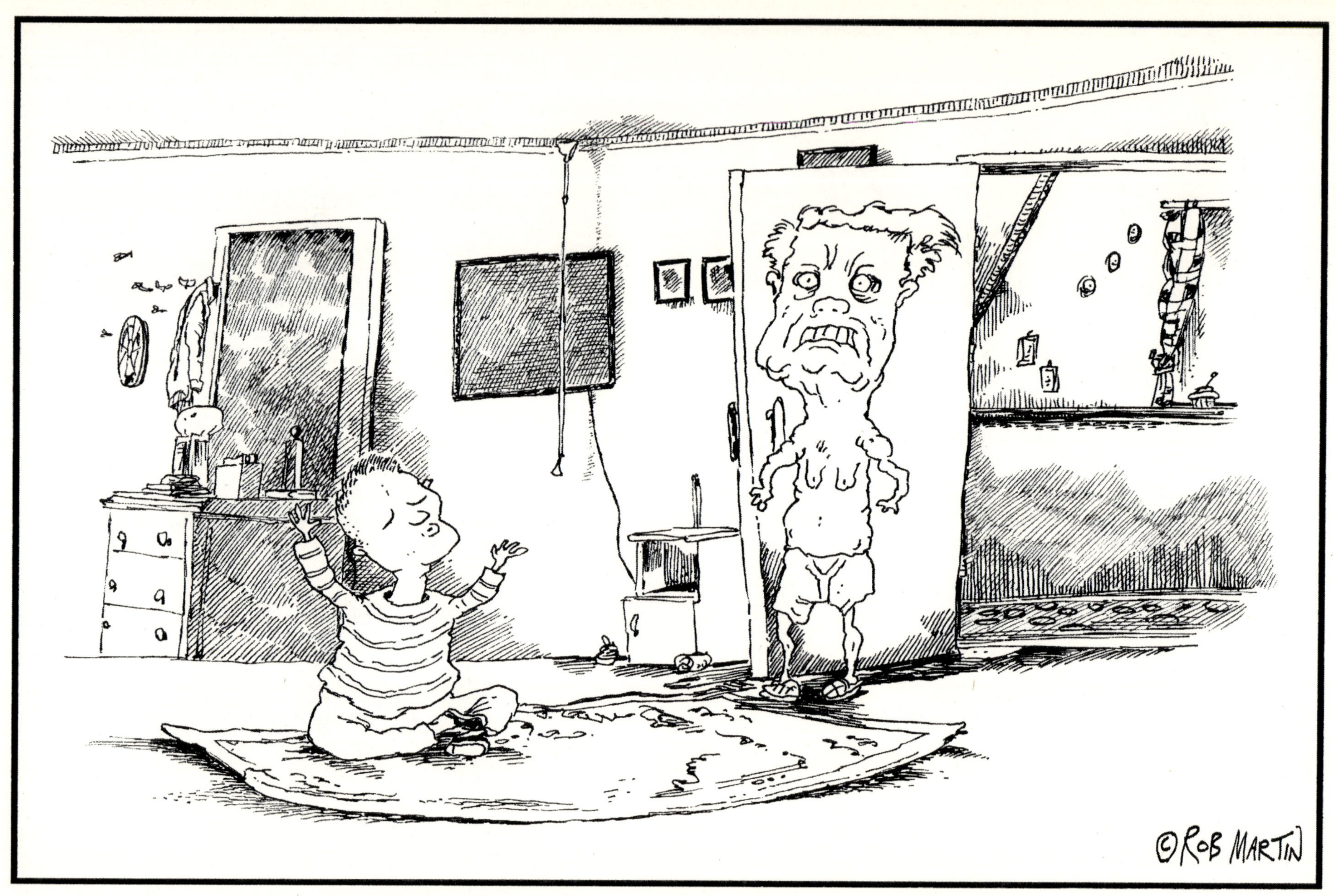

Fed up of living with his aggressive Father - Neil tries his best to fly a way on a magic carpet.

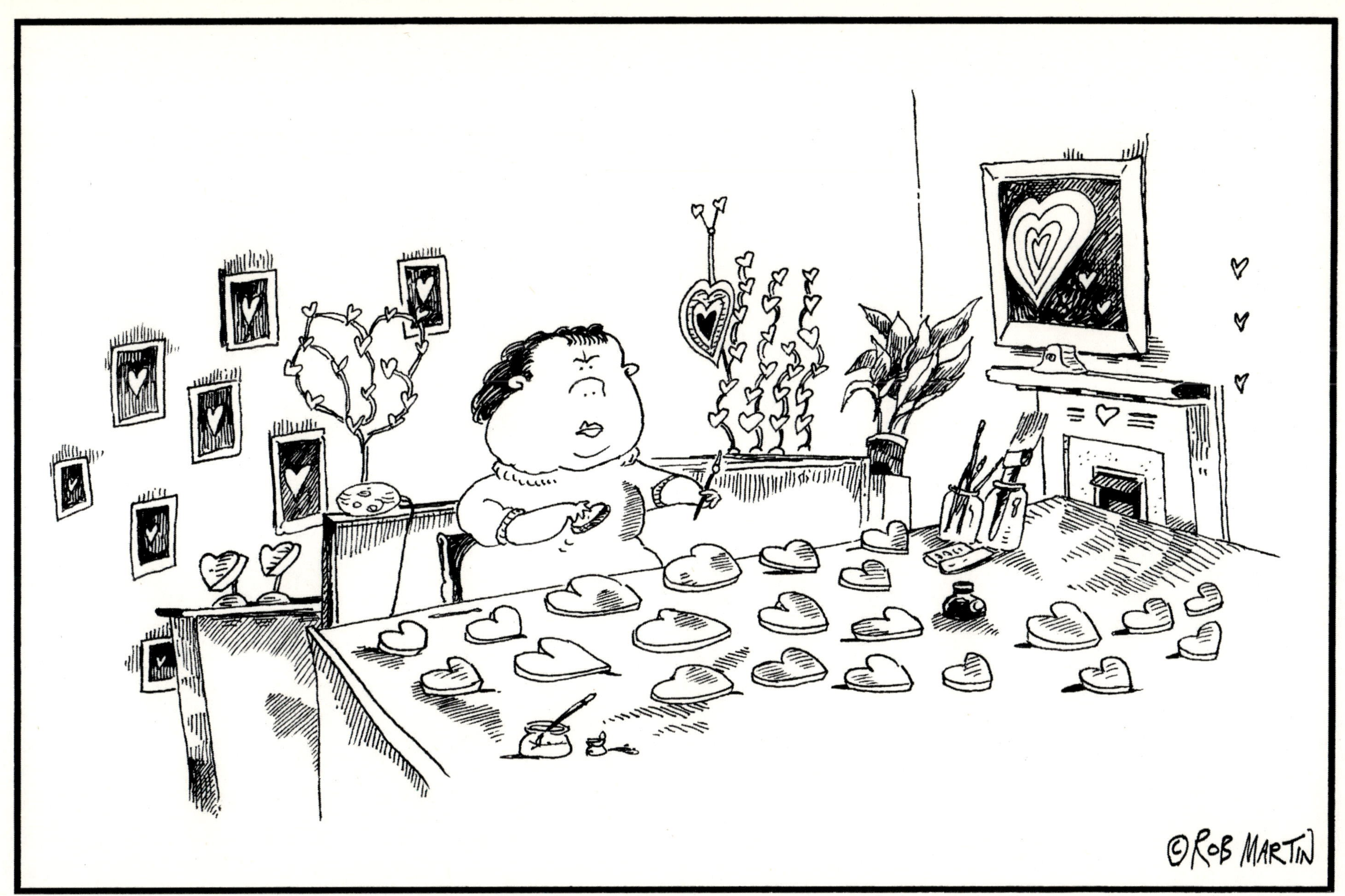

Sociopathic woman making clay hearts.
Doesn't care. As long as it makes money.

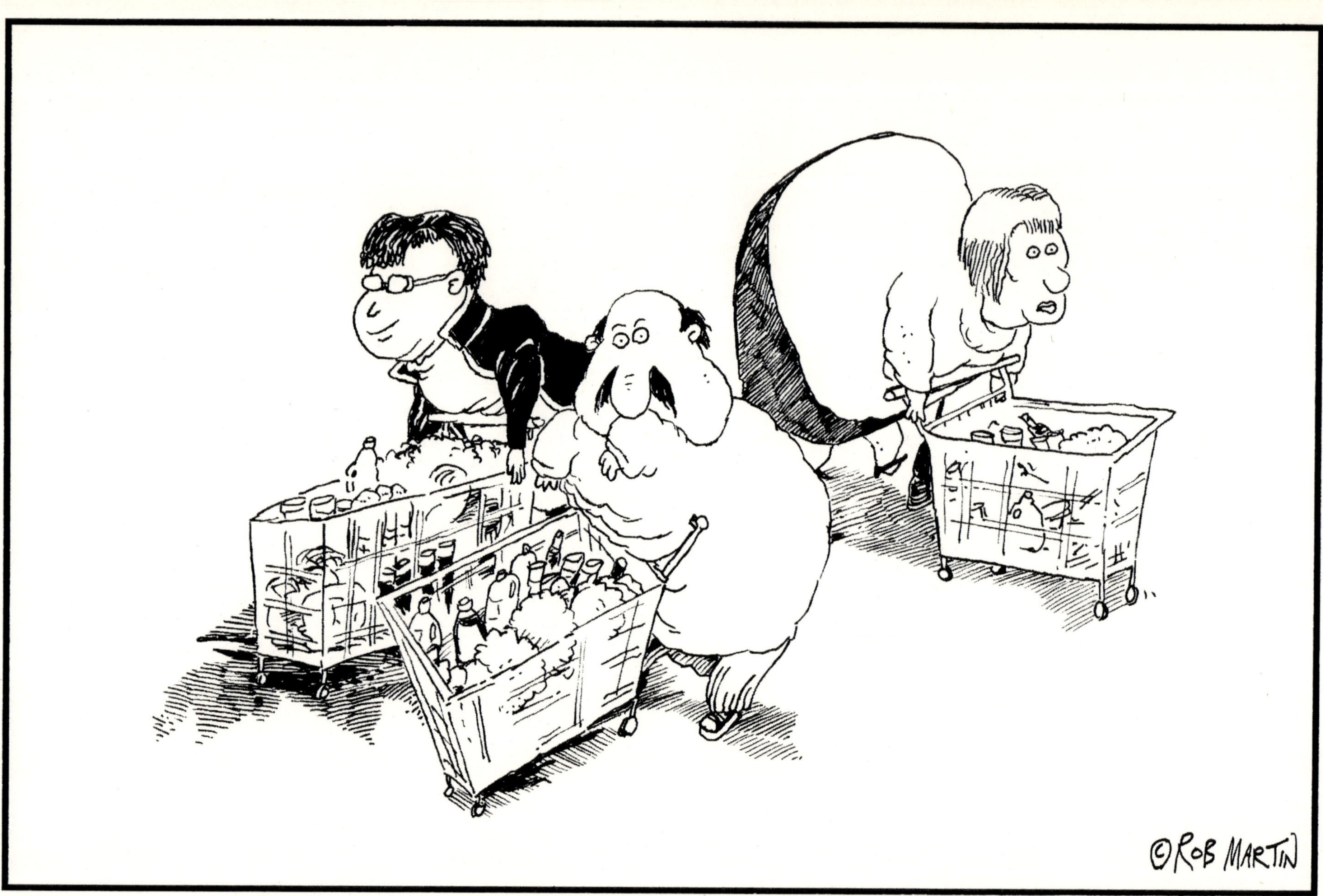
©ROB MARTIN

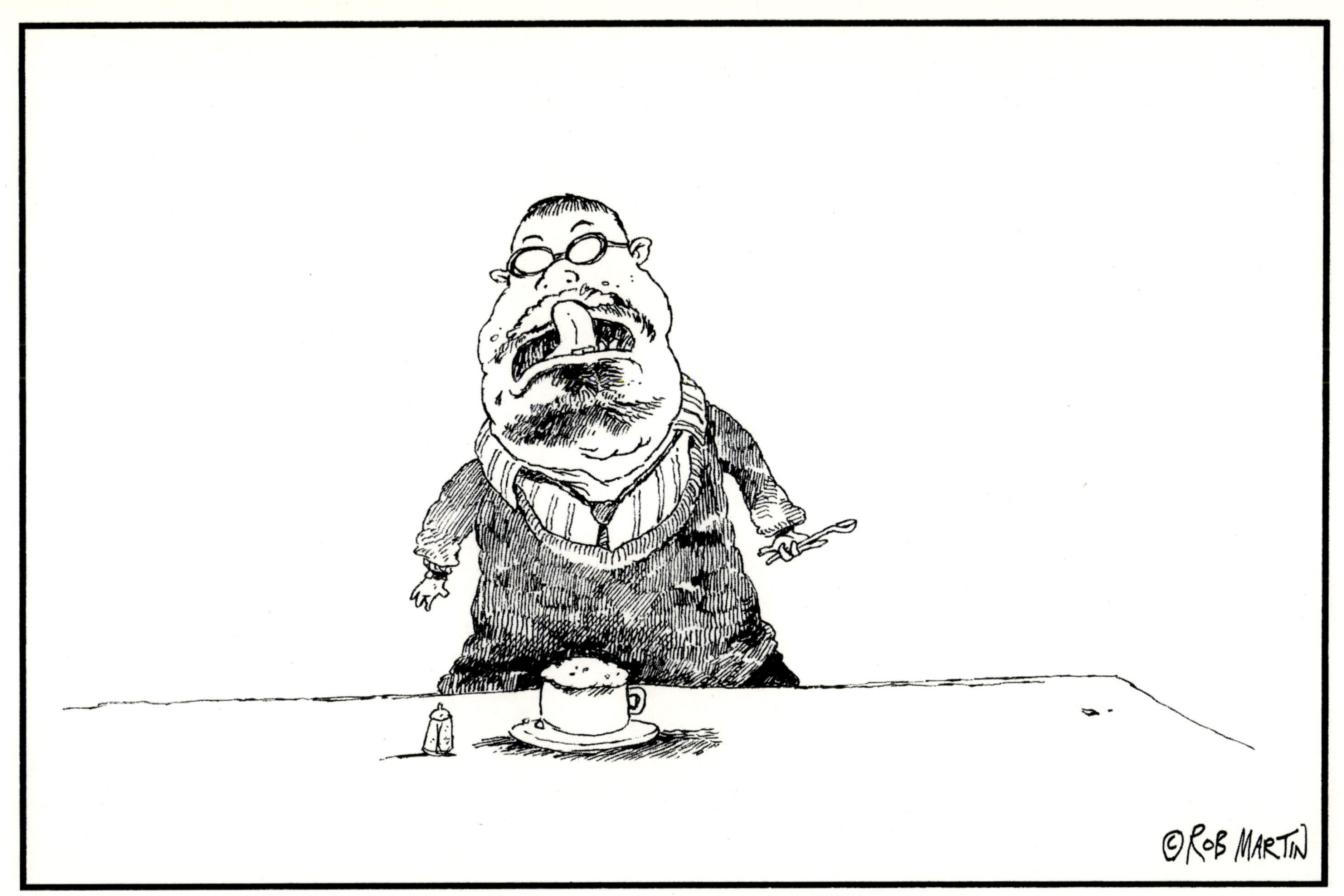

Clive licks frothy coffee from his top lip.

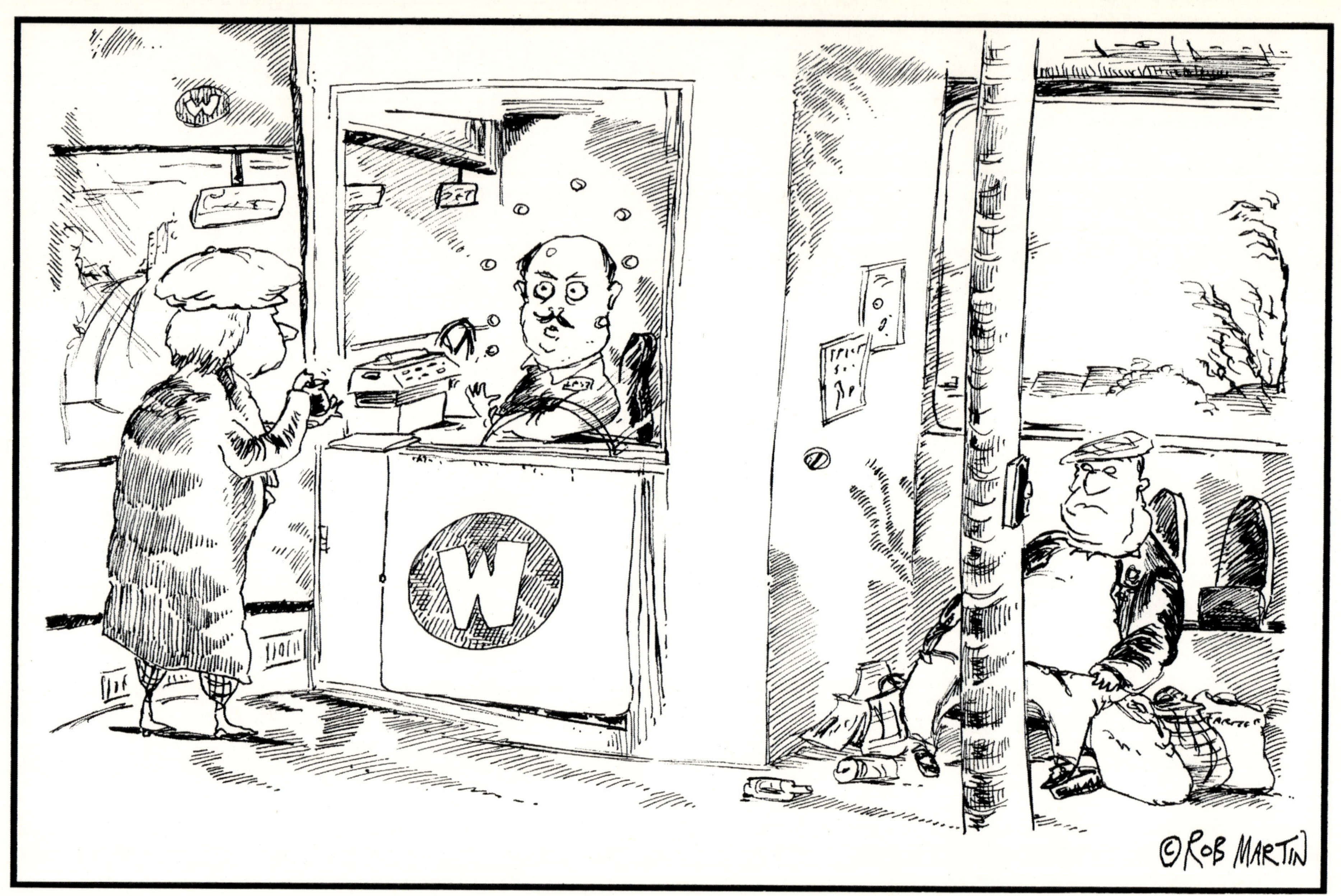

An arrogant bus driver complains that his bus is always late, because the public are slow at paying.

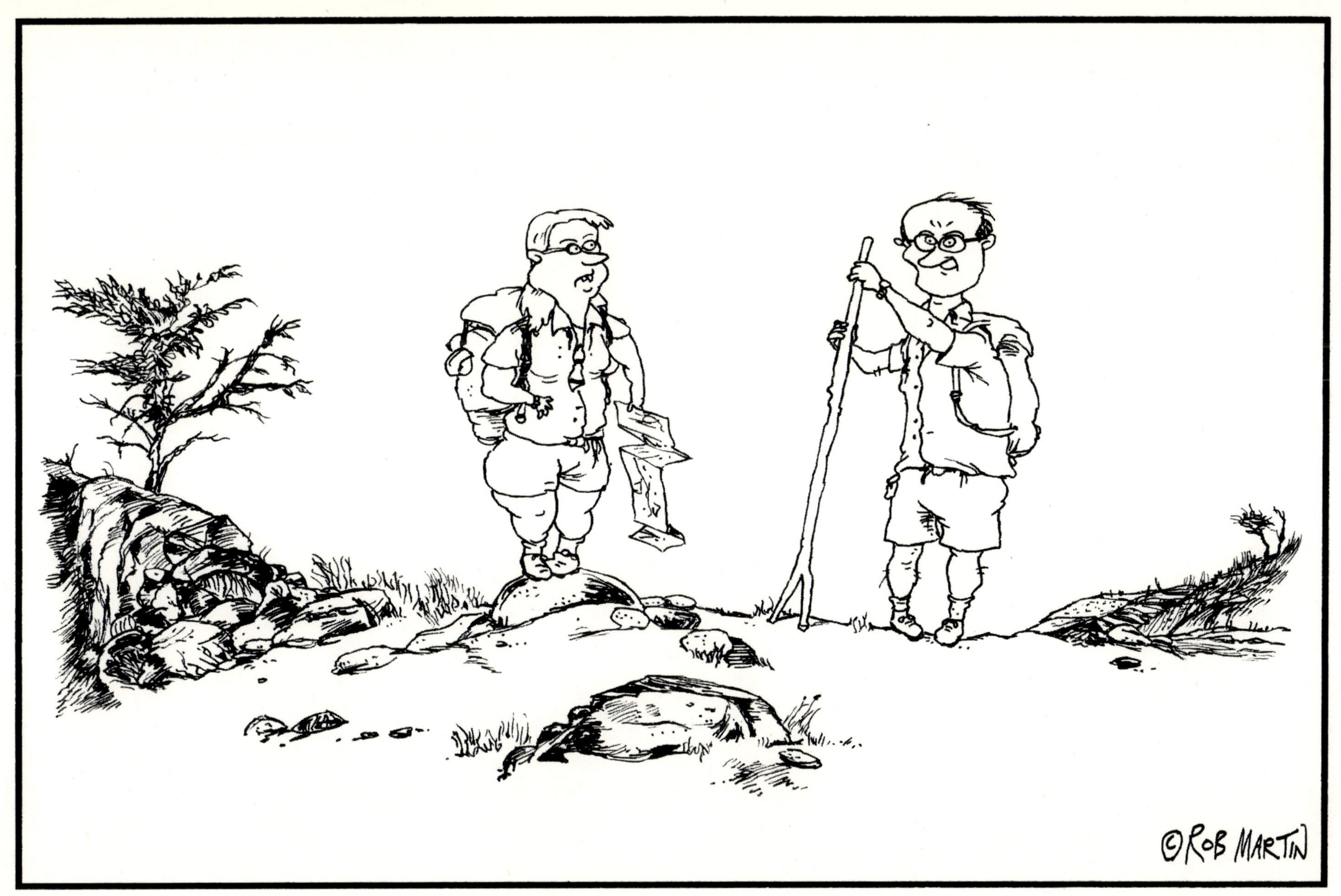

Not wishing to suffer a Snake bite. Ralph decides to poke every tuft of grass on the moor.

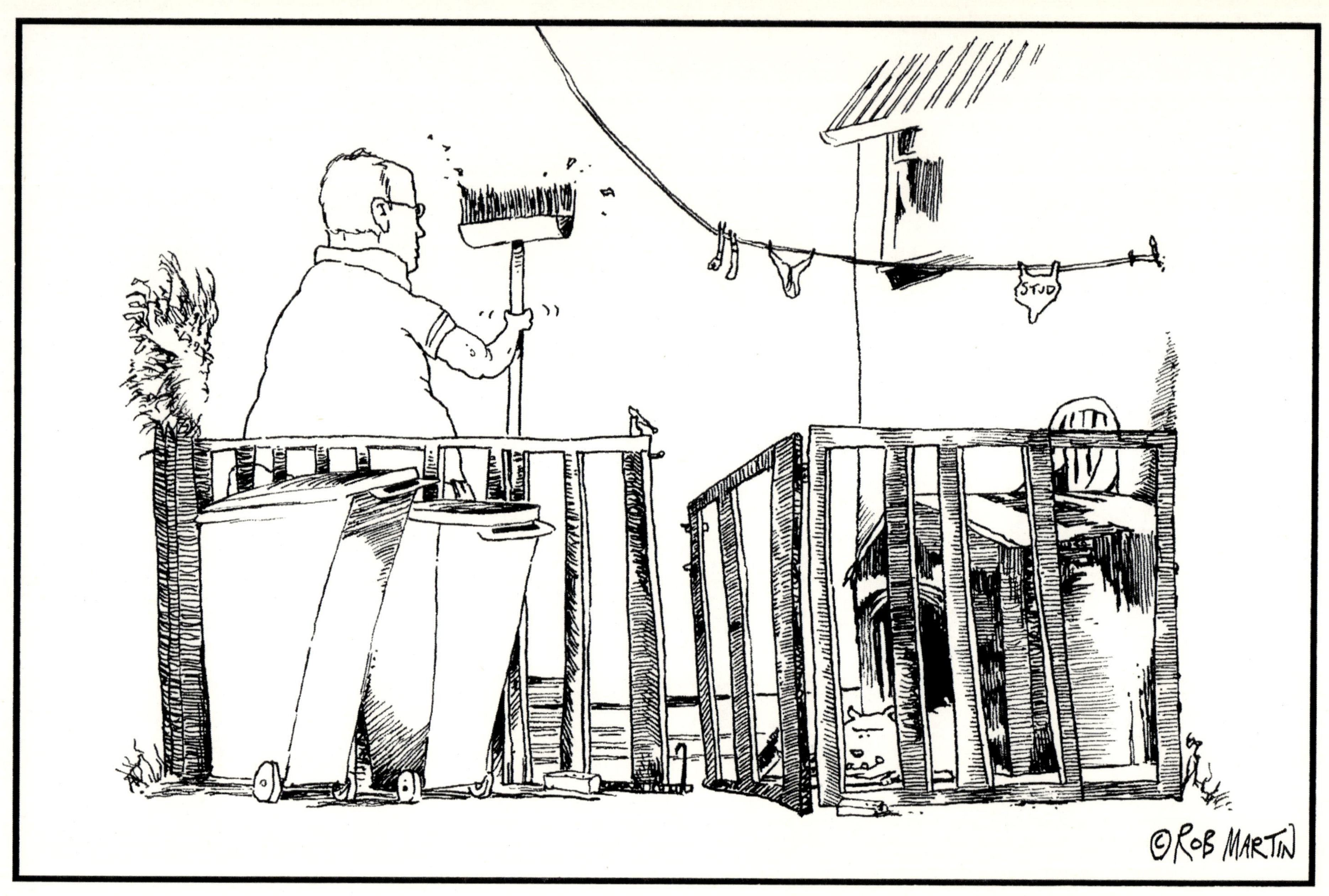

On a Sunday morning, the man at number 43 bashes his brush.

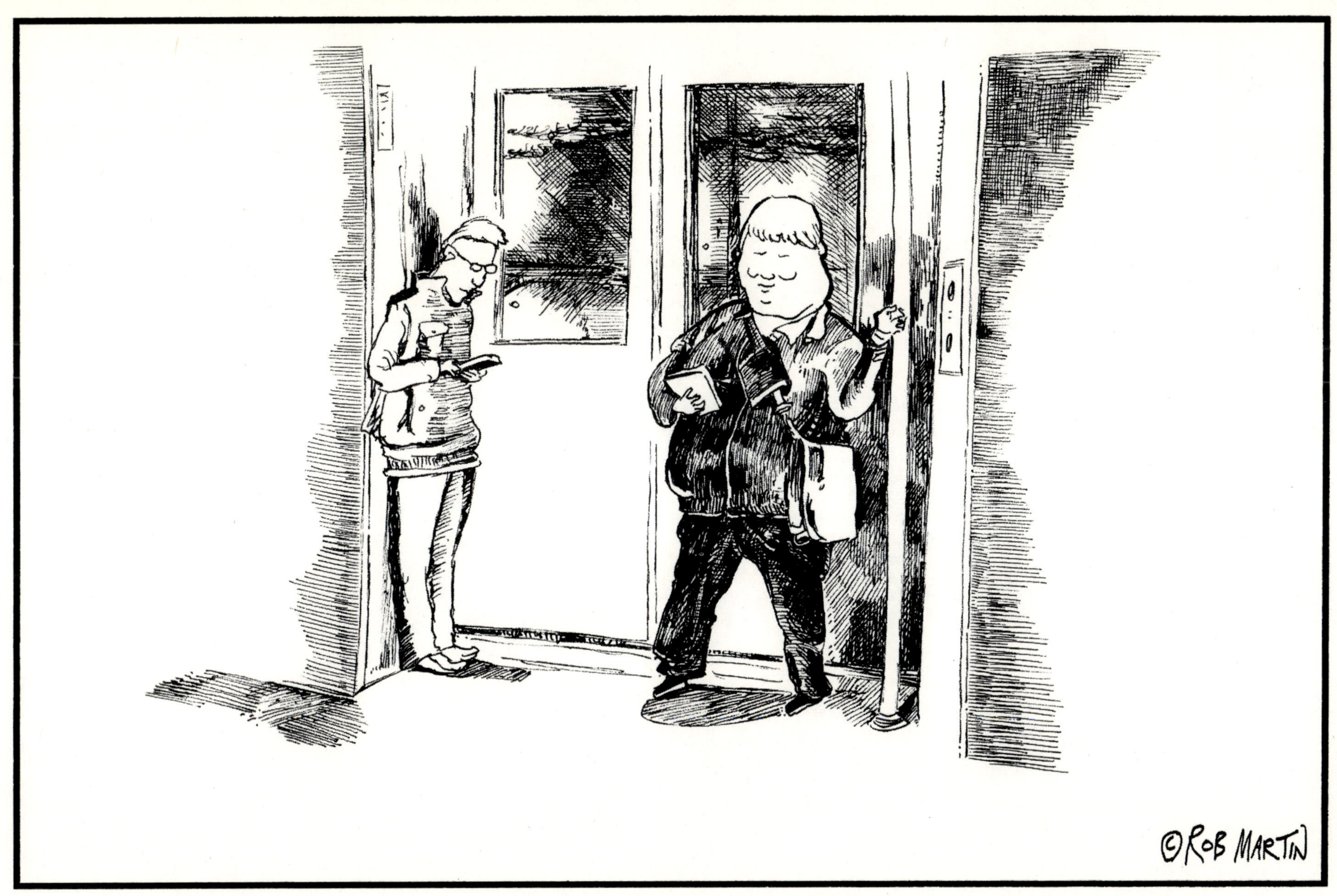

Blocking the train doorway, two men are engrossed reading electronic books. One reads about quadrilateral parallelograms whilst the other, pies.

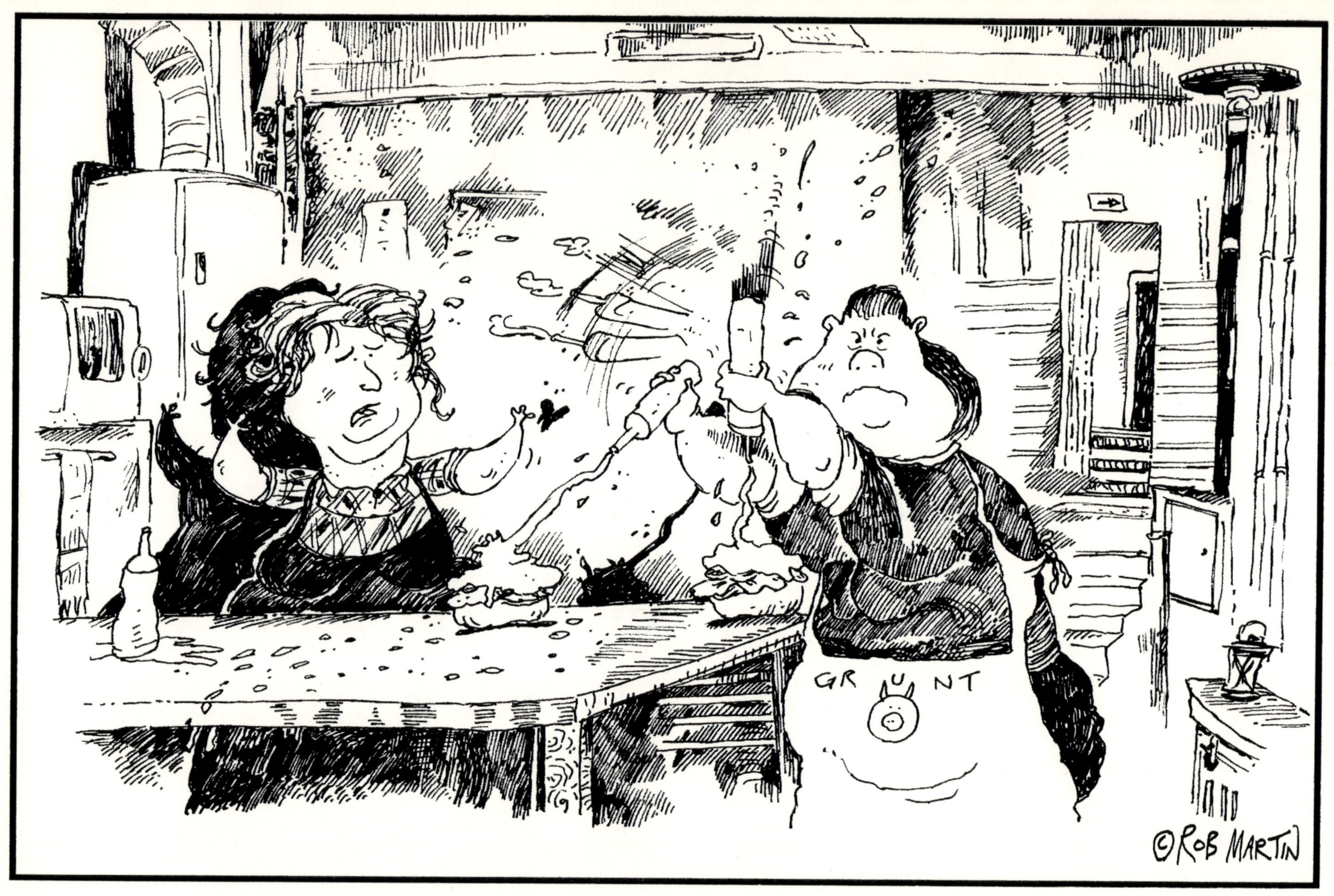

Angry with the World. Paula squirts all the salad cream thinking of her last love.

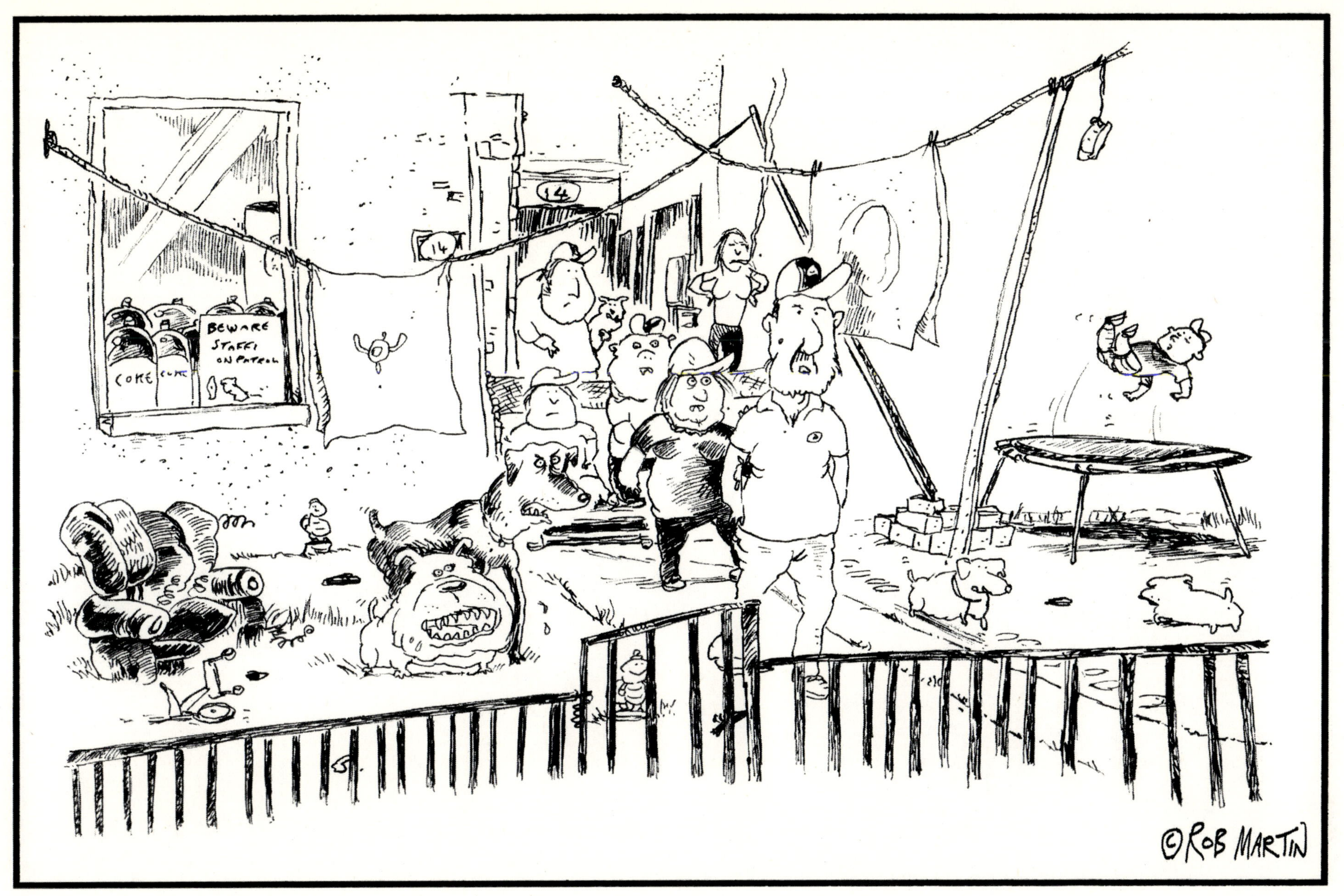

The family at number 14 wait for a flat screen T.V. to be delivered.

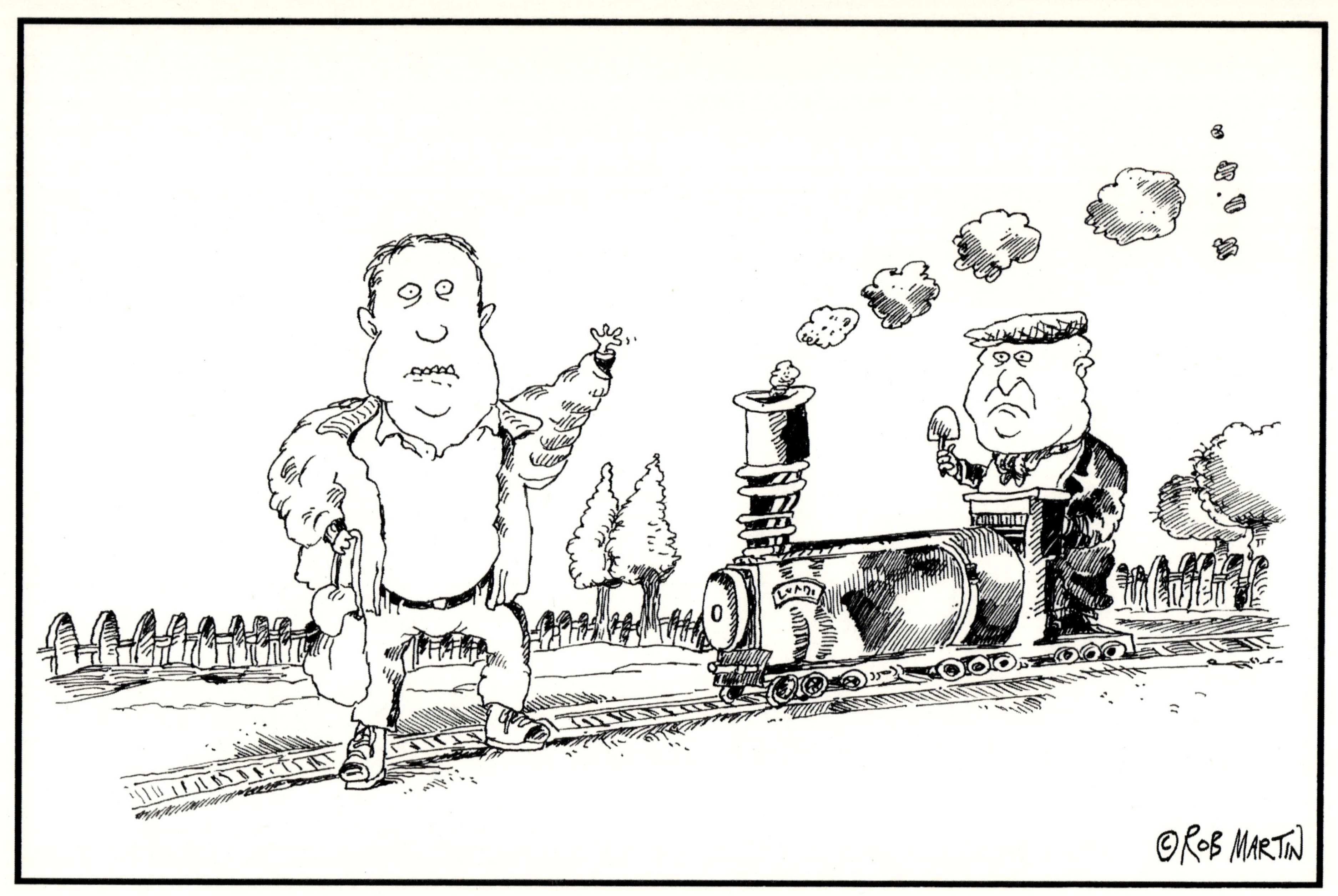

Having had a bad day, Steven decides to stand on the train line at the 'Model Engineers Society'.

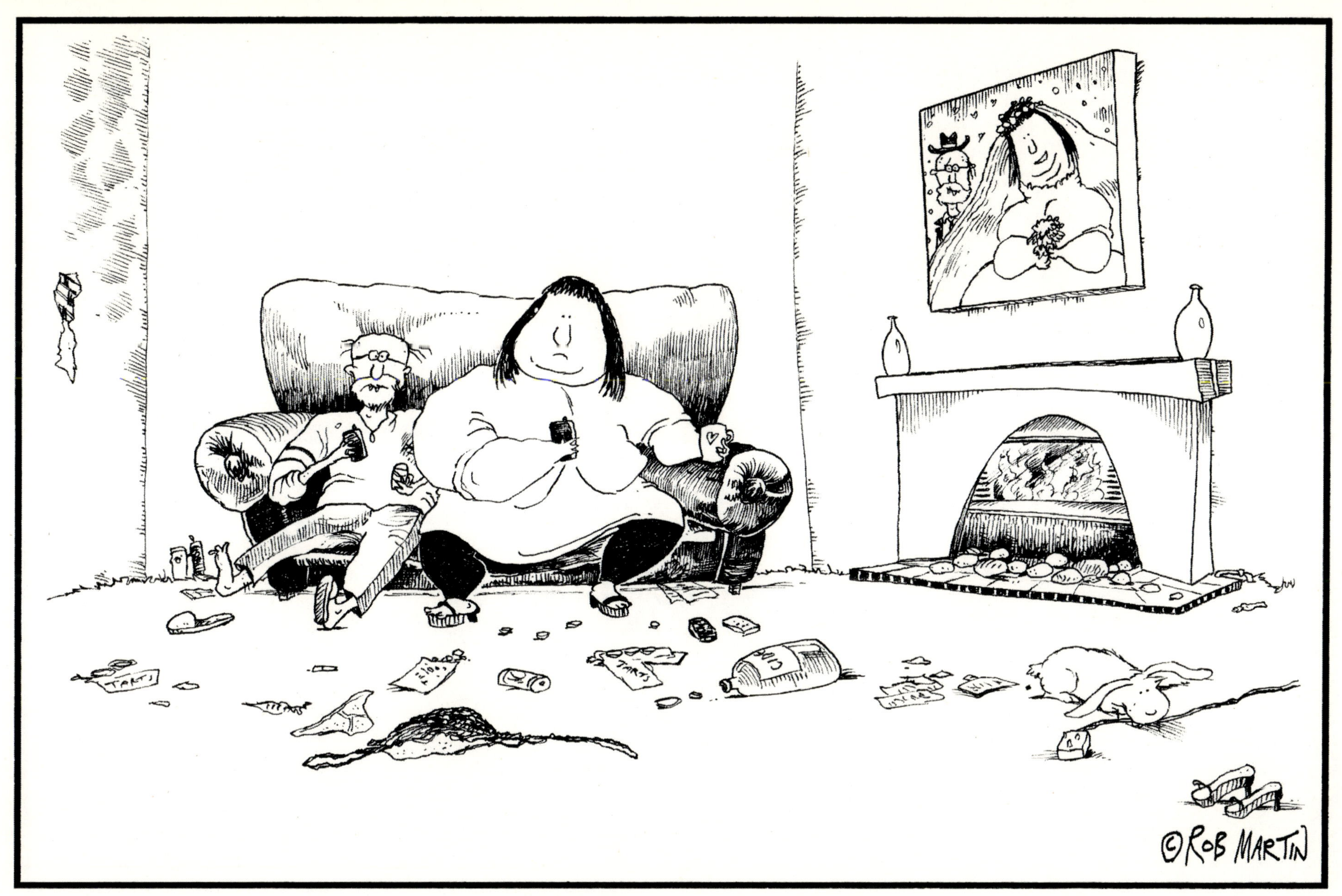

A year after the marriage.

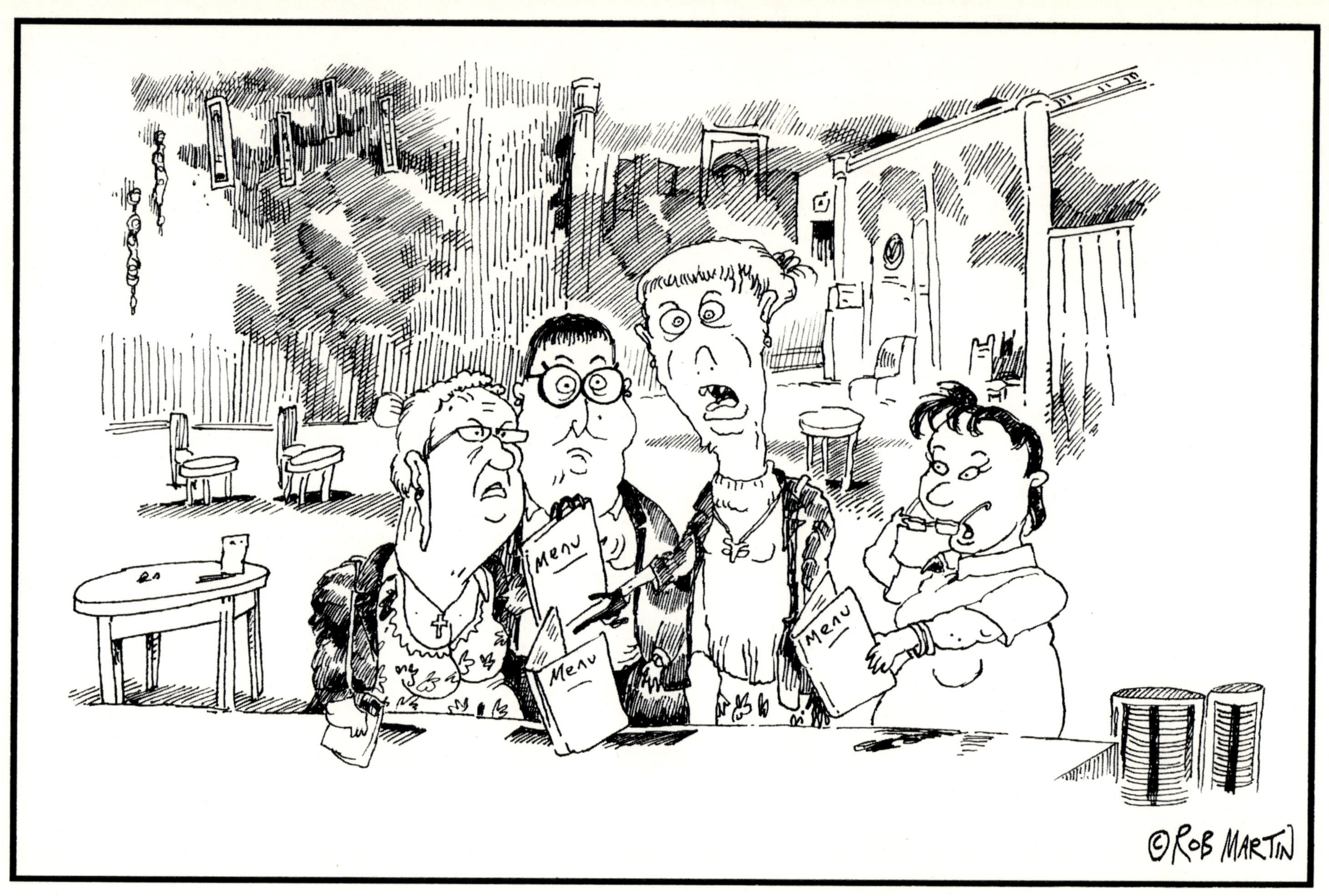

"Is the broccoli steamed? £17.95 isn't that absolutely marvellous?"

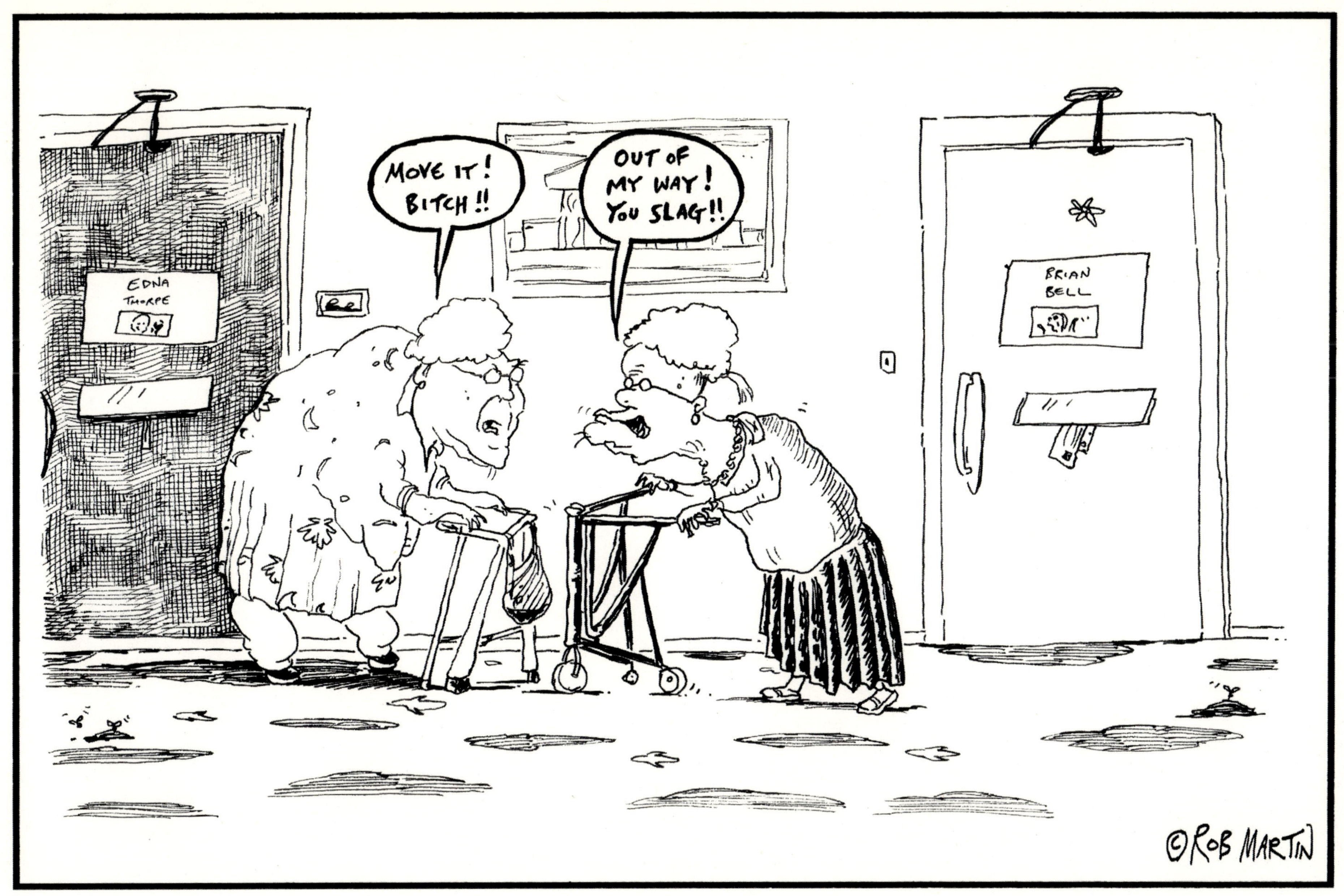

In the care home, two 82 year olds block each others right of way.

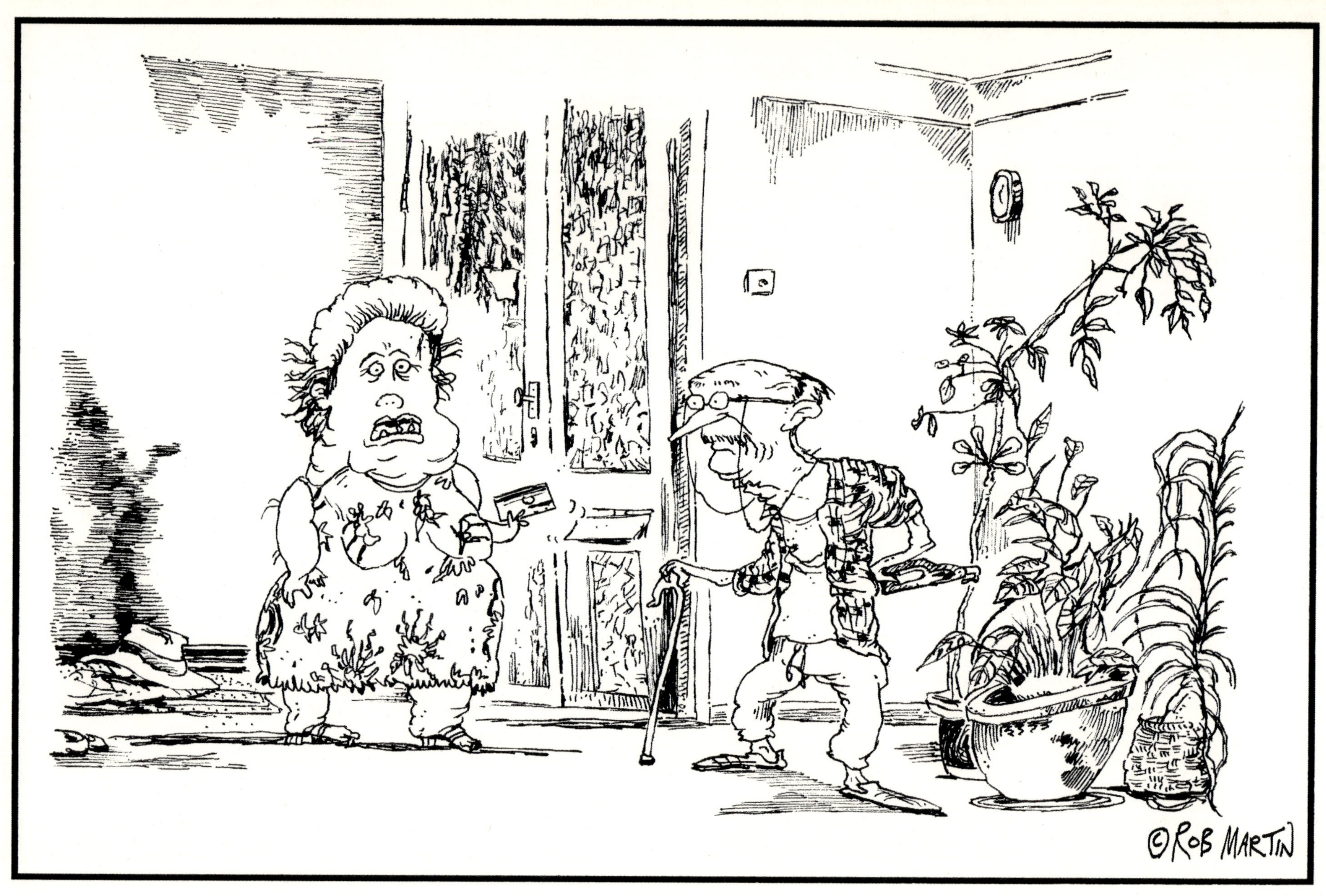

"Exactly who is Madame Fluffy Legs?!... Humphrey!"

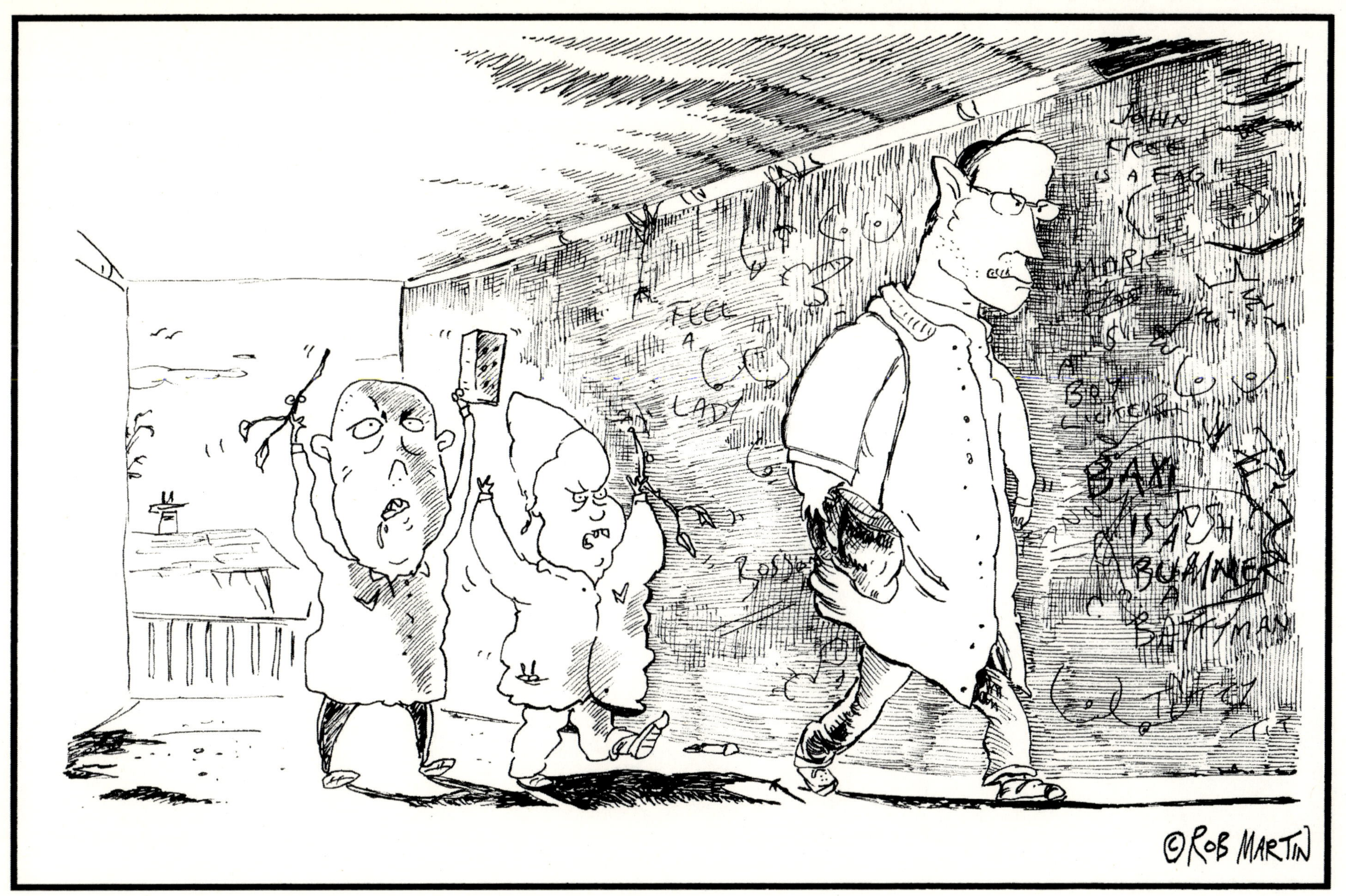

Two nine year old boys threaten a forty year old man
with a twig and a brick.

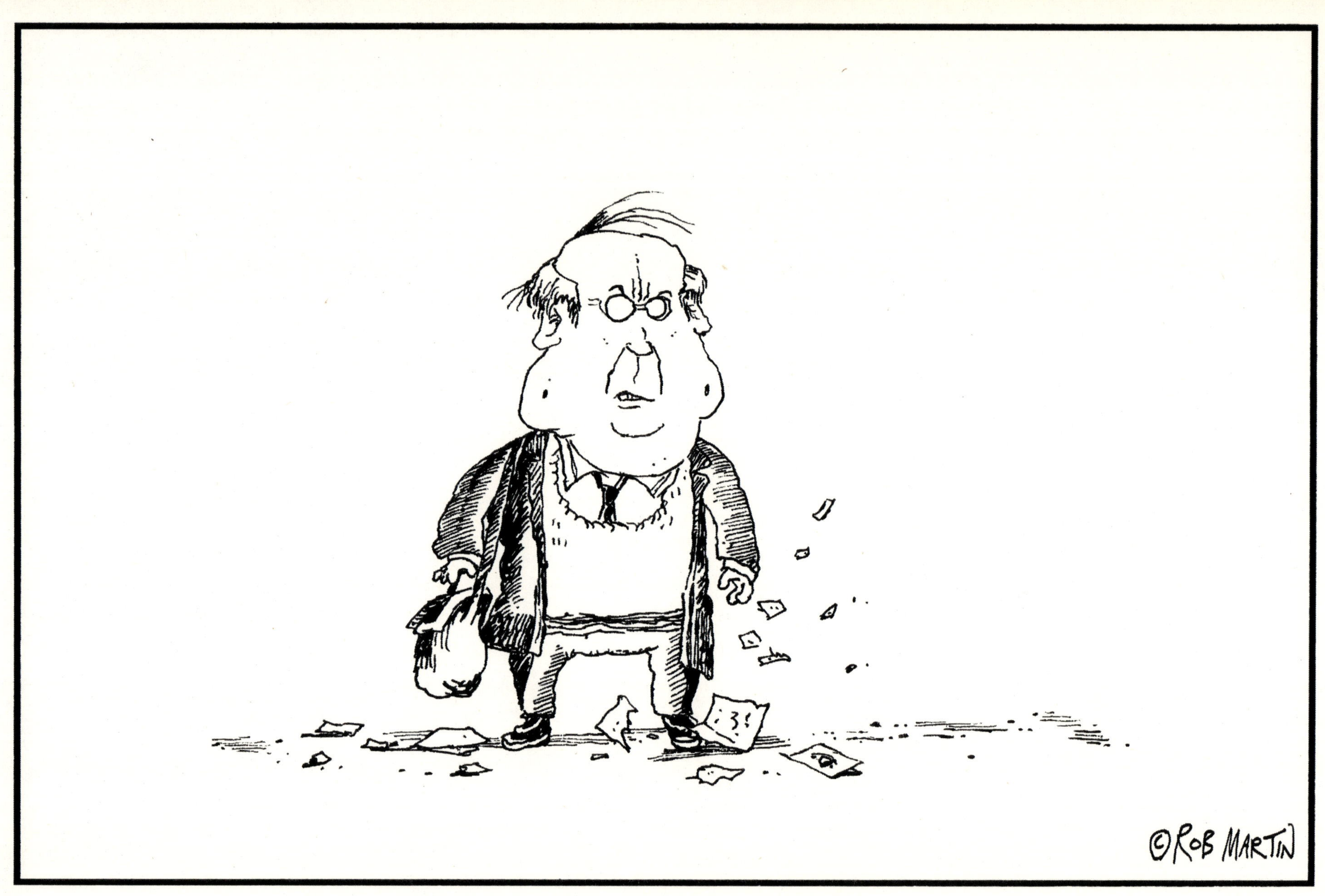

An office worker rips up his 'Have a Happy Retirement' card.

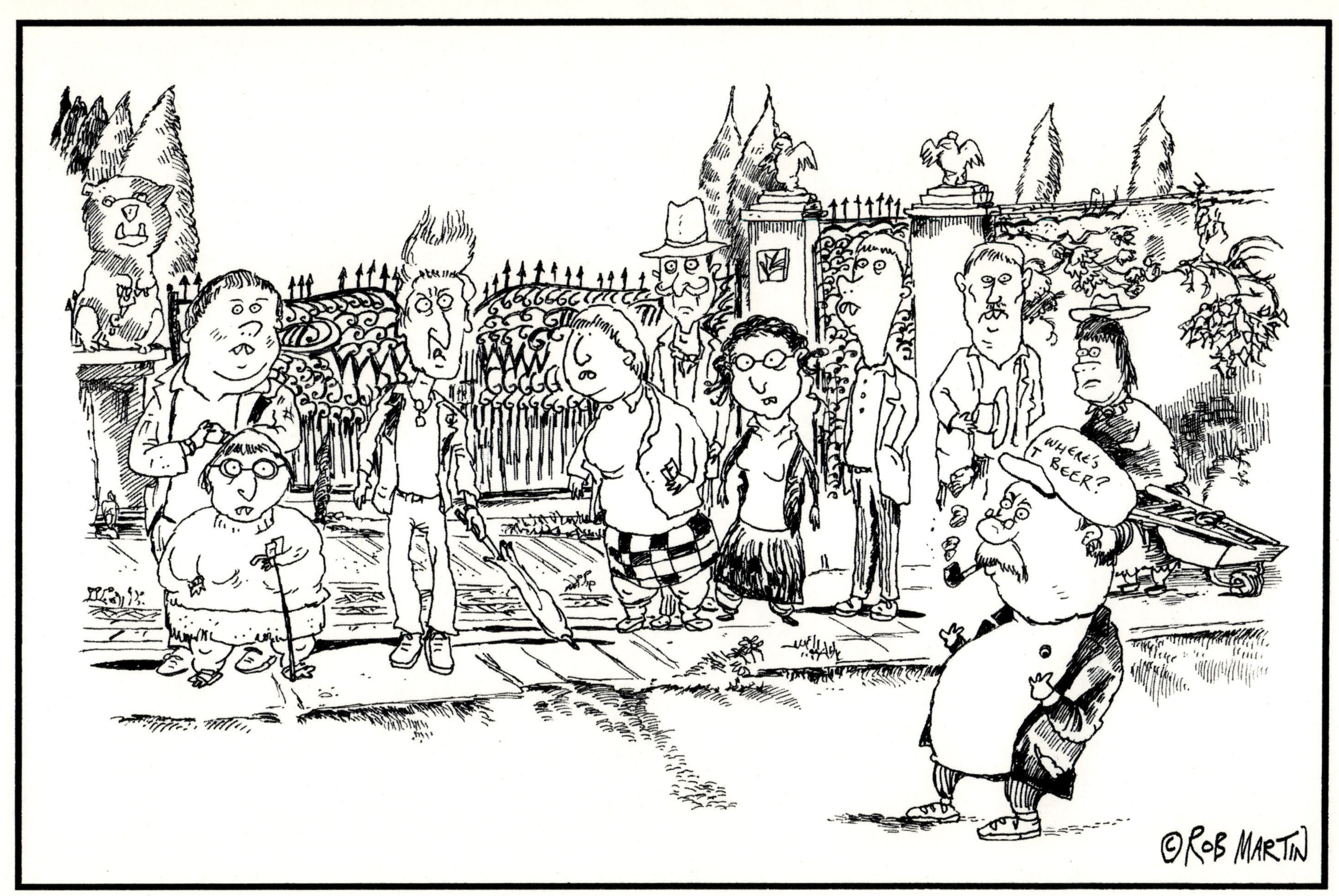

"Are you lost?"

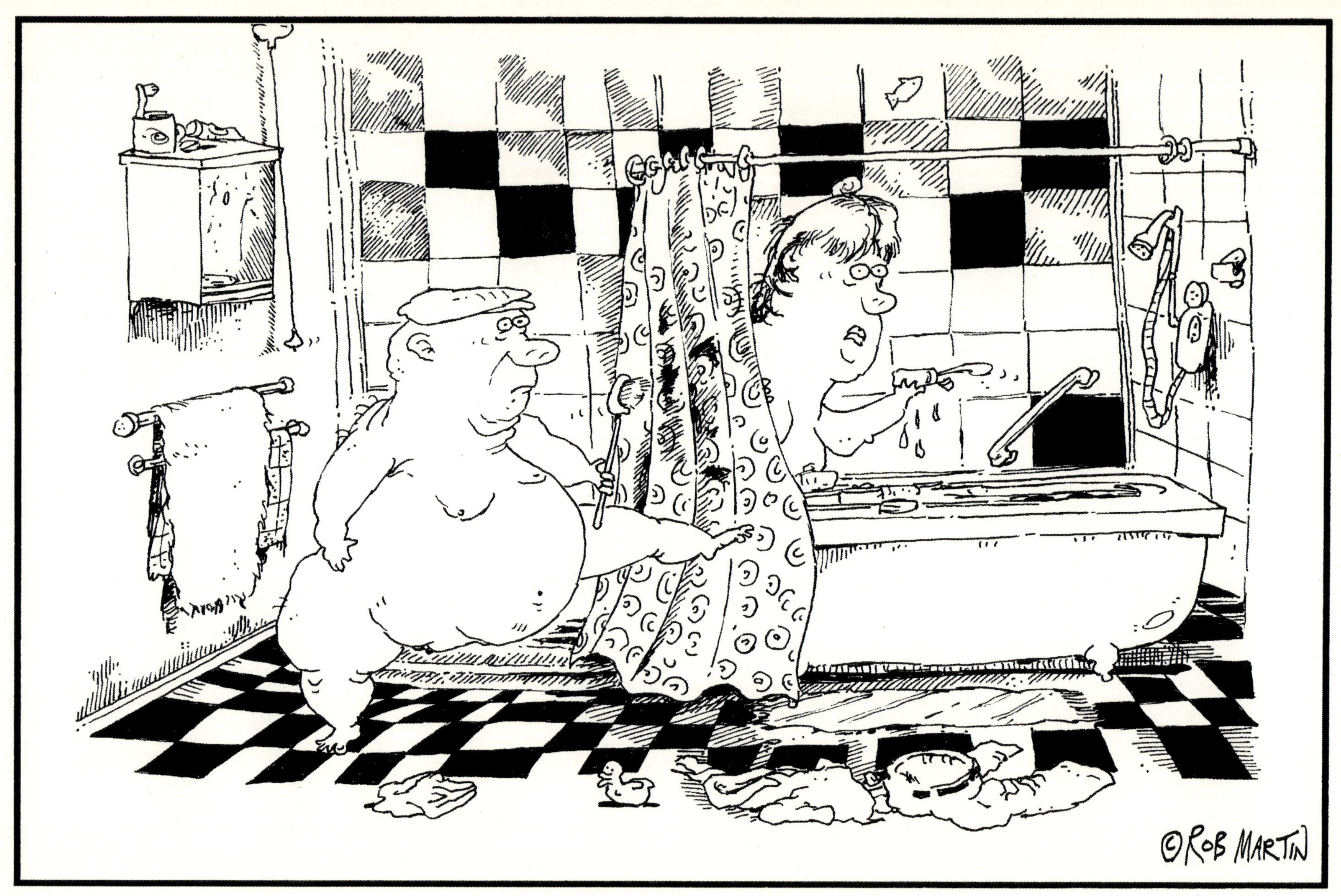

The Farmer and his wife at 7 P.M. on Sunday night.

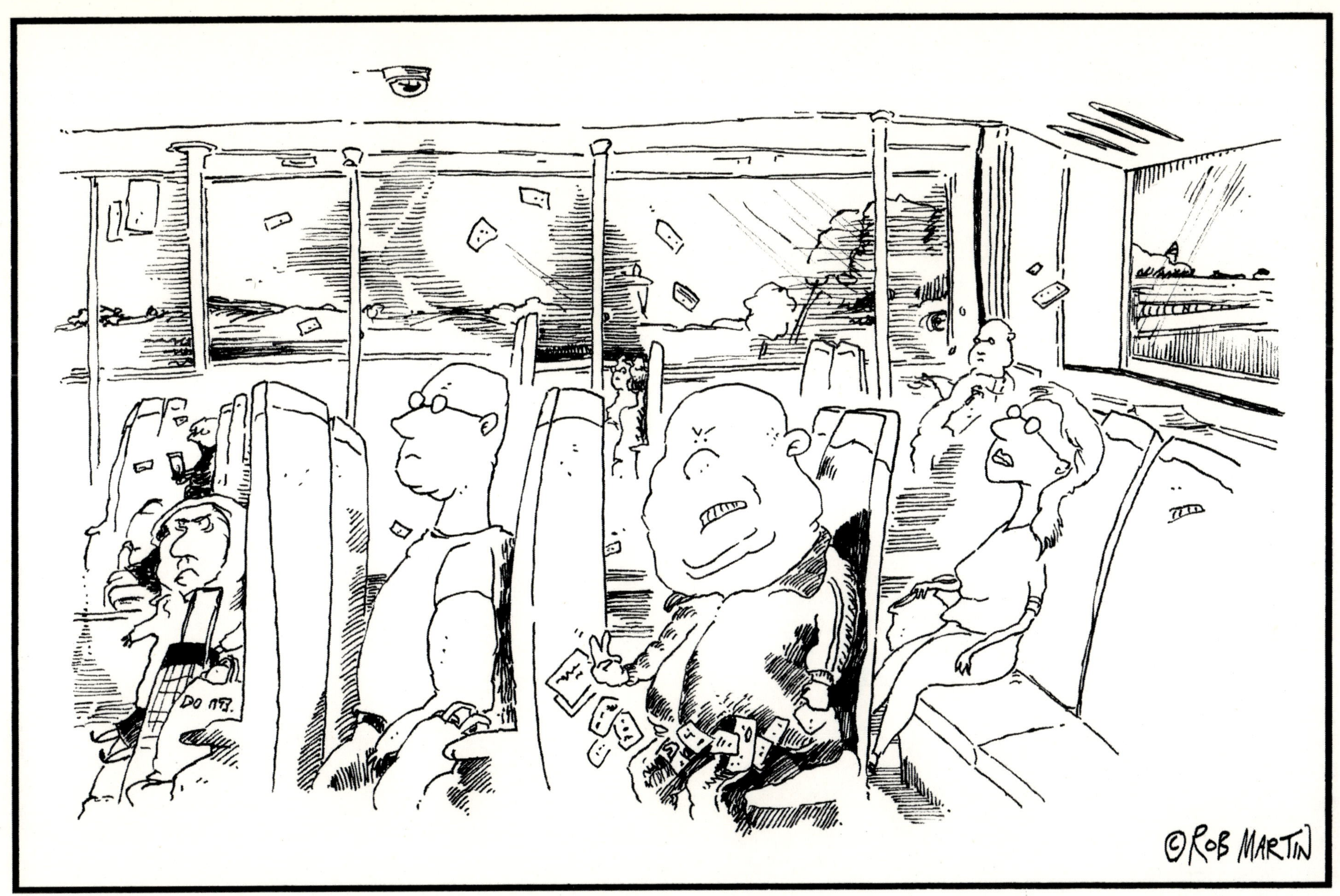

Having spent all his money on losing scratch cards, Geoffrey decides to hurl abuse at them.

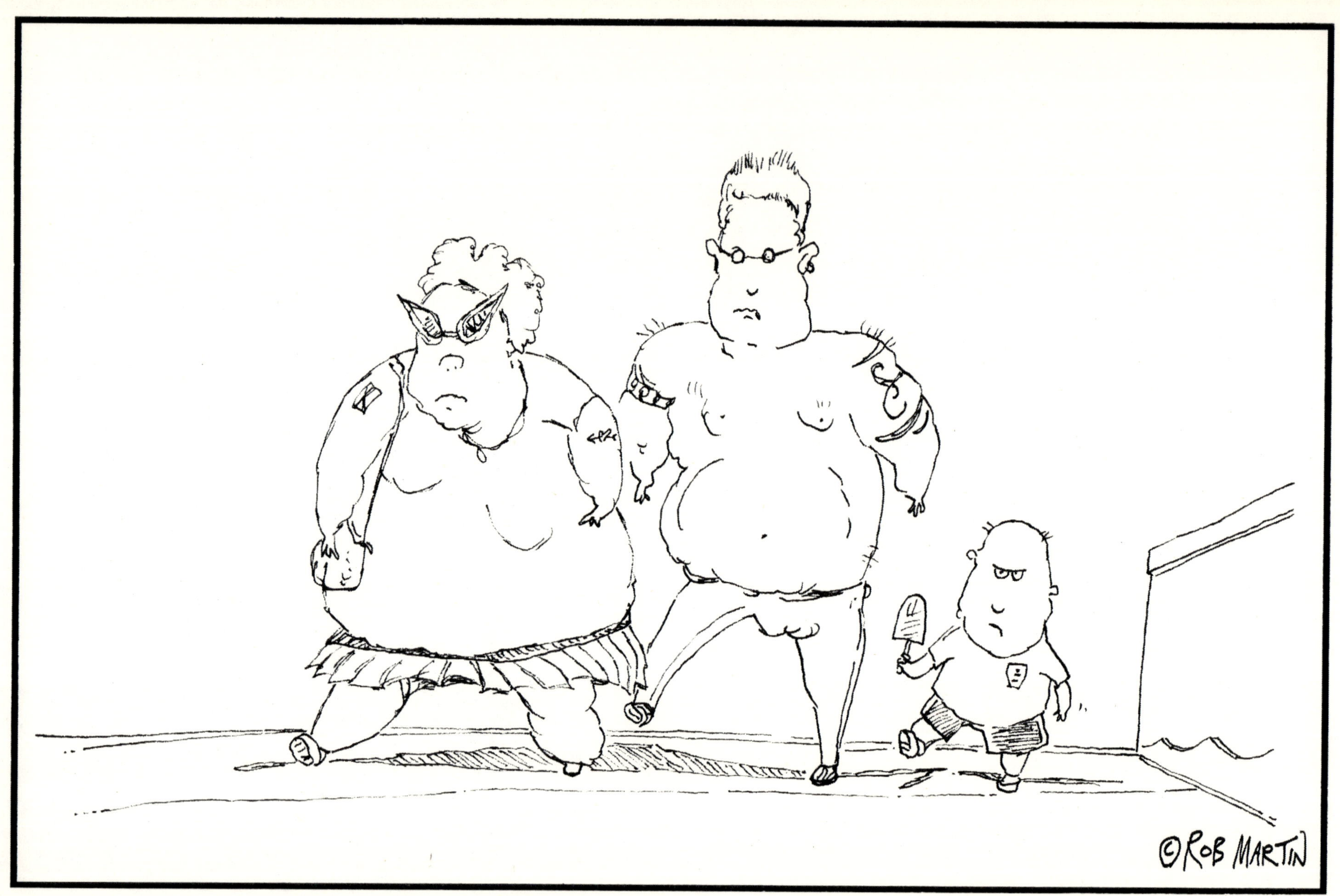

The grunting family on holiday.

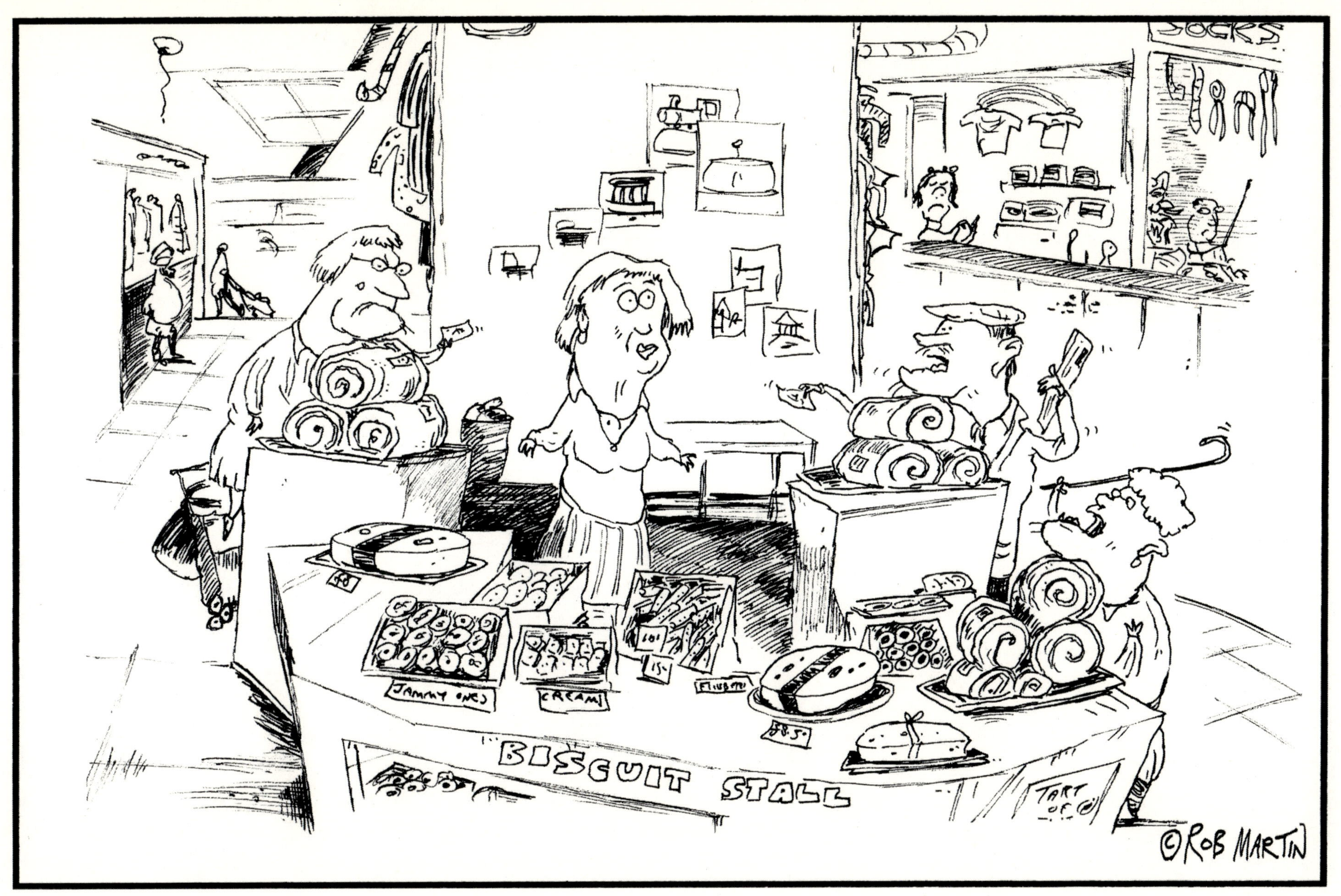

Pensioners descend on the biscuit stall at 10 a.m. prompt.

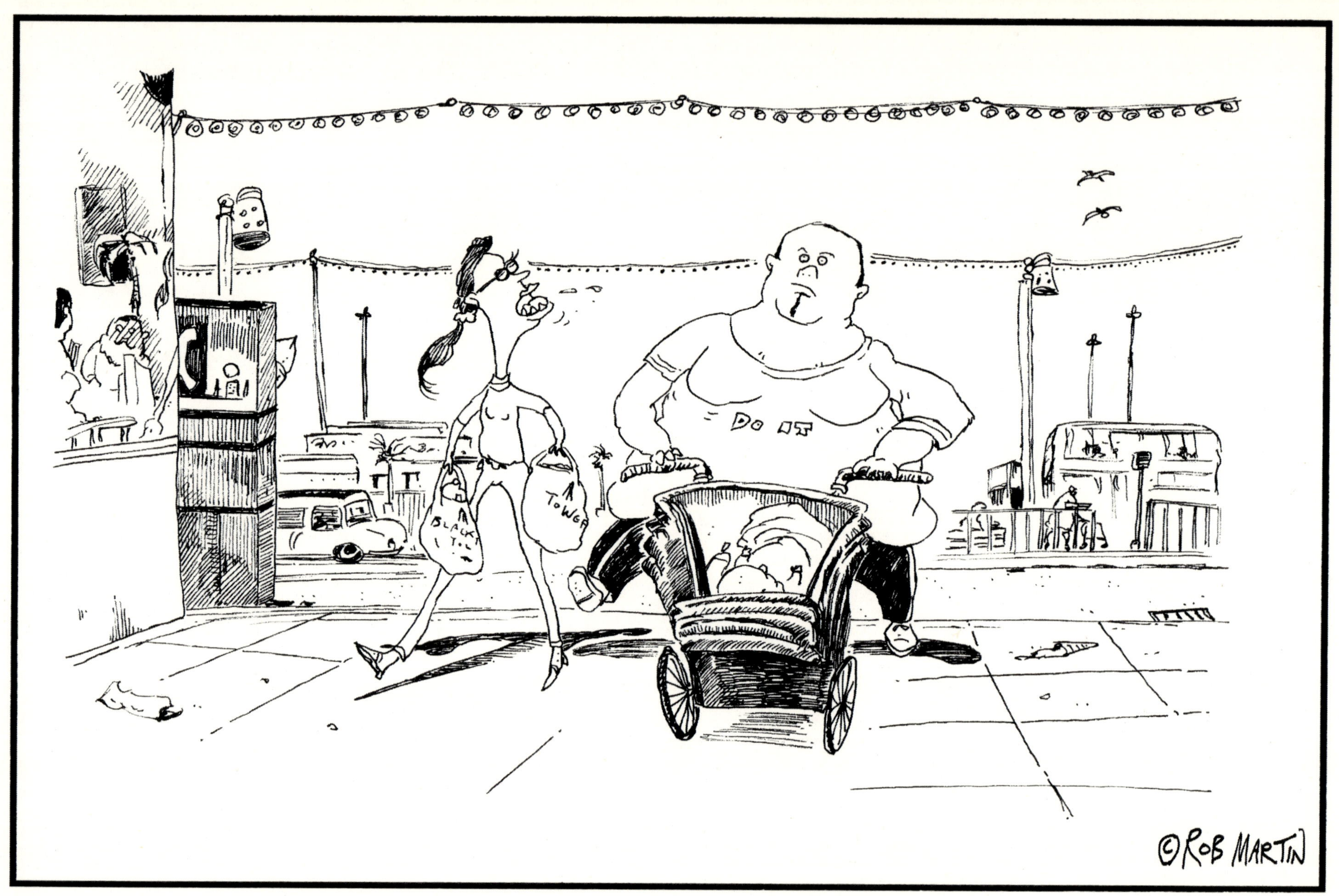

Man with bigger breasts than girlfriend.

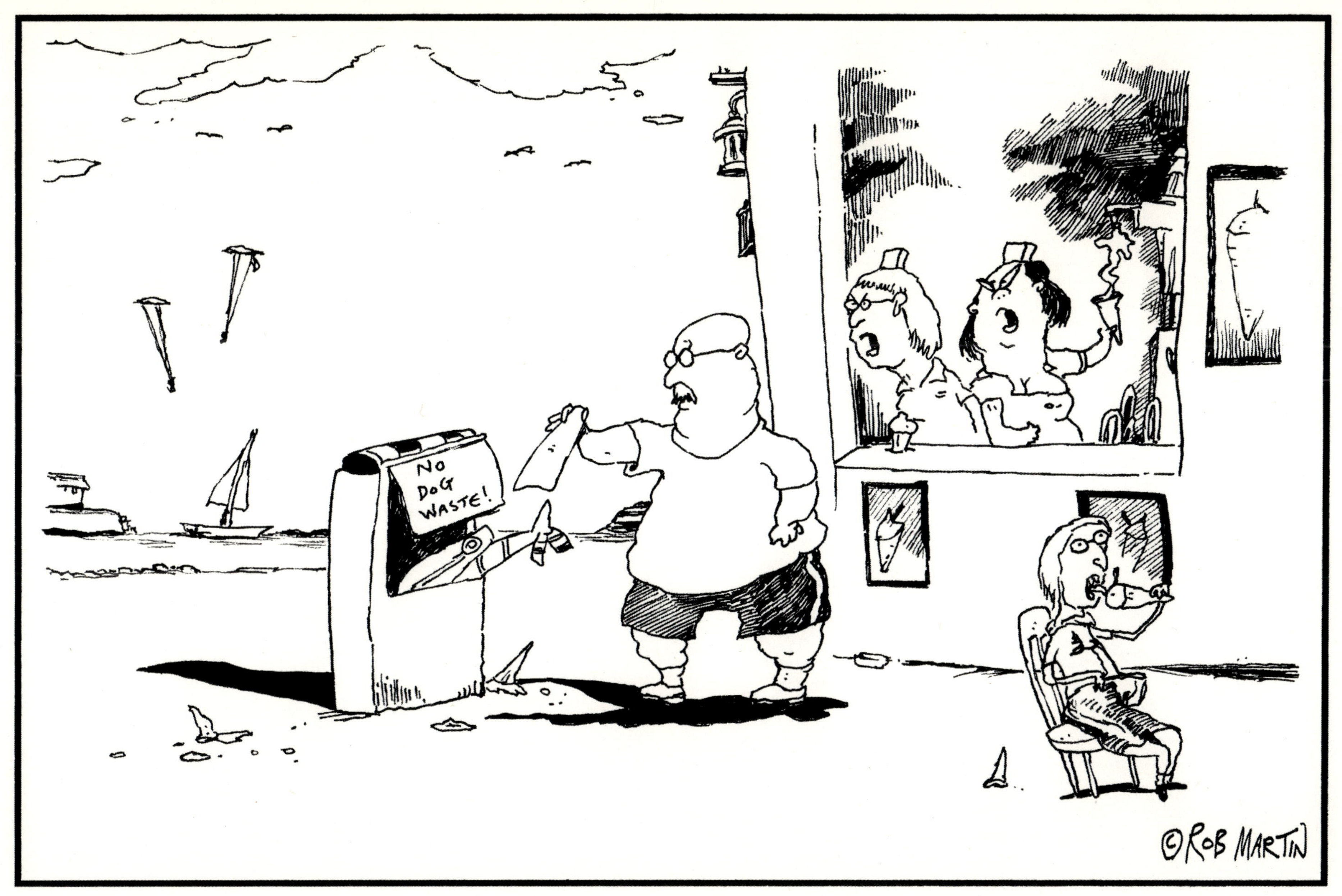

"Hey!! You can't use our bin!!" Shout the ice cream women.

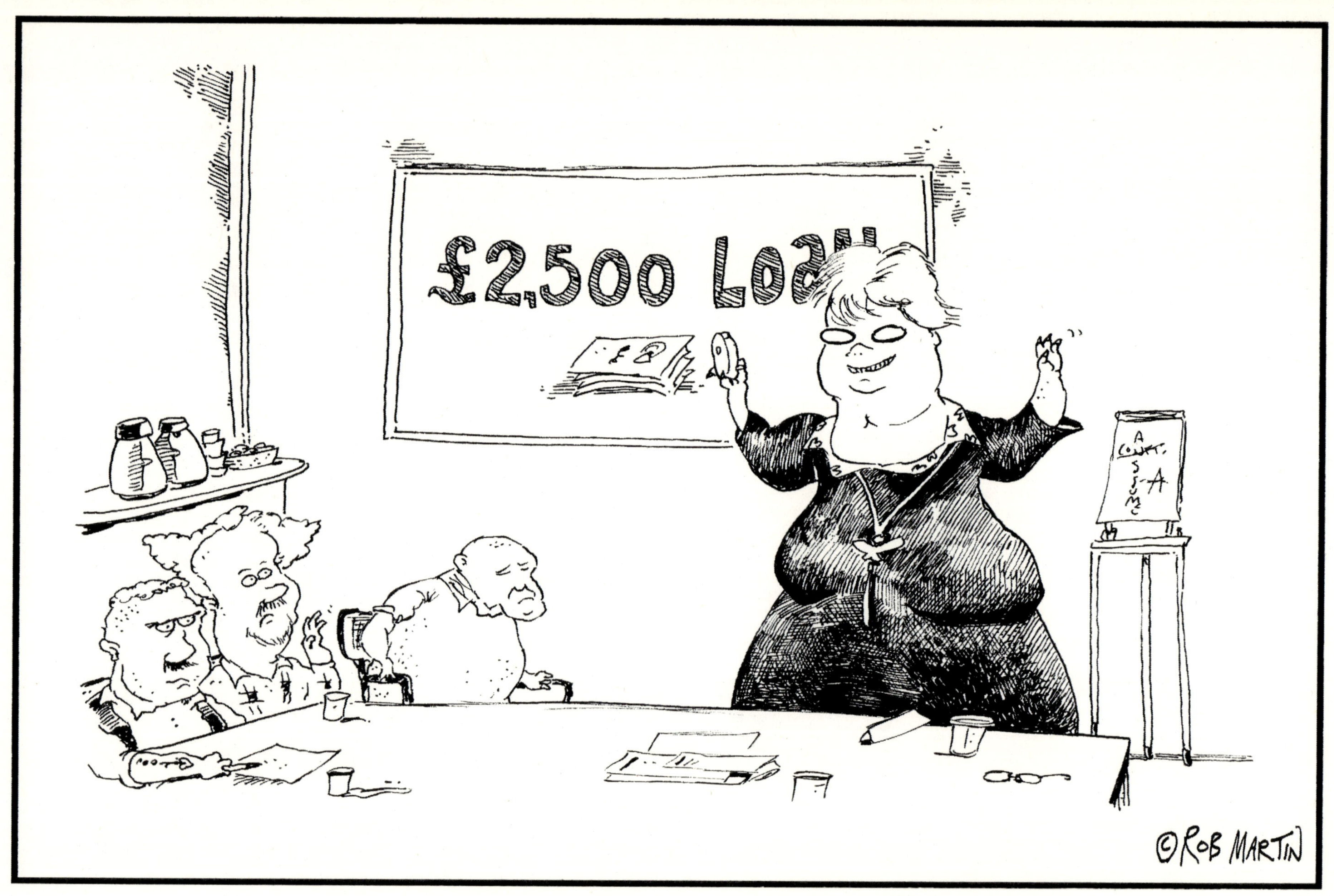

Agnes Thribble tries her best to convince a group of unemployed people, to take out a loan and become freelance wheelie-bin washers.

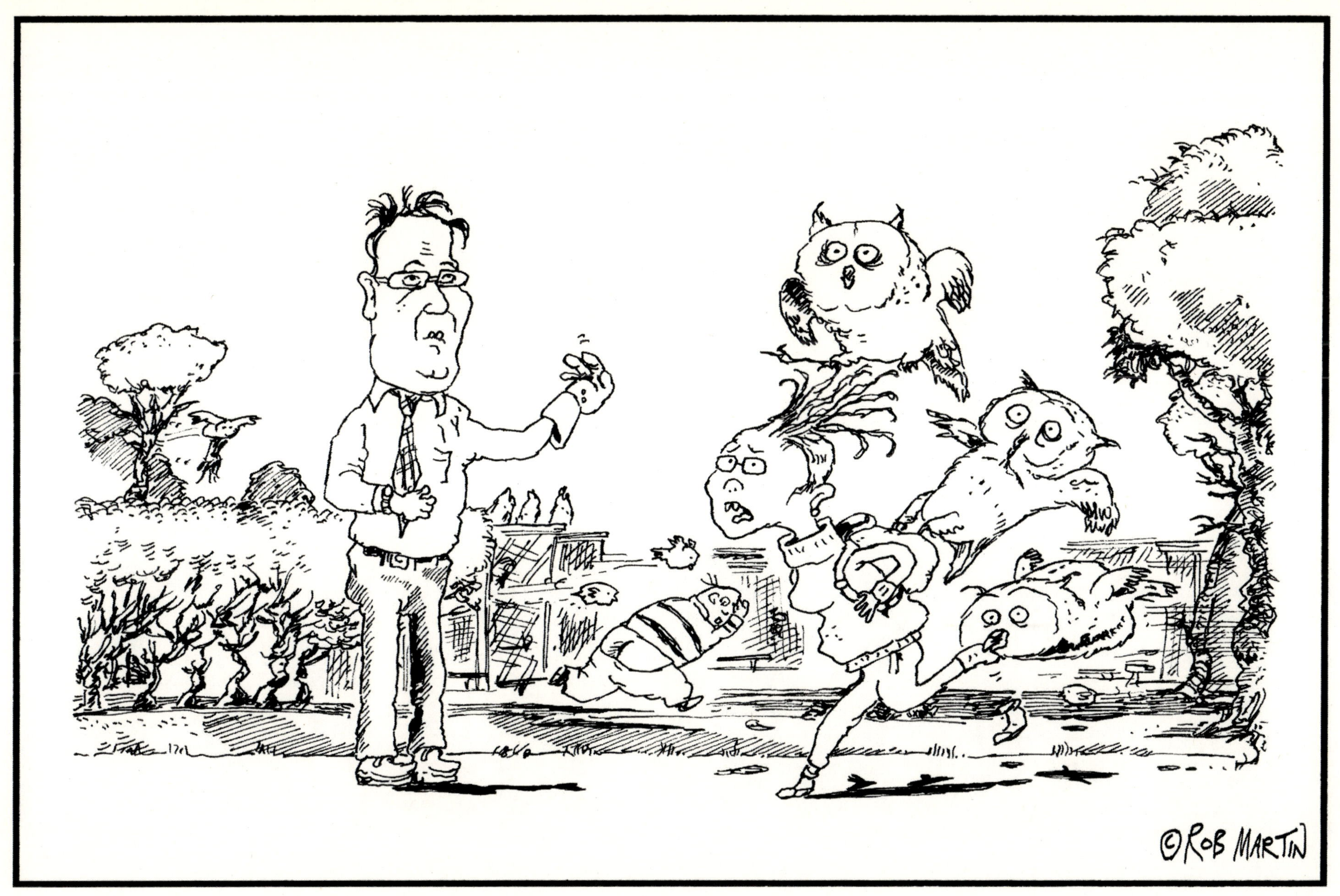

Having sacked all his staff at the Owl sanctuary.
Andreas tries his own hand at flying the Owls.

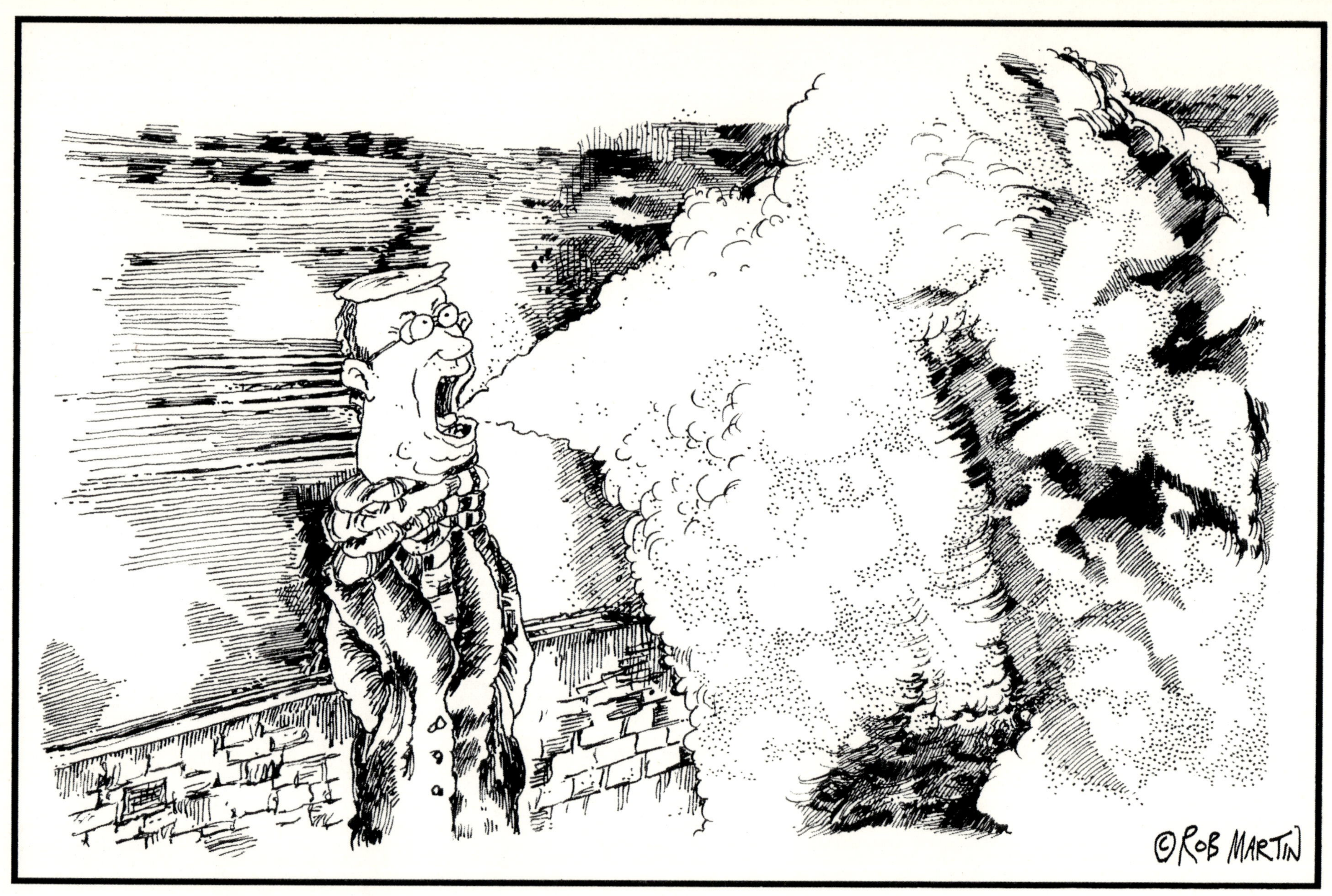

On a frosty morning, a man yawns causing a plume like a steaming kettle.

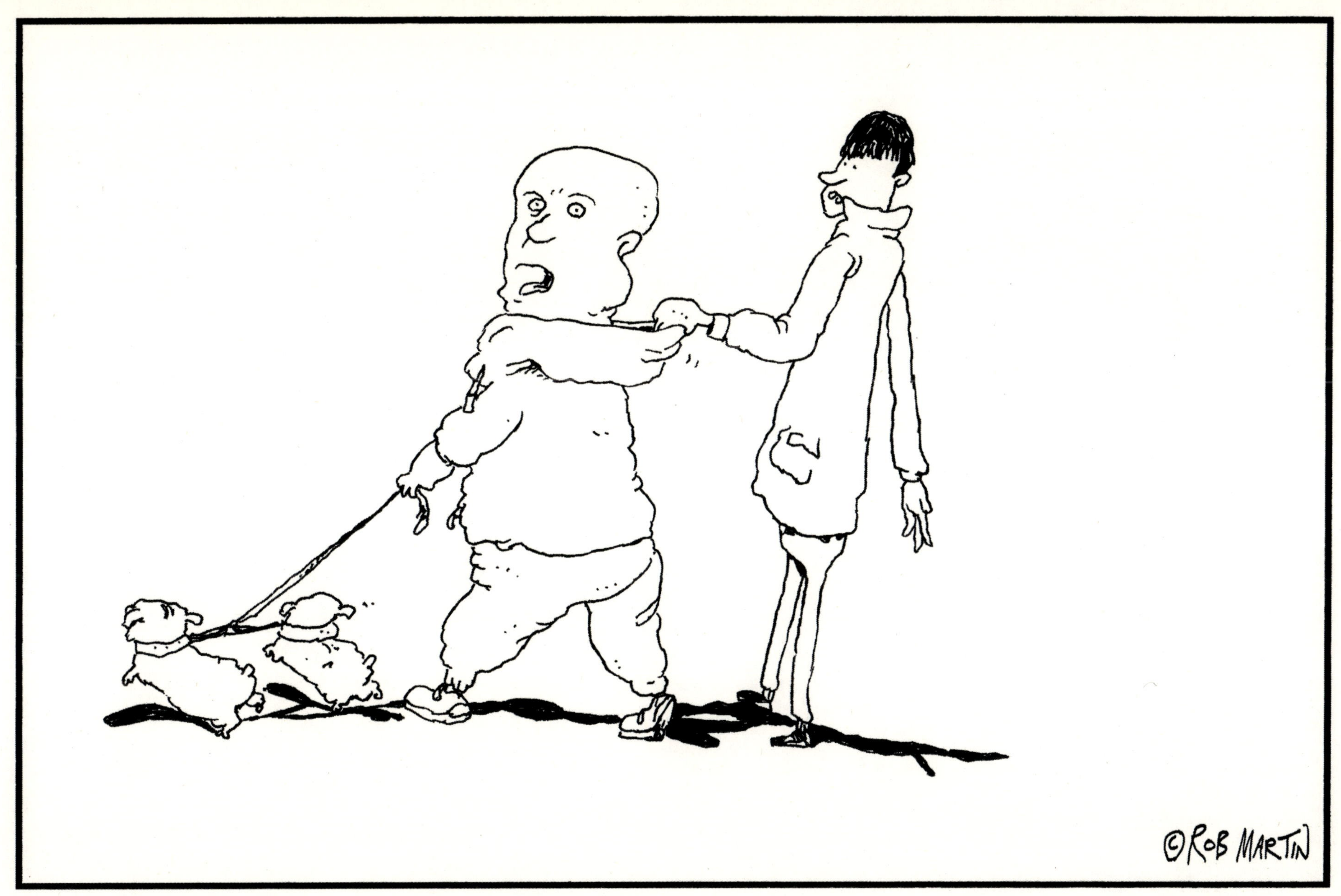

Needing attention, the beanpole son pulls on his Father's hood.

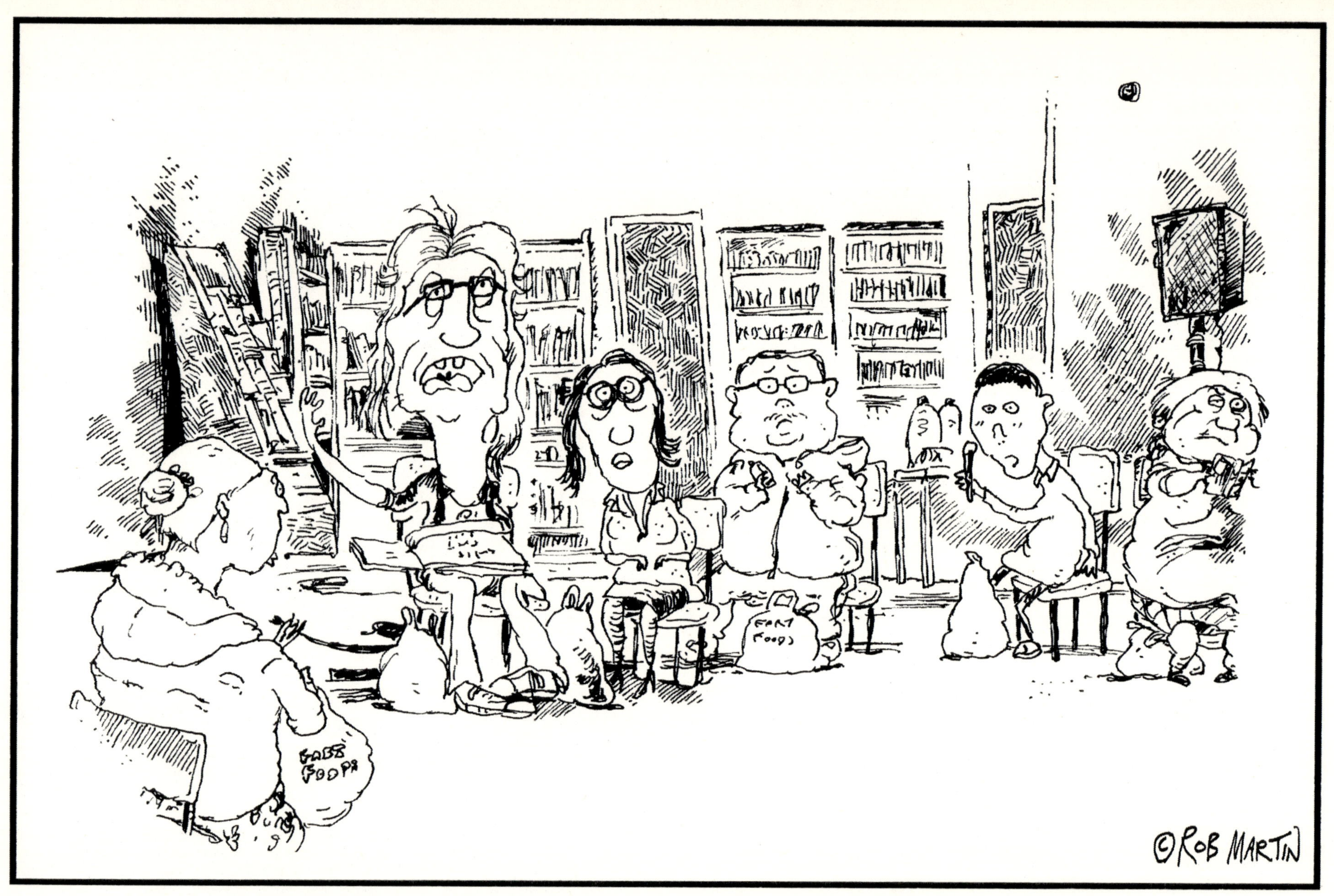

In the library, shy nervous timid folk meet and display deep woes, cheese smells and anger through poetry.

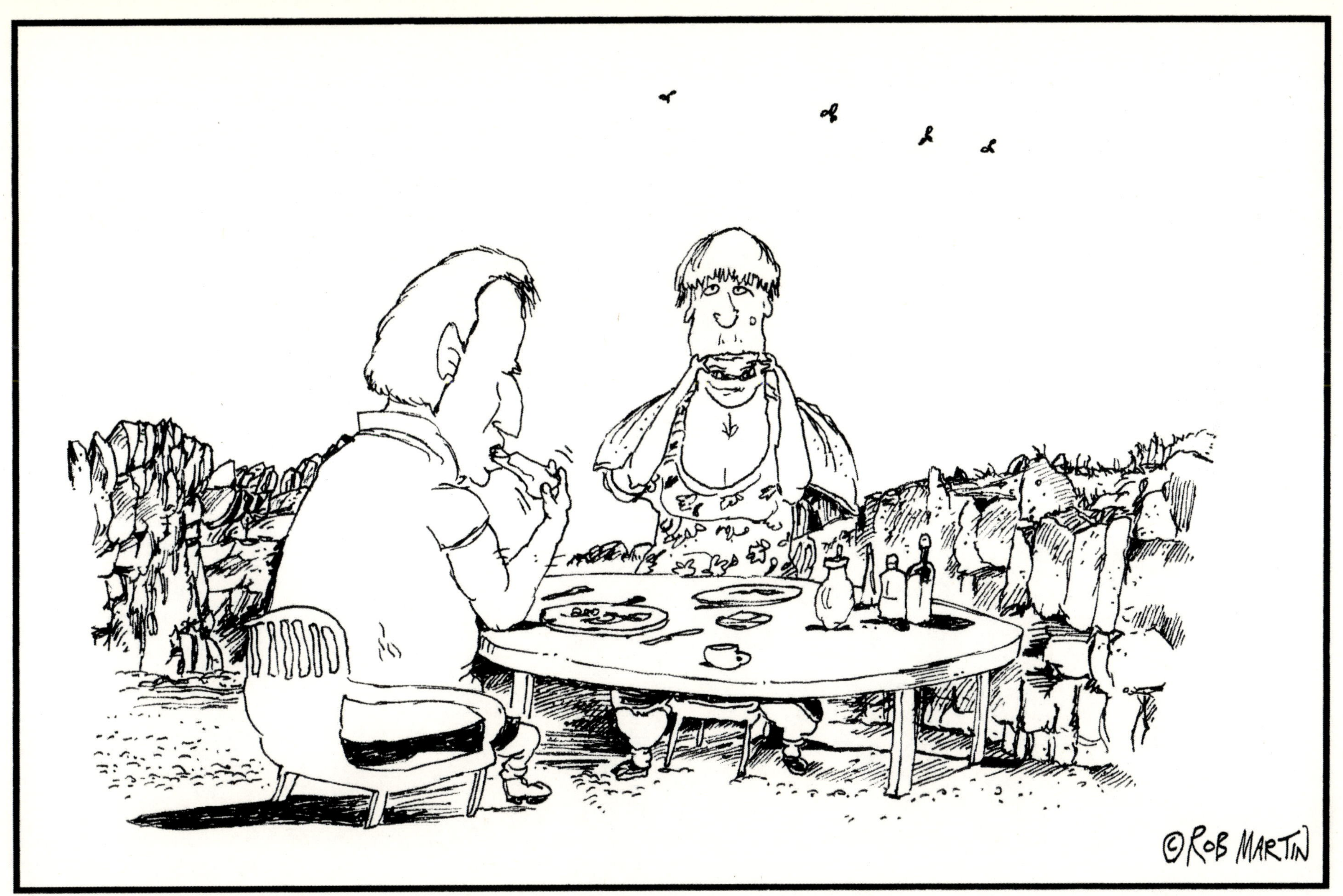

8 years after the marriage.

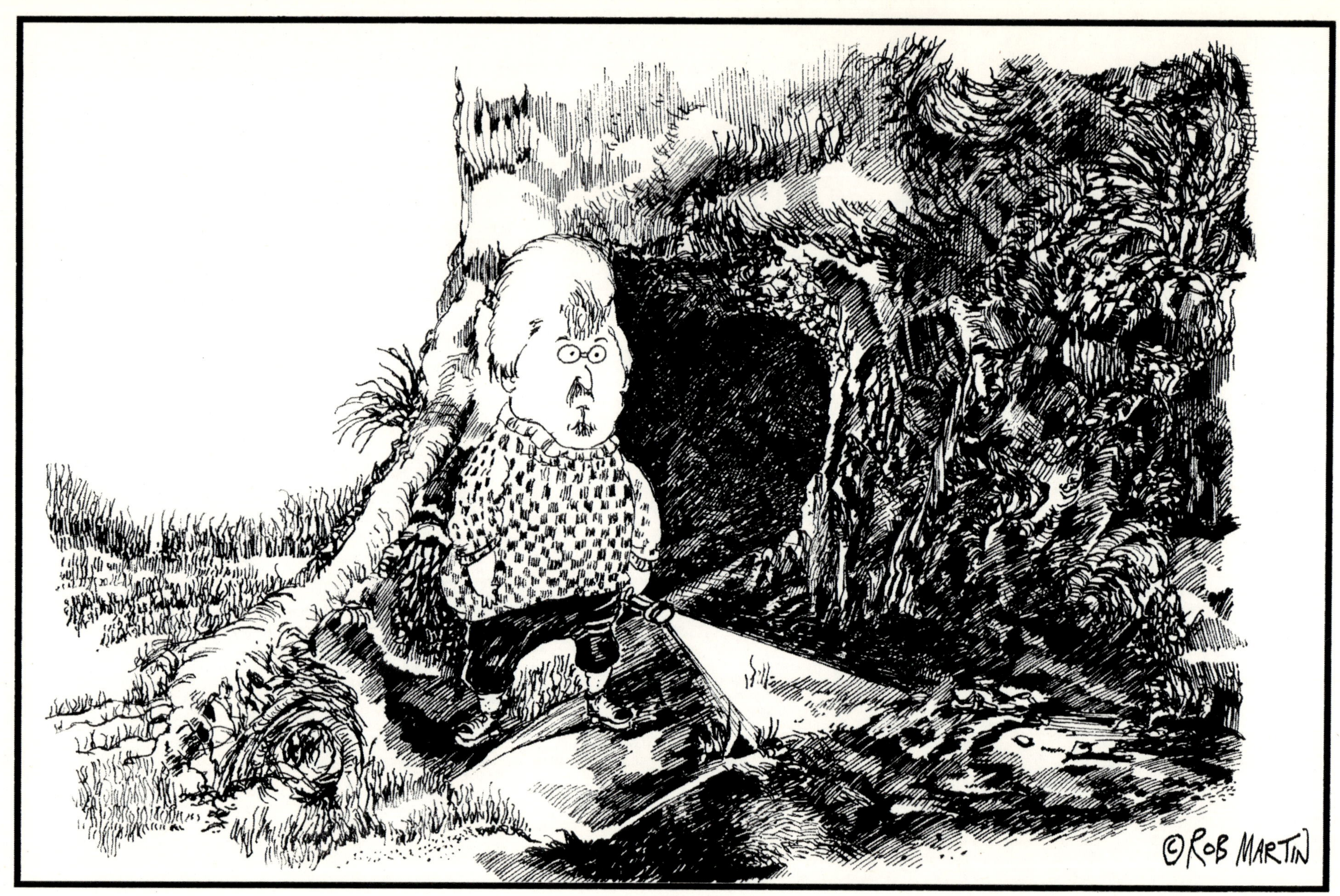

Slowly shining his torch to the ground. Paul 'Bemused' Bumstead believes he's just found the Tooth Fairy's Castle.

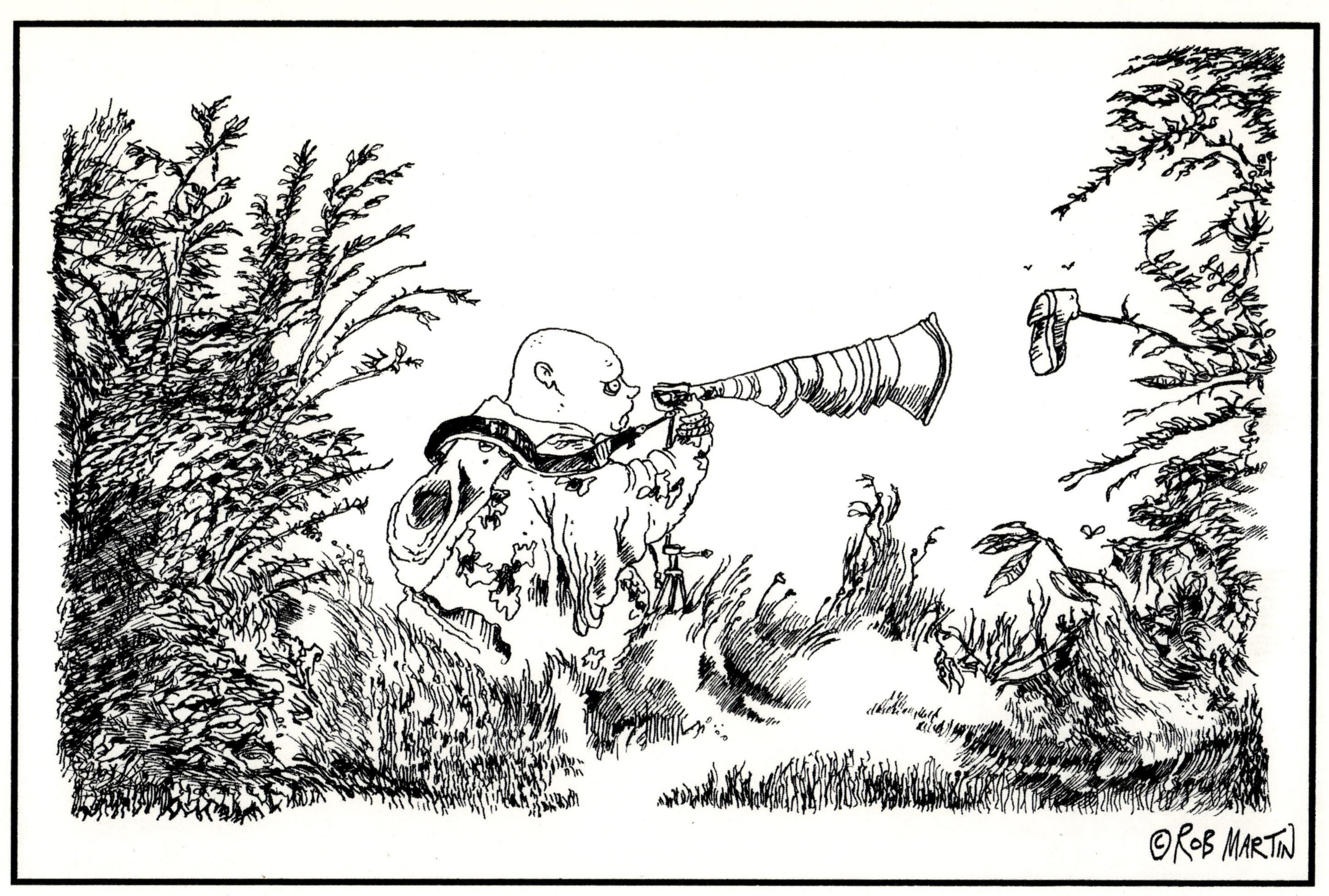

Amateur nature photographer, Bummy Trogg goes hunting for a Stag with his £8000 lens.

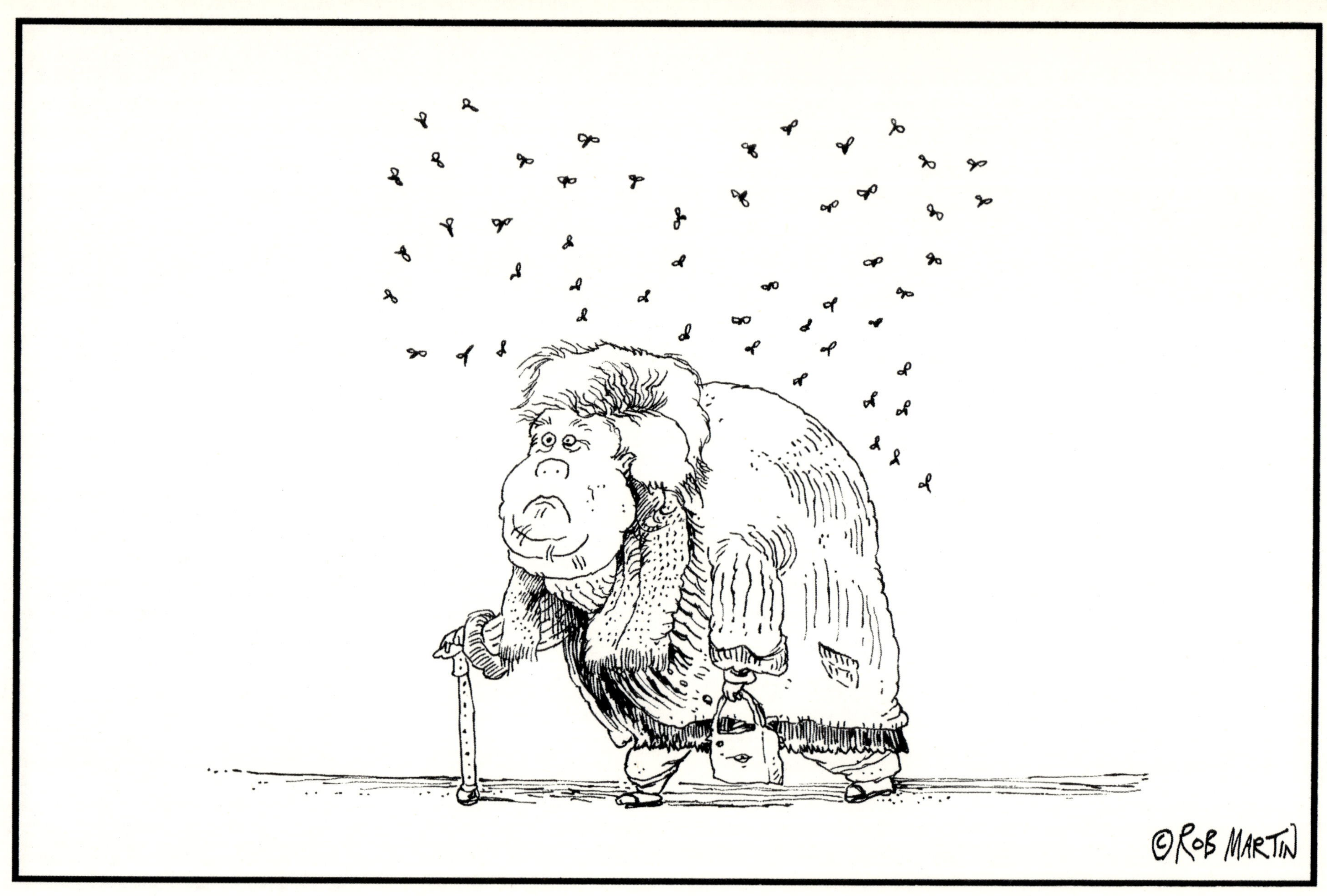

Swarming flies mistake old Mrs. Trubshaw as a moving pile of dung.

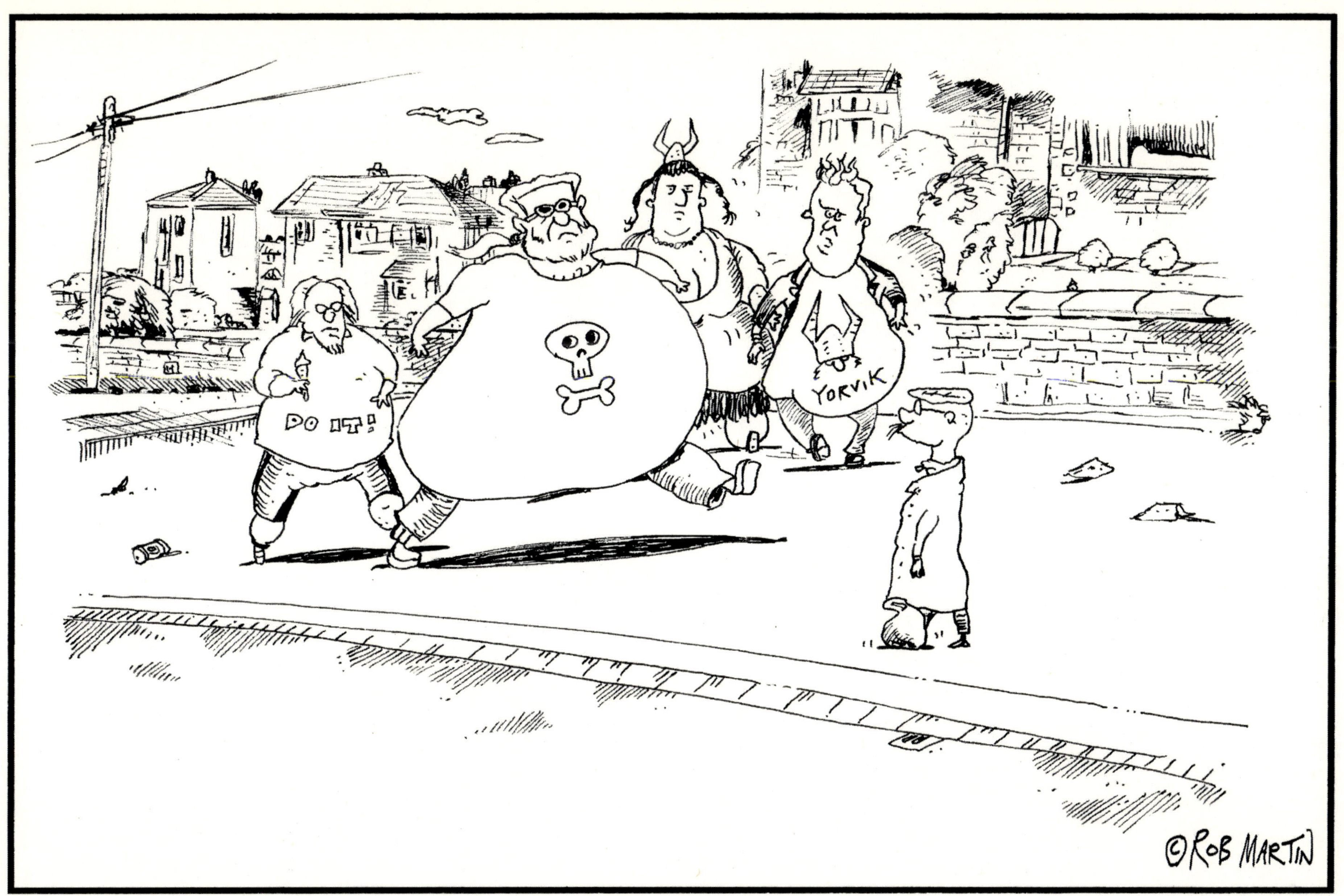
DO IT!
YORVIK
©ROB MARTIN

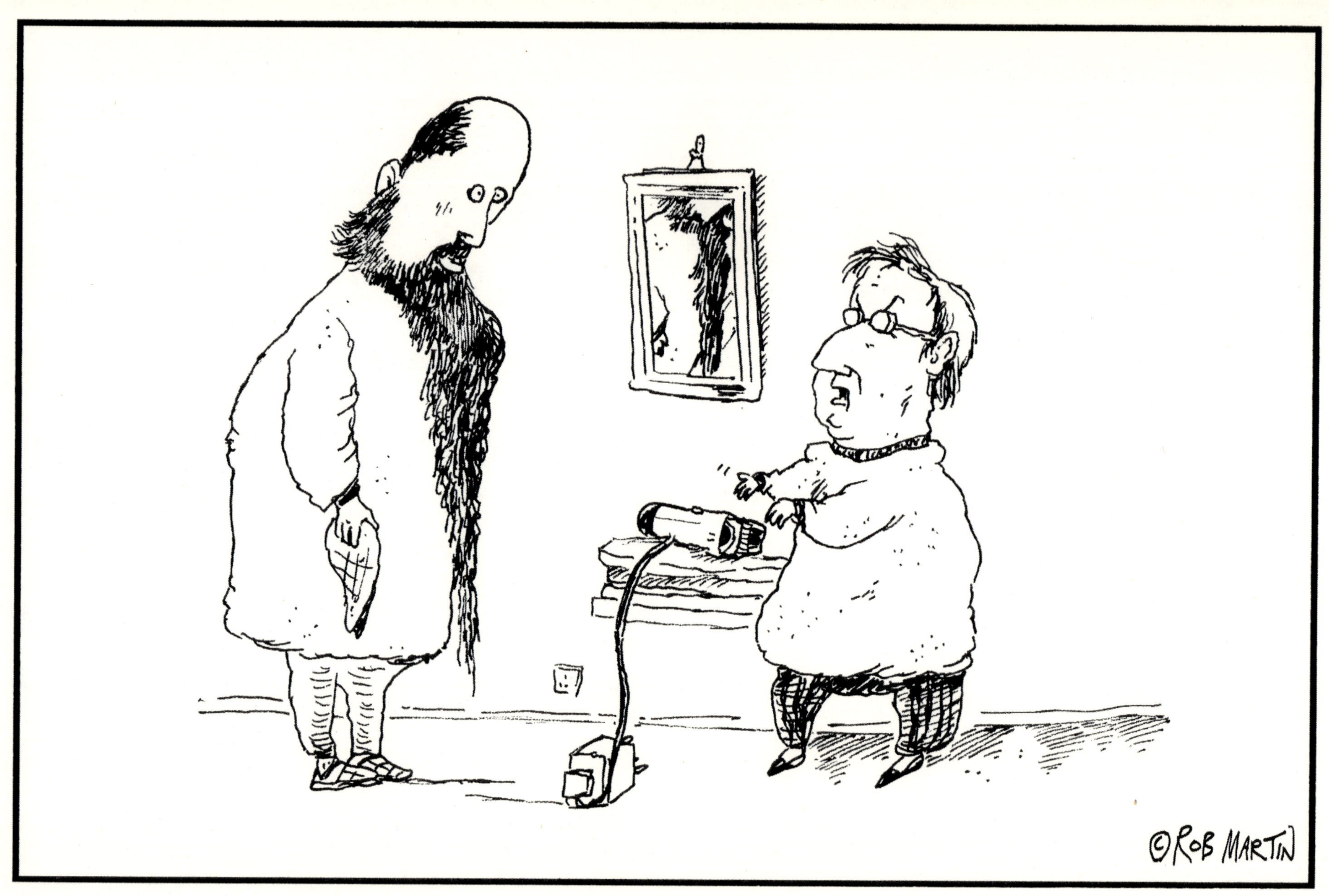

A mother shows her son, the fully charged
beard trimmer she has just found.

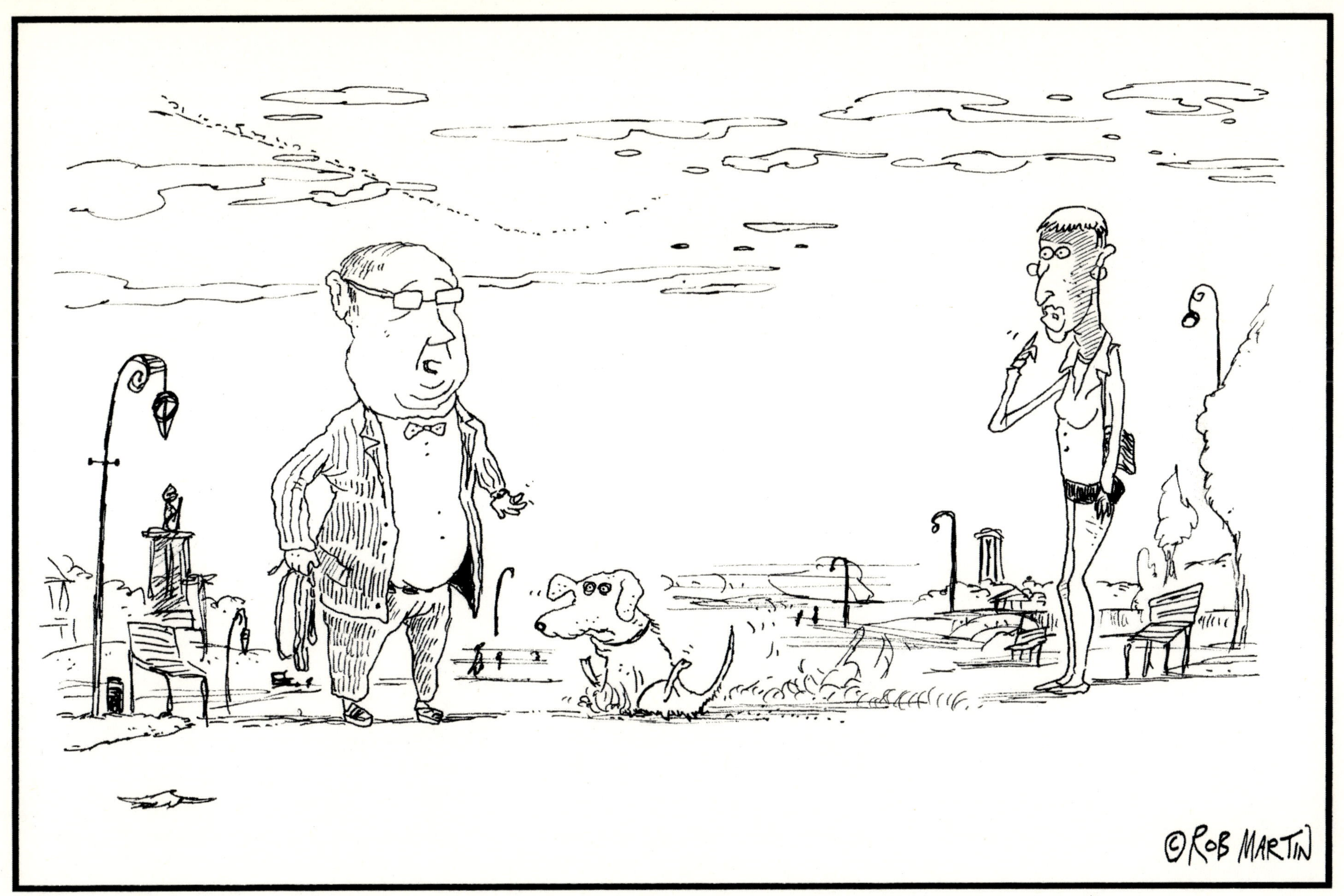

"He has trouble with his anal glands!"

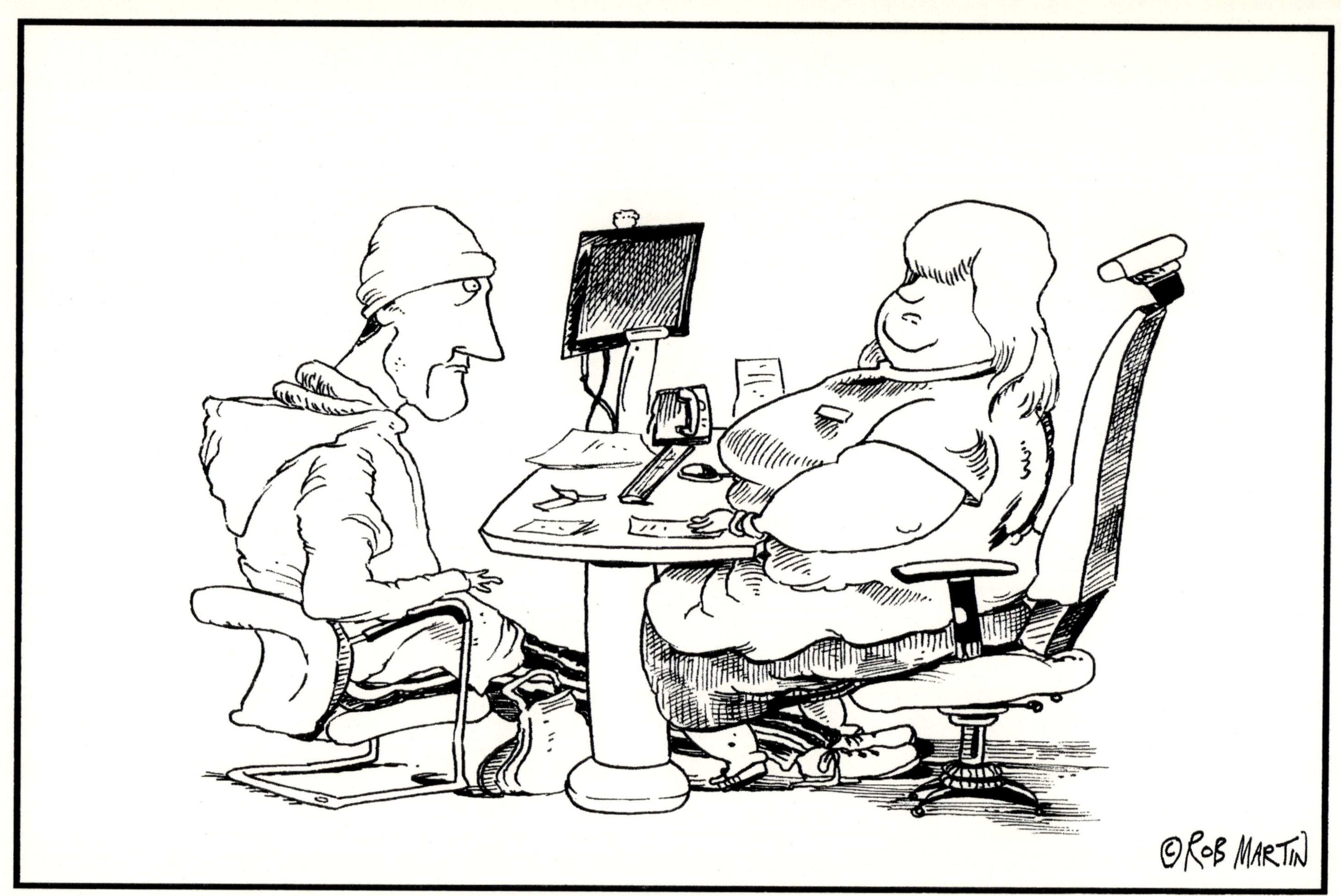

In the jobcentre, customer and adviser play footsie
whilst discussing internet job searches.

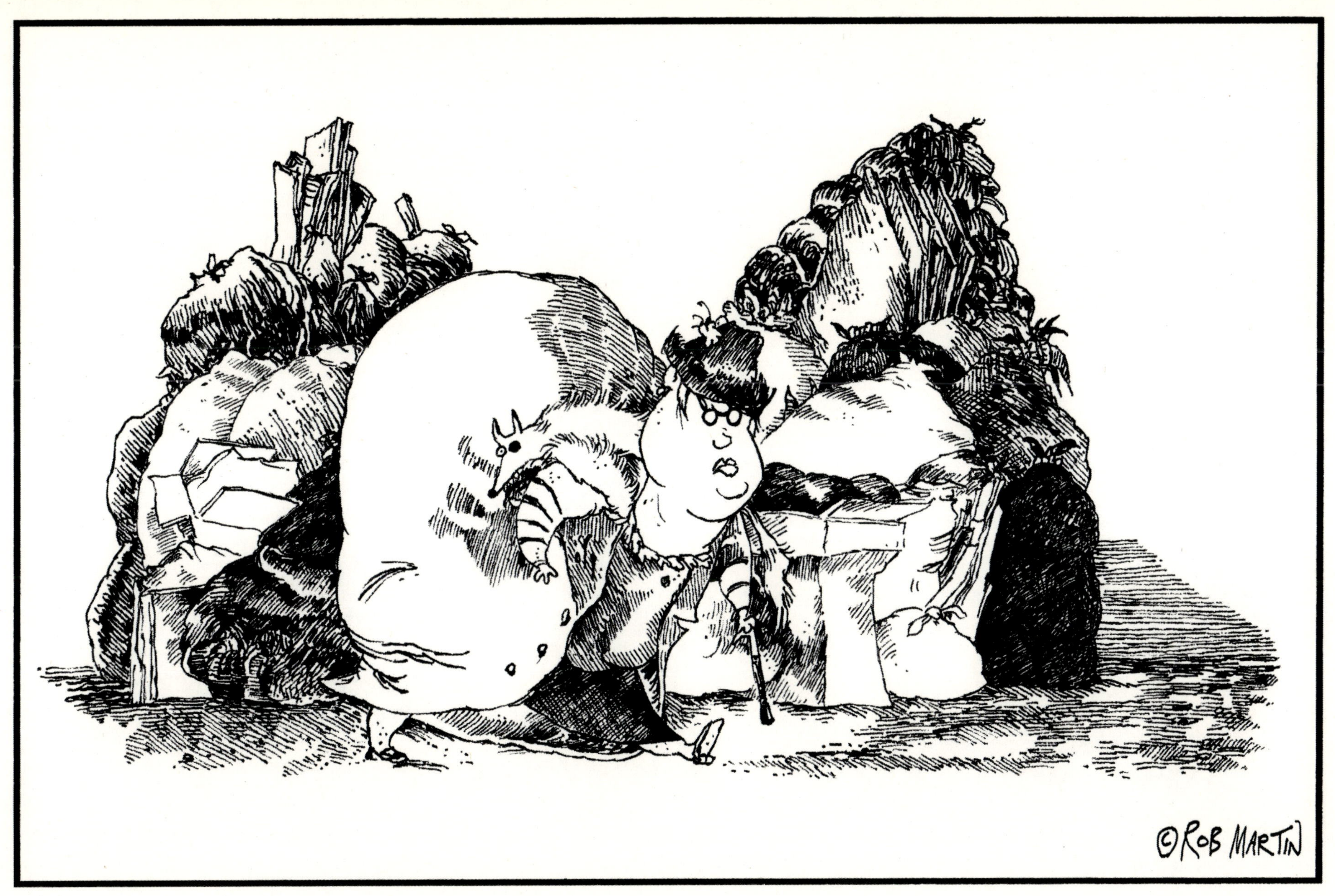

Mrs. Meekly hobbles past piles of tipped rubbish. Unaware, that she now resembles an old bin bag.

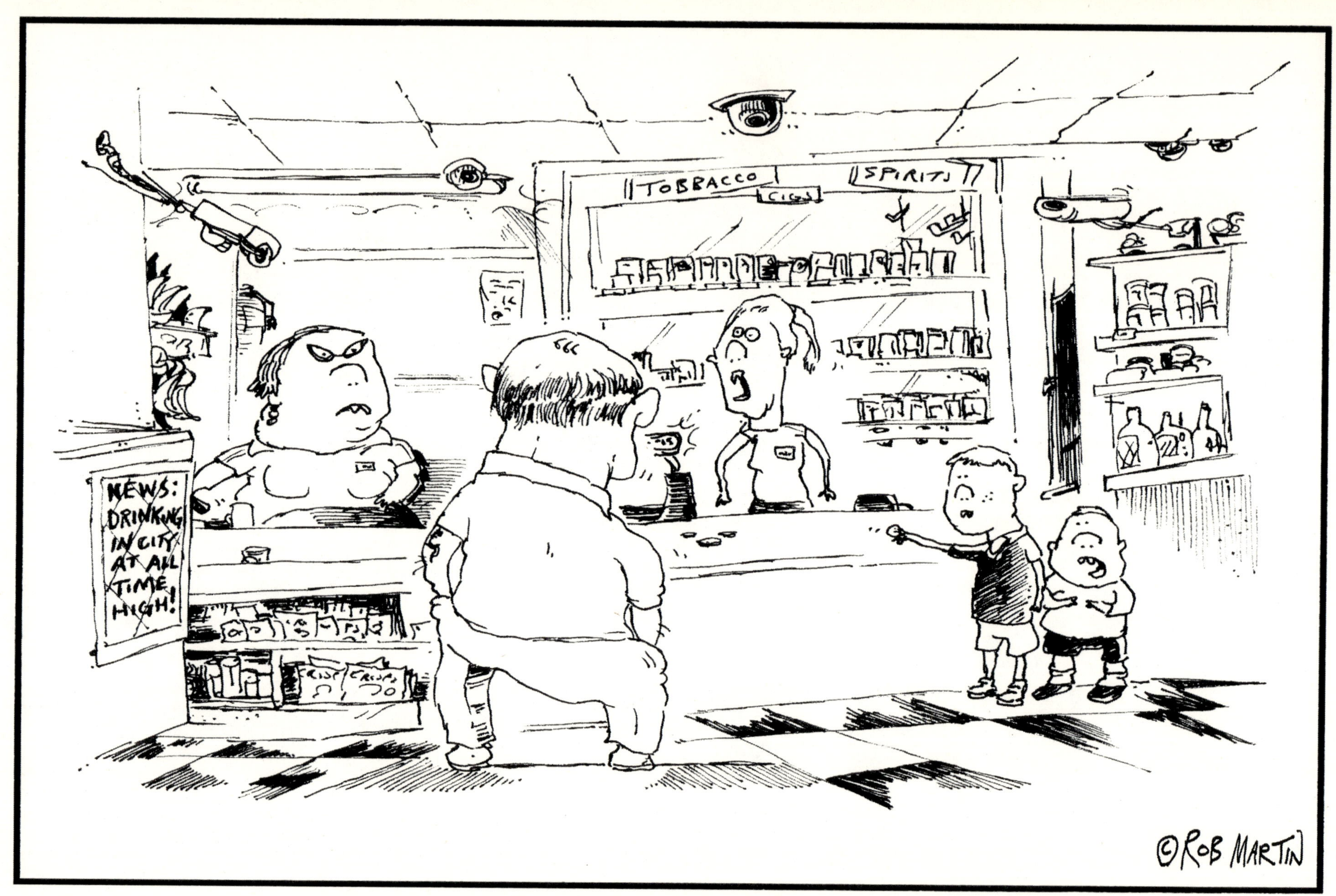

A heavily drunk man wants another bottle of cider, but is 21p short.

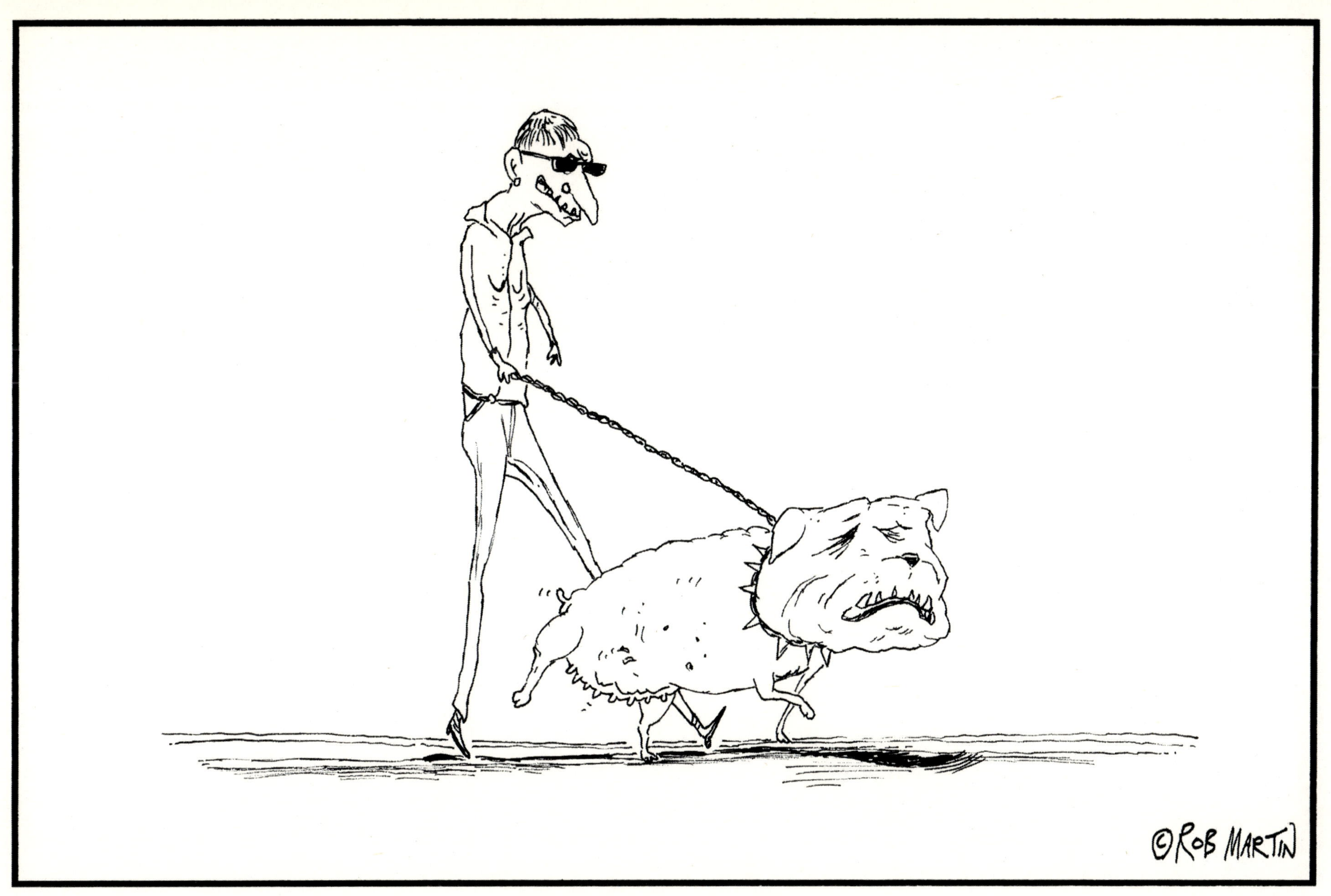

Two ugly things go for a walk.

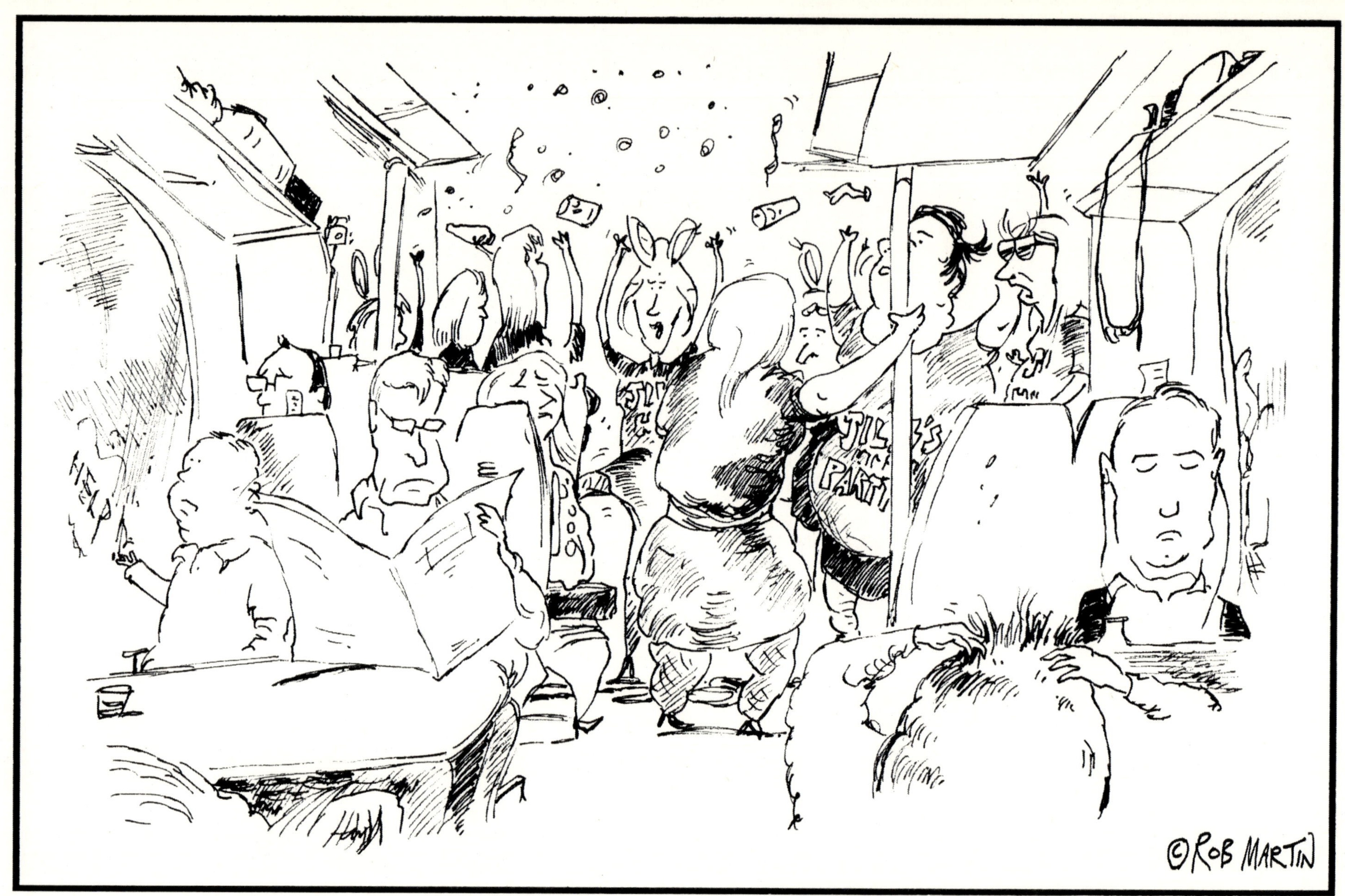

Hen party on the train.

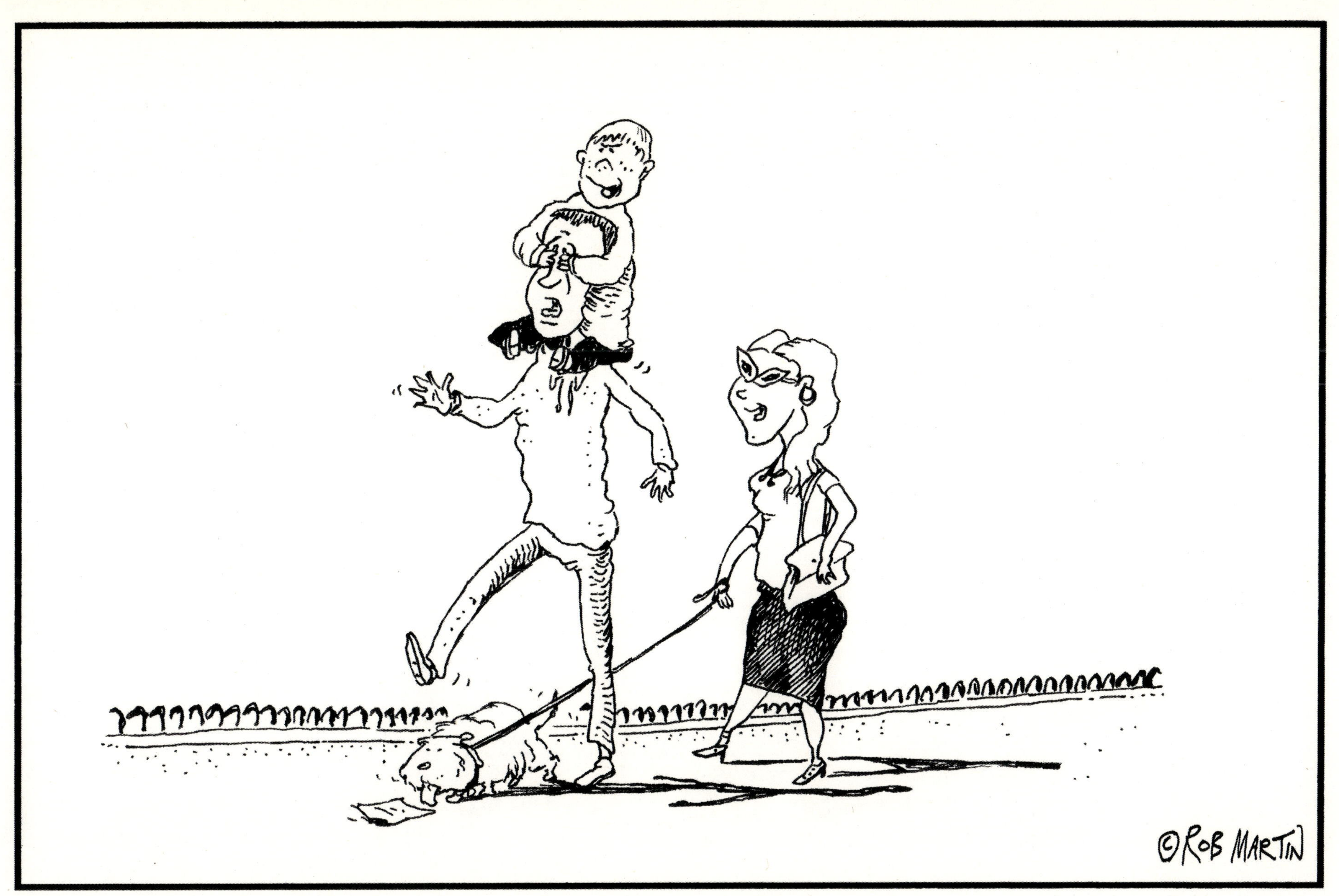

Six year old Ben, tries to pop the eyeballs of Nigel, Mum's new boyfriend.

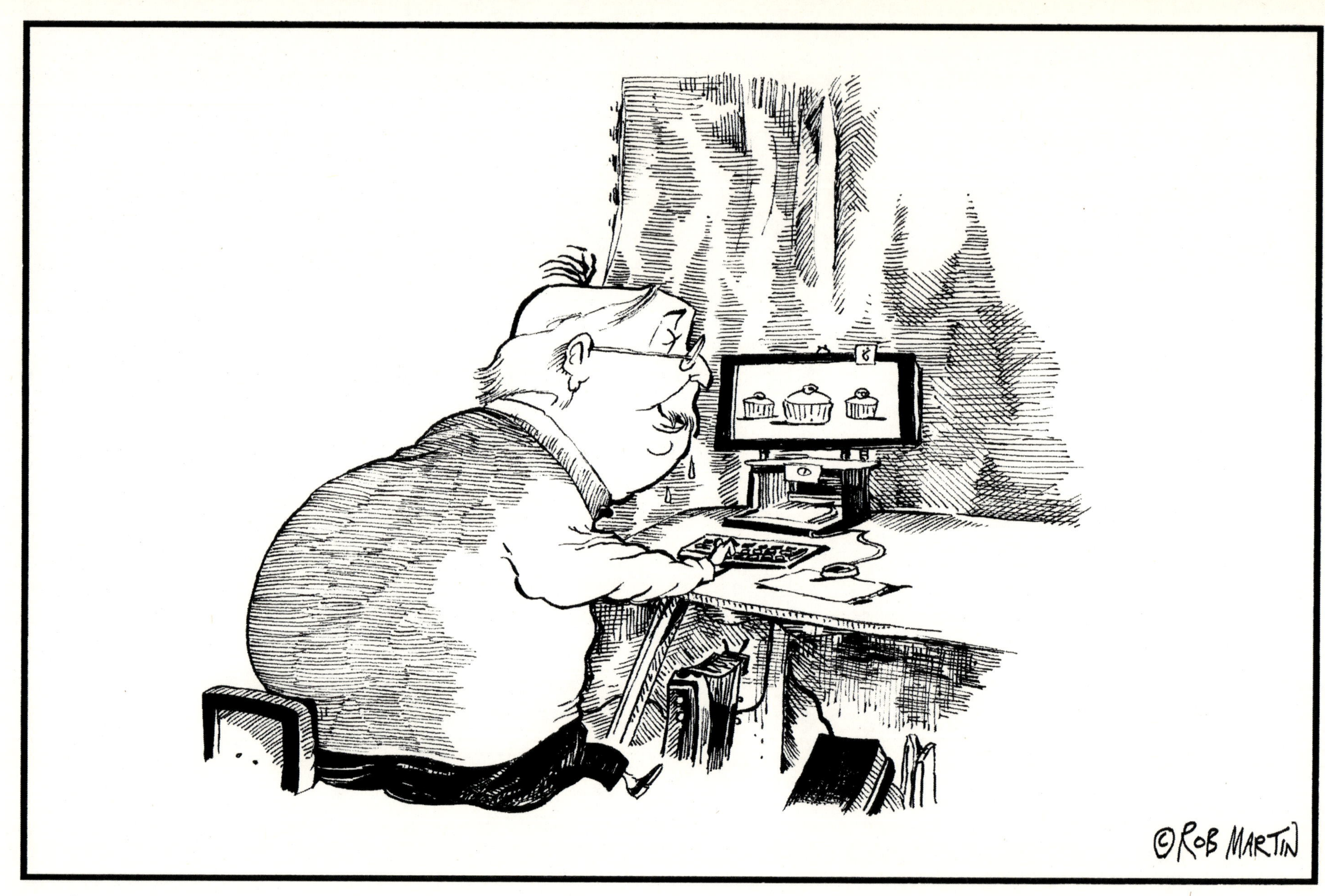

Mr. Treacle salivates and drools over a film about buns.

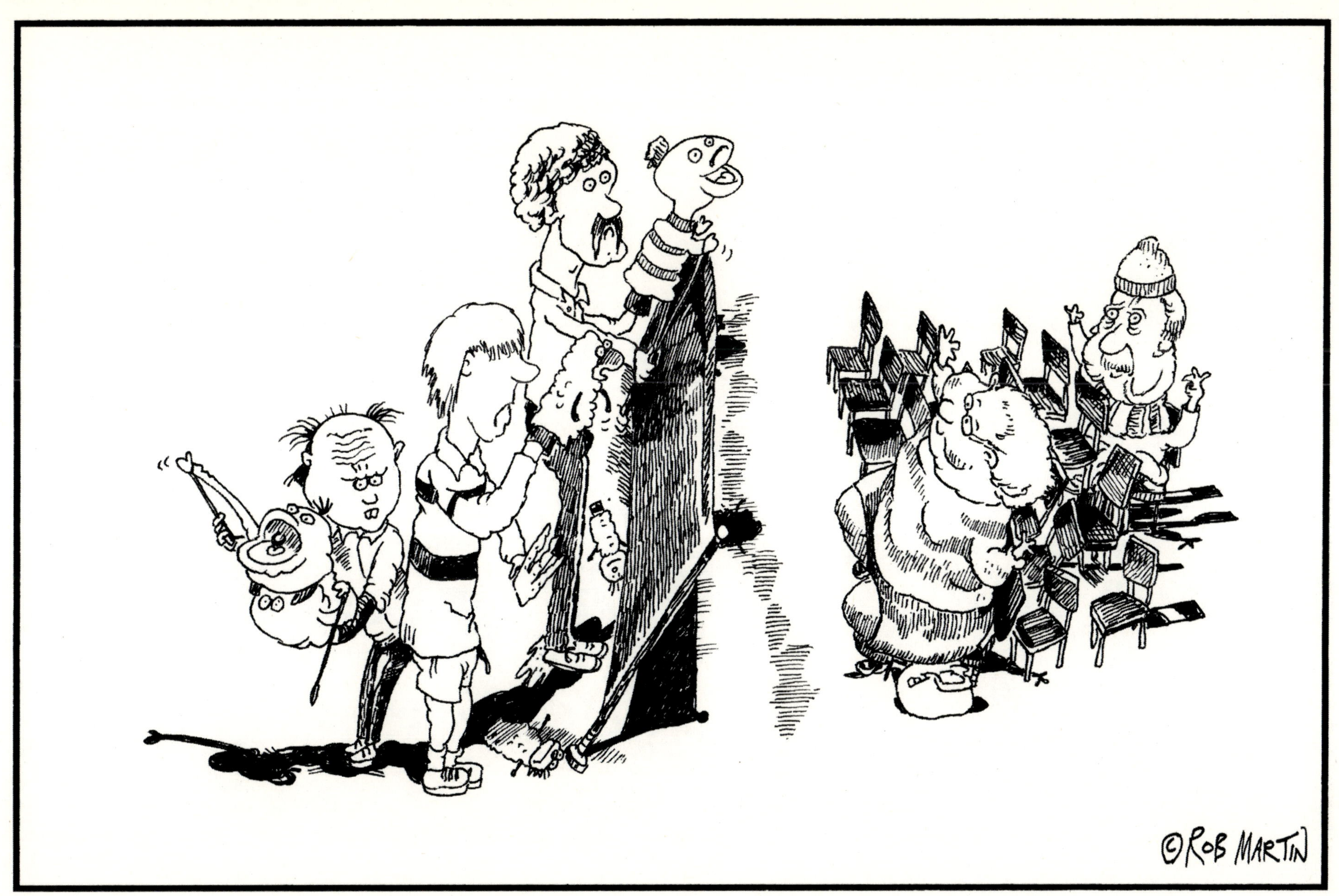

It was at this moment, Duncan realises he doesn't enjoy enjoy puppeteering Zamquox the Lemon anymore.

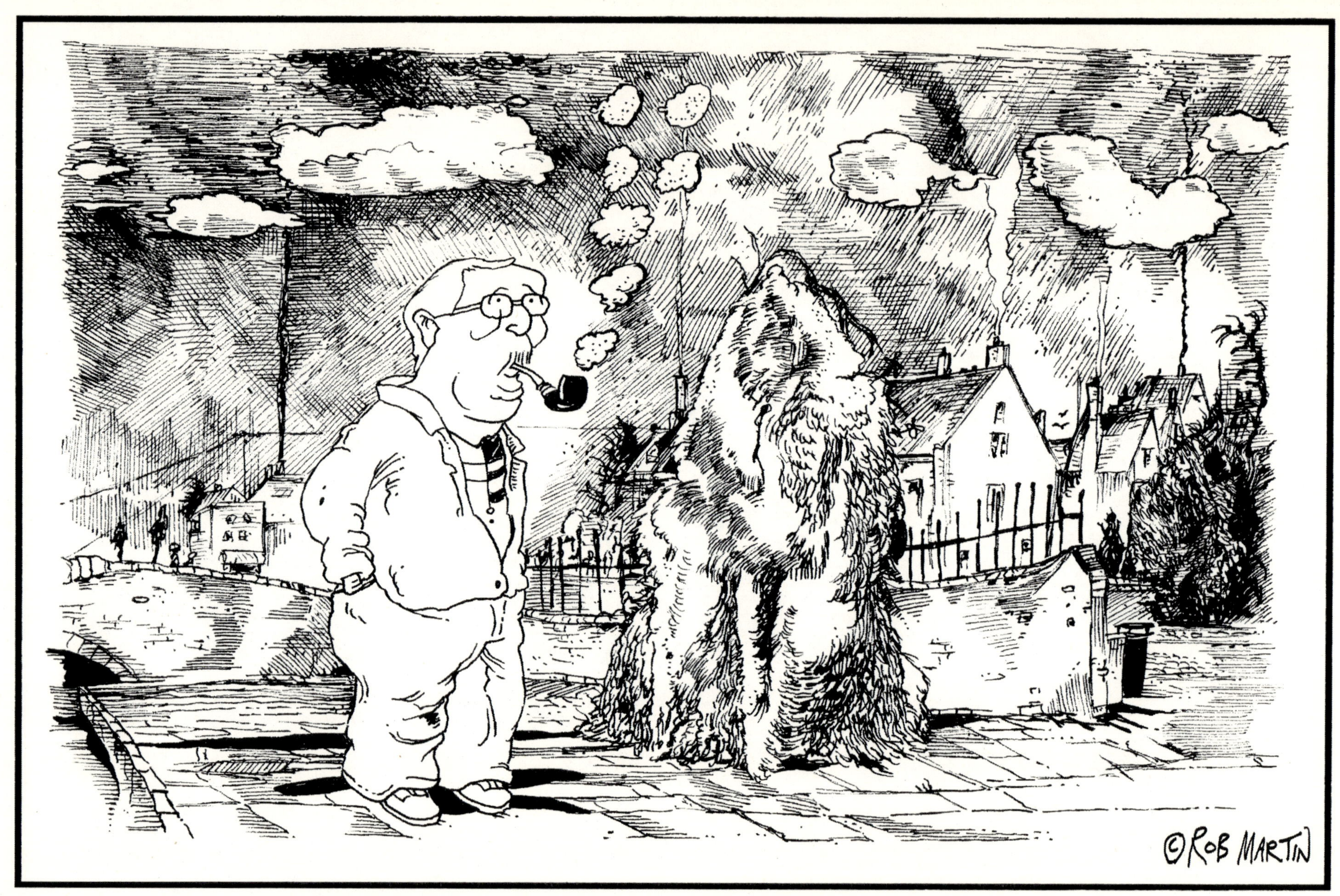

John considers the genus and composition of plants. Mainly he thinks about Dahlia, with its tuberous roots.

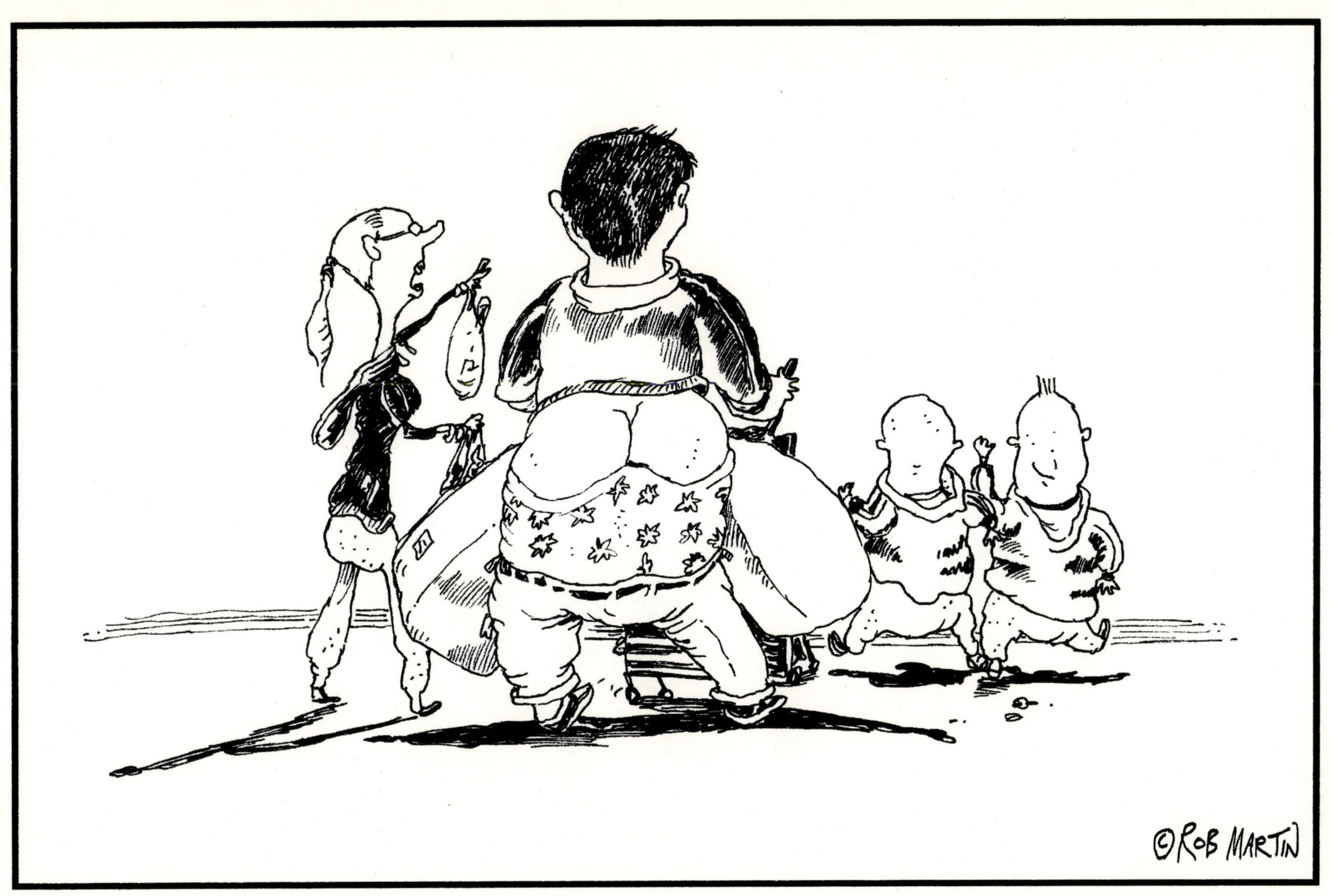

Man with bigger breasts than girlfriend. Pants slip down balancing a mattress.

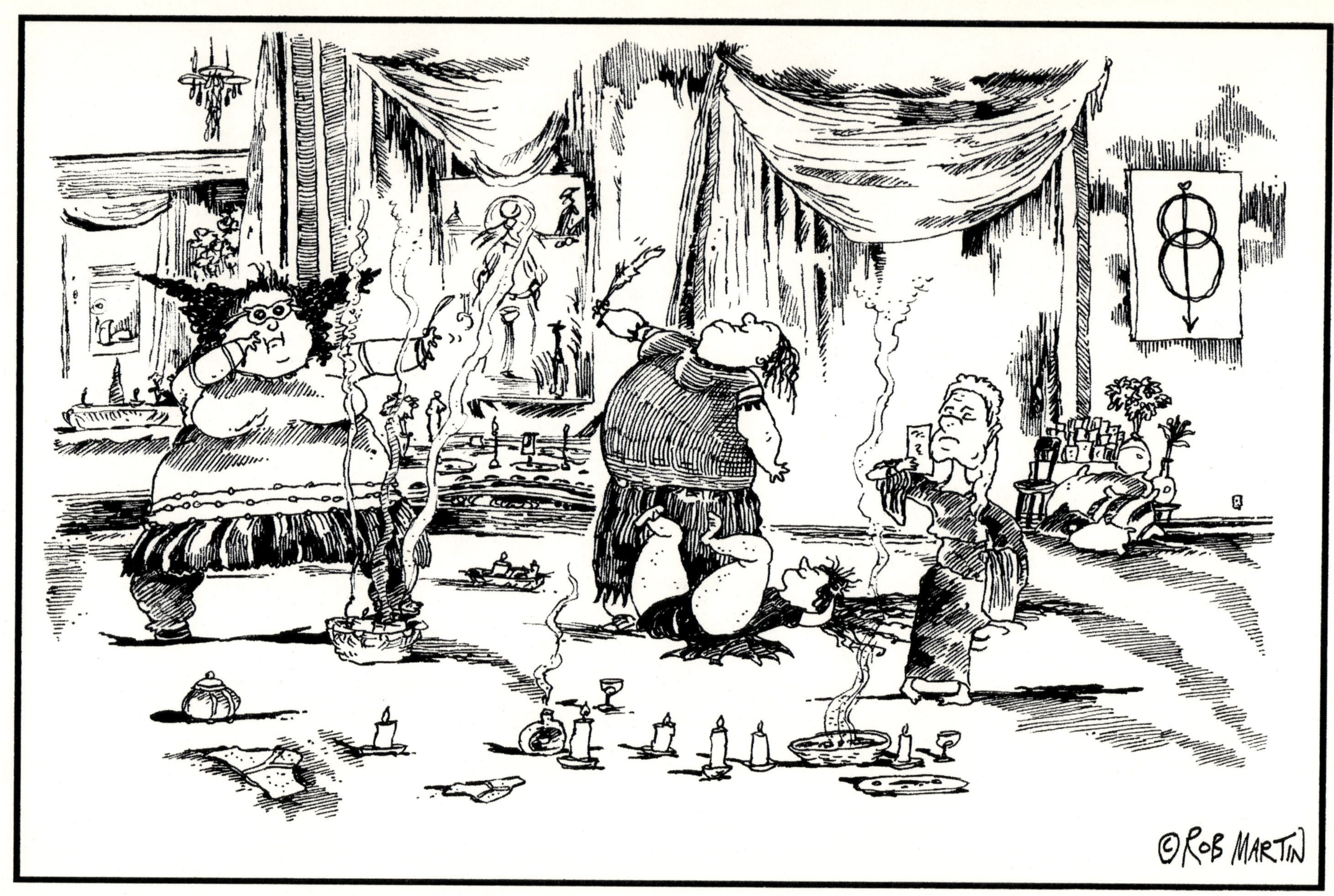

In the Goddess Temple, women and transvestites do a fertility meditation on the bright purple carpet.

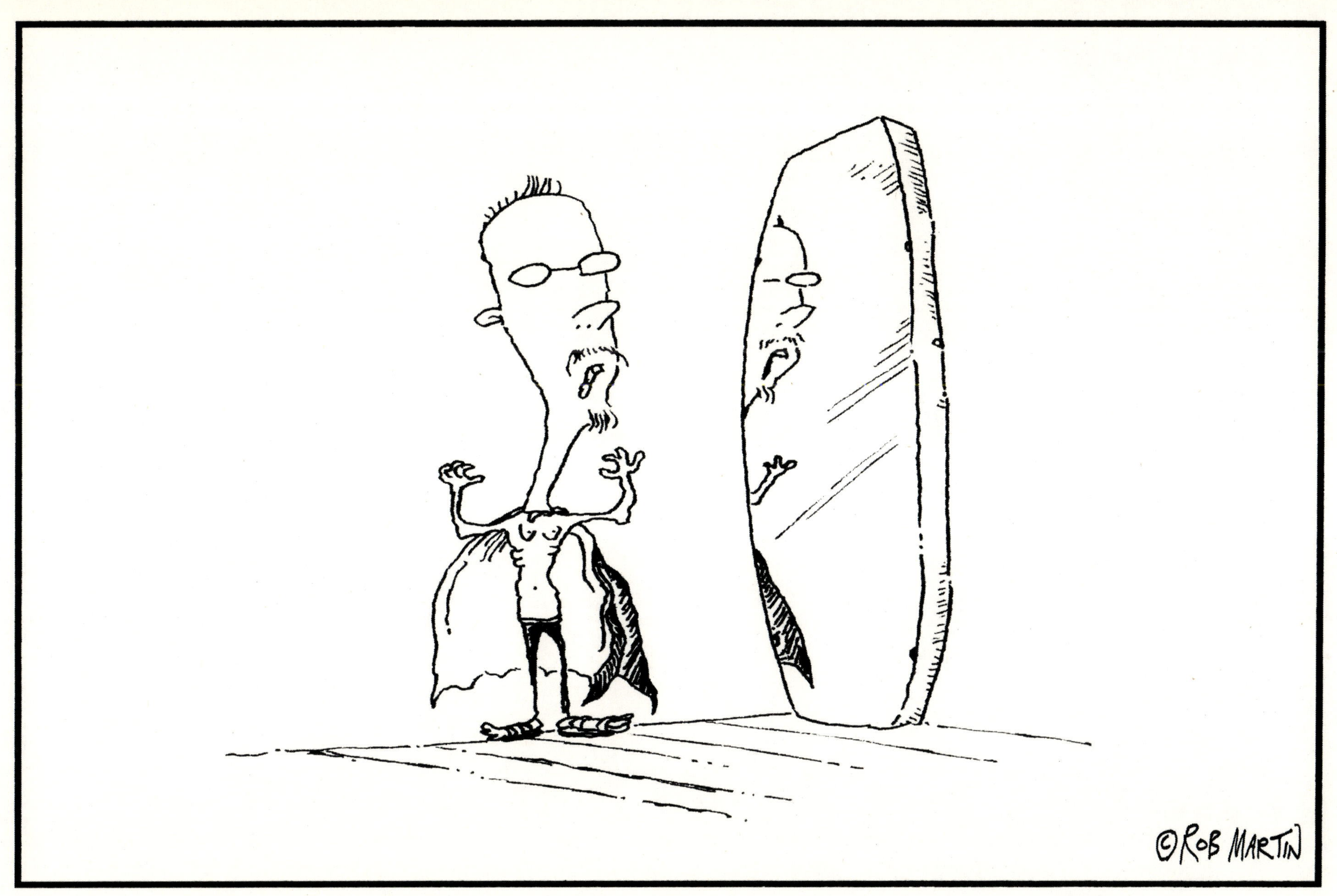

Is it a bird? Is it a plane? No, it's a comic shop owner lacking Vitamin D having delusional flying ideas.

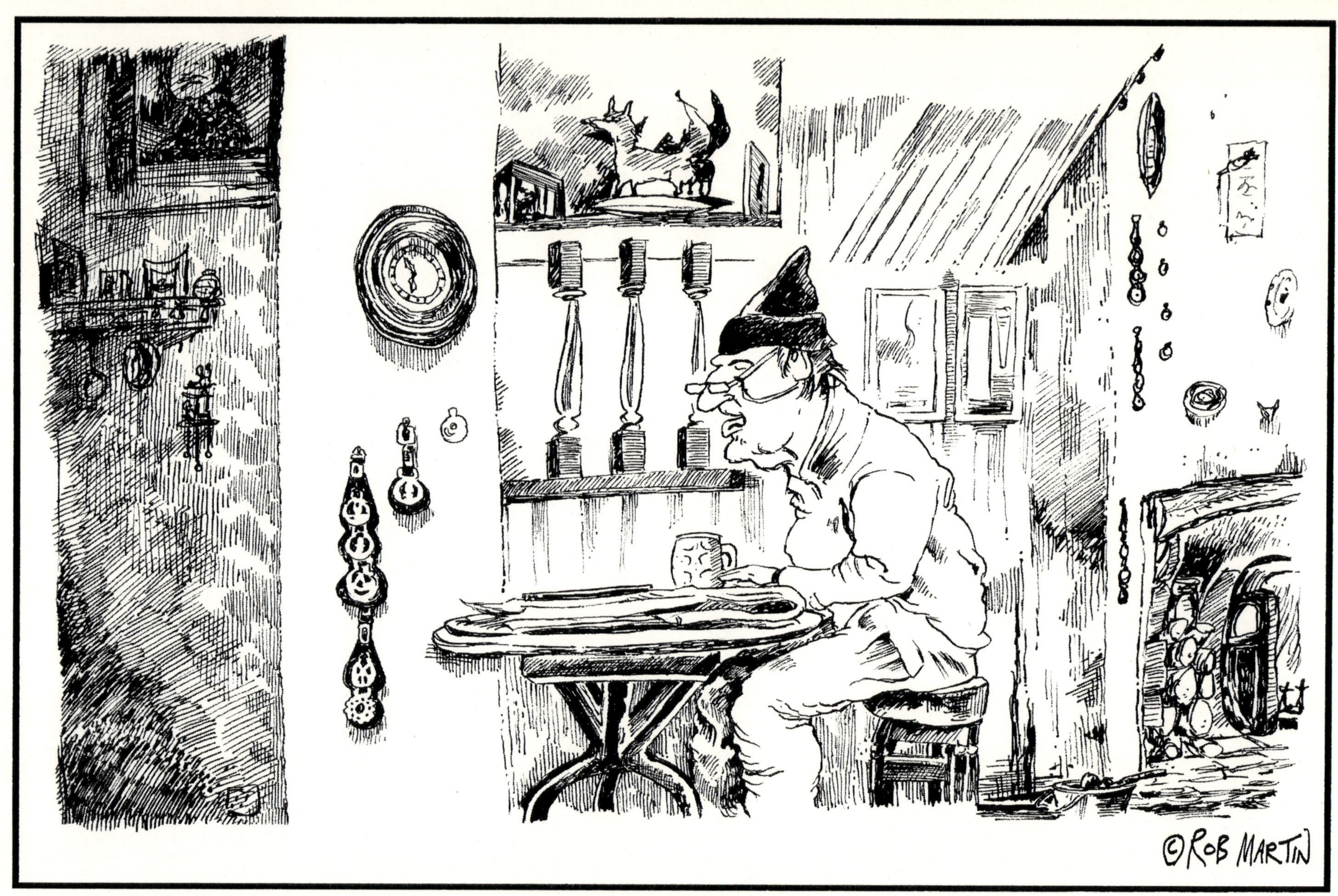

Mr. Stolon considers spoonerism as a word for 4d in the crossword.
"What is e.g. half-warmed fish or half-formed wish?"

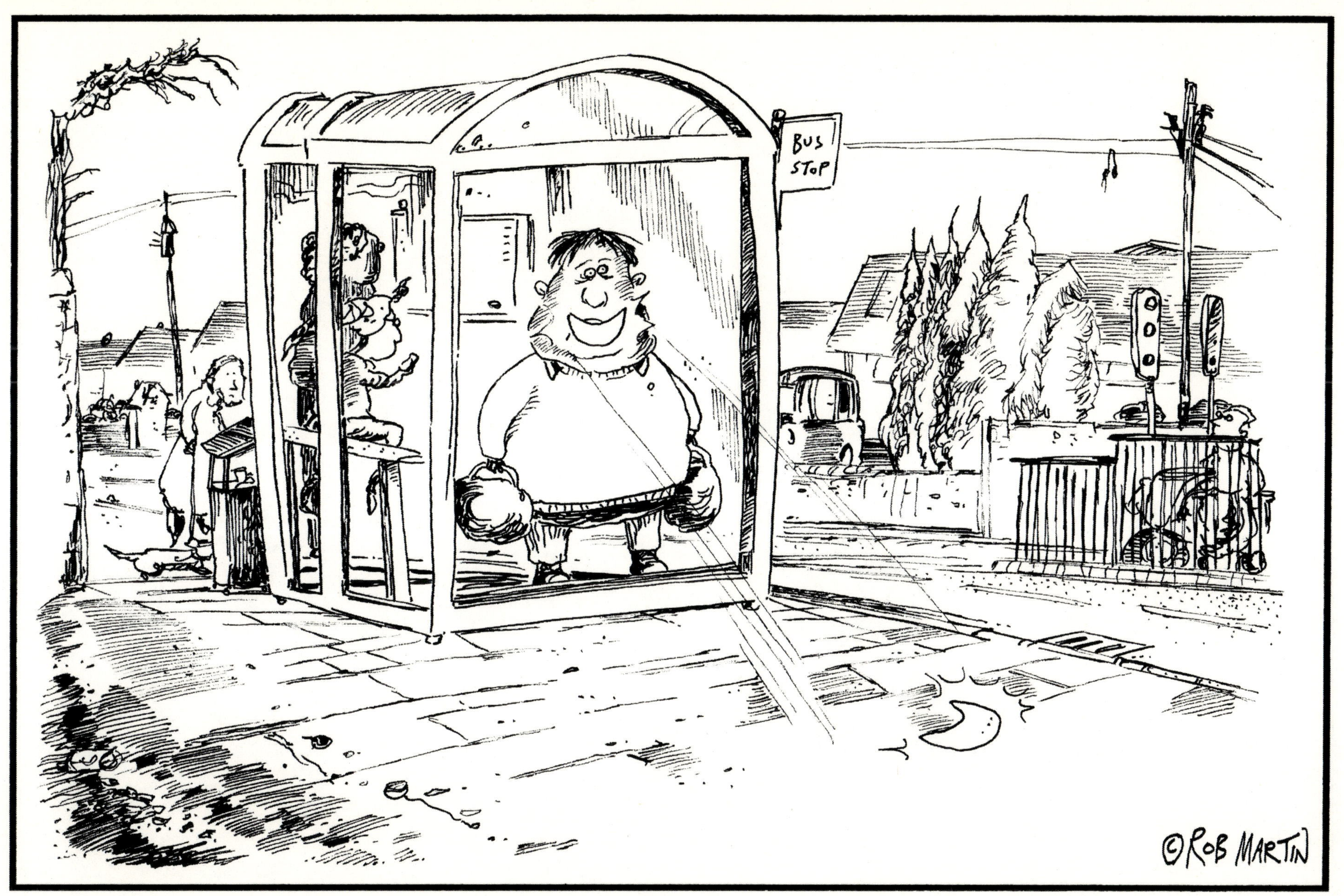

A reflection of melting gum in the noon sun, makes a miserable man appear happy.

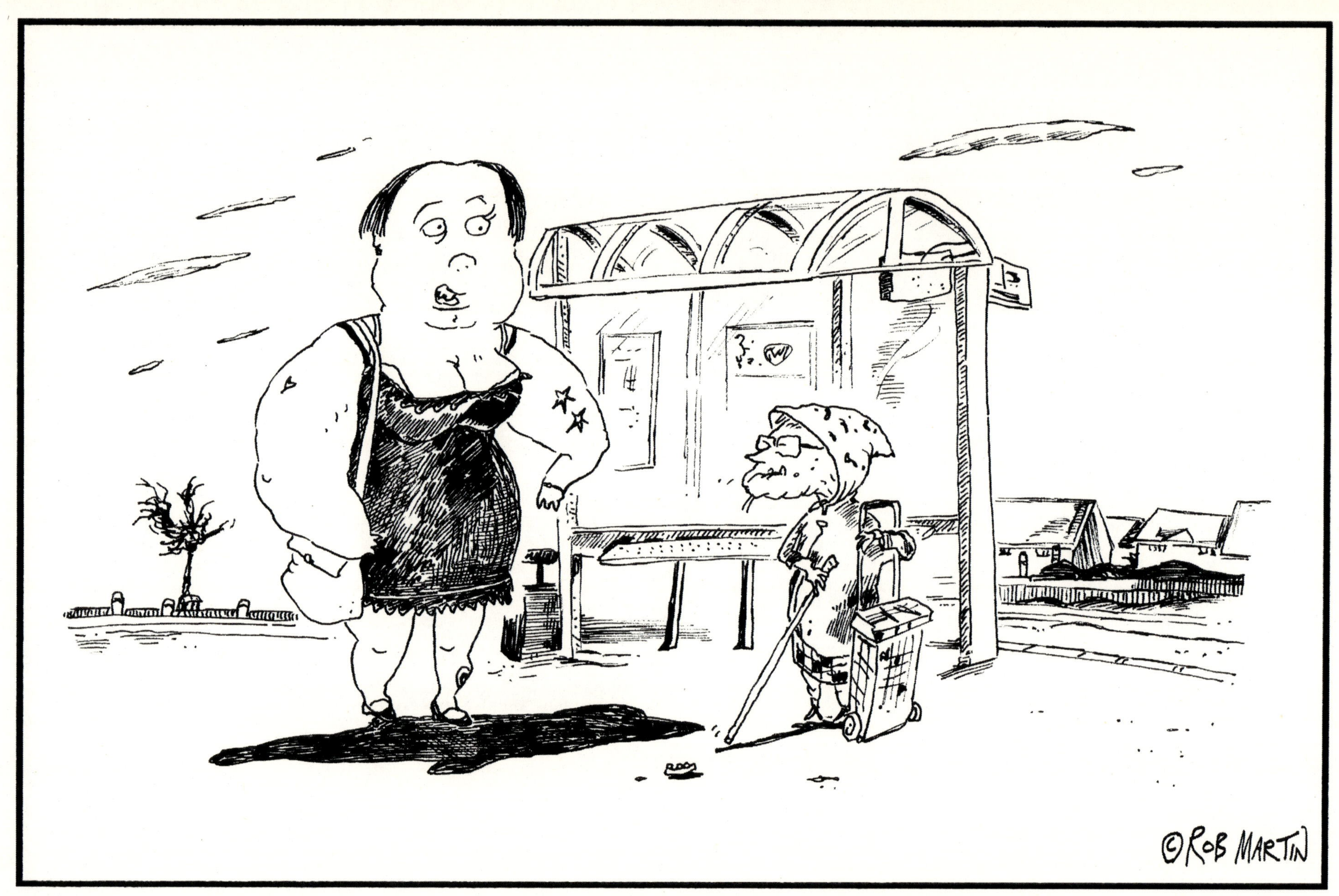

A big girl at a bus stop, talks to a blind old lady.

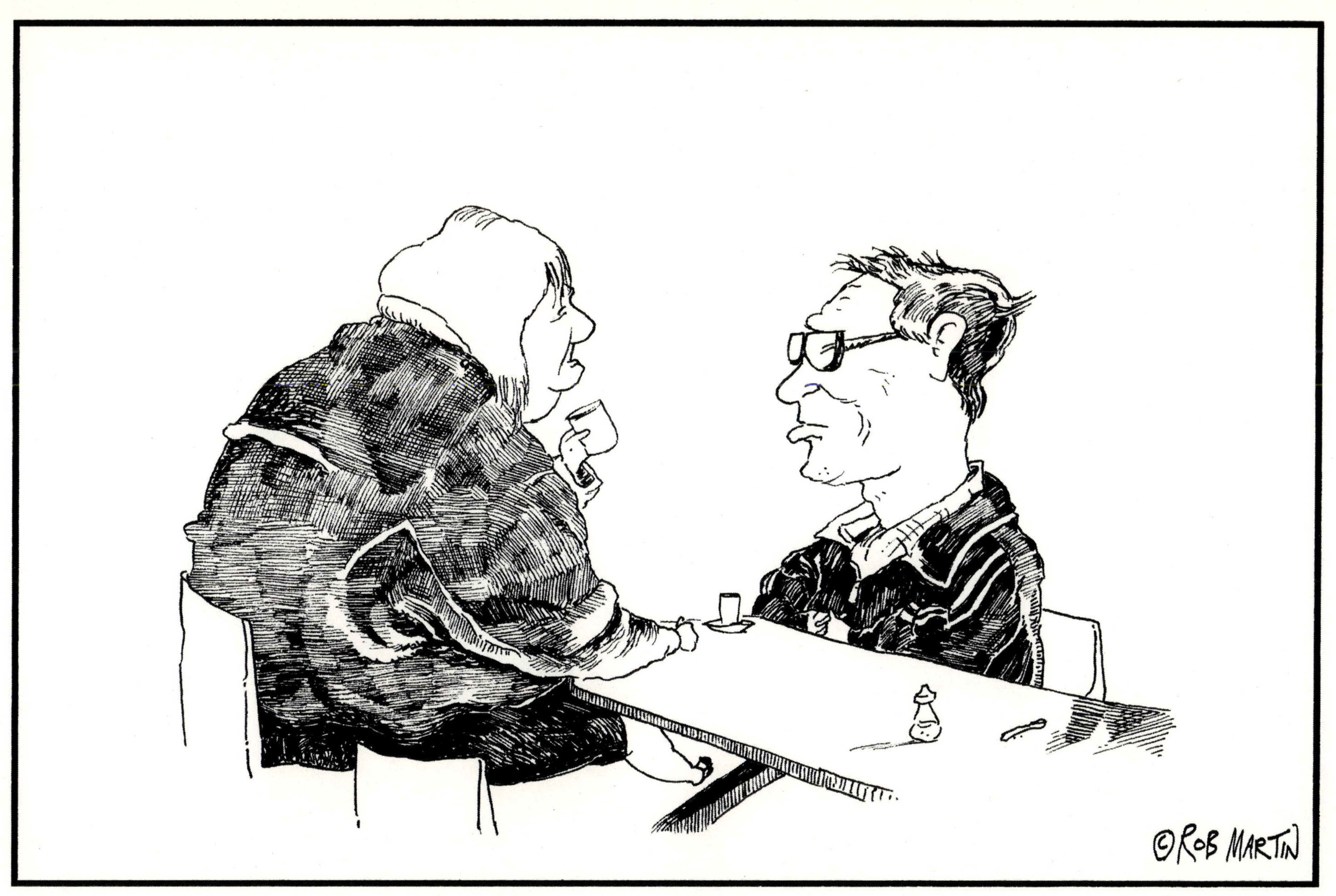

A couple in love, discuss visiting a chocolate factory.

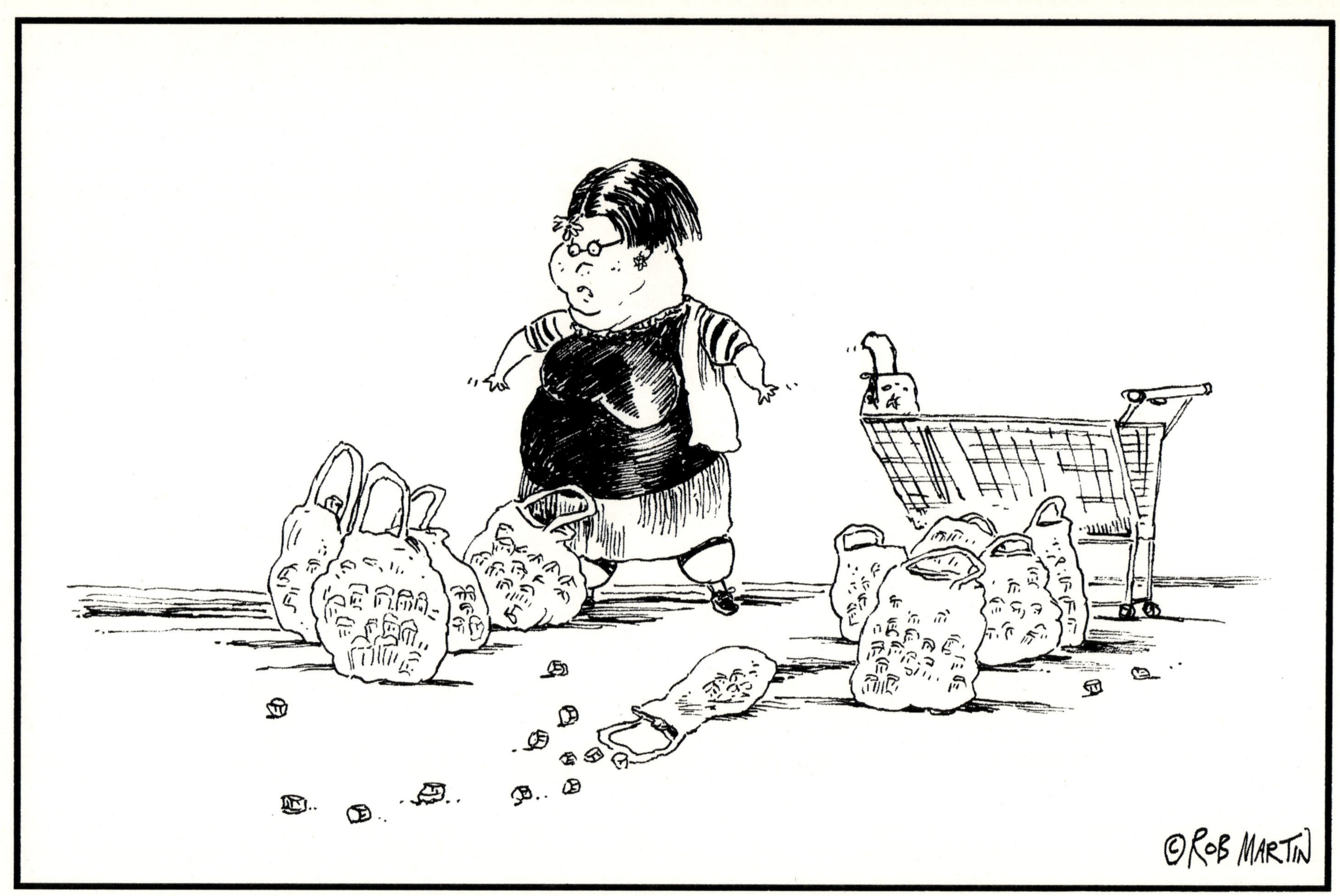

A girl having bought all the muffins in the supermarket, has trouble thinking how to get them all home.

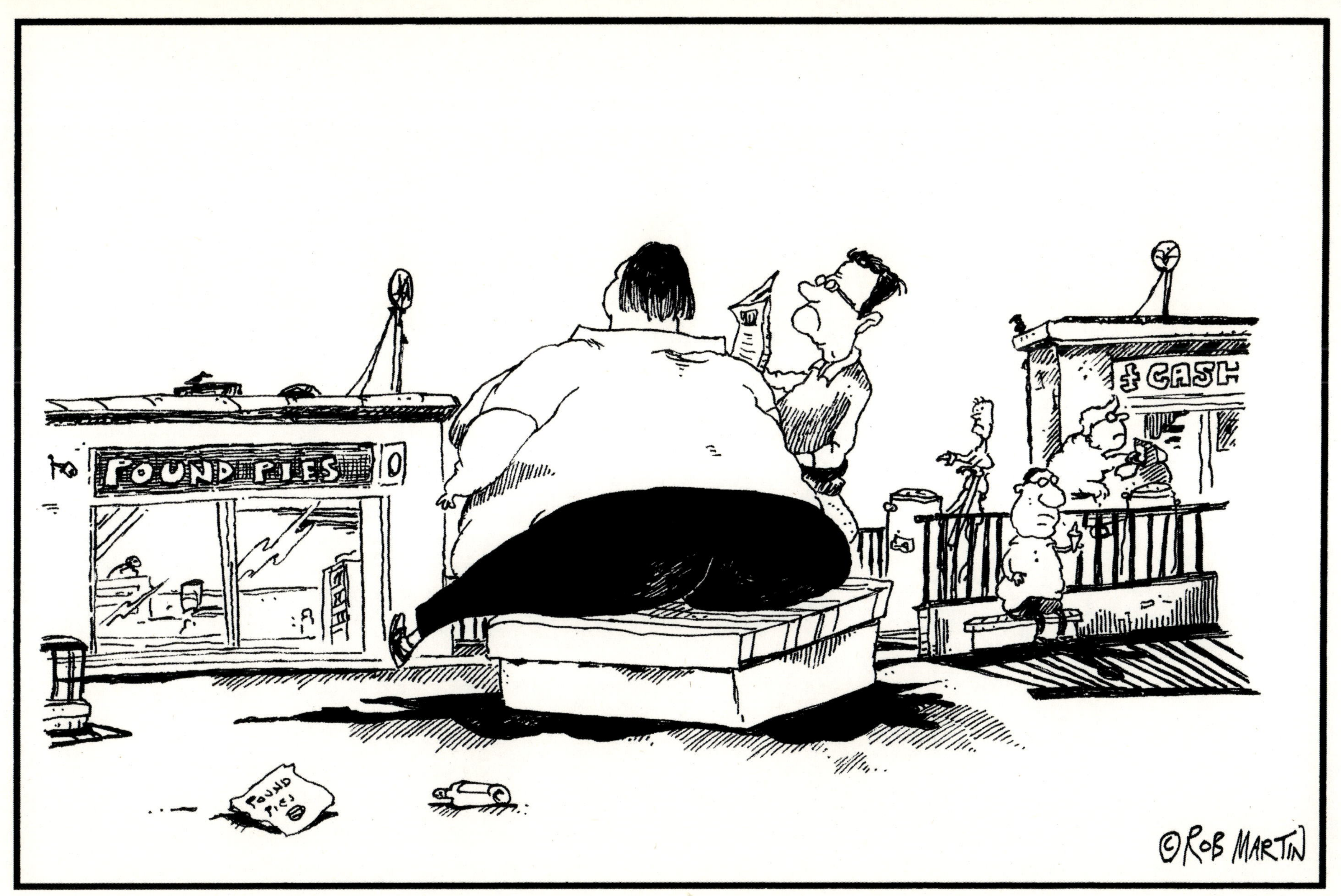

Jerry and Merri consider two pies for a pound.

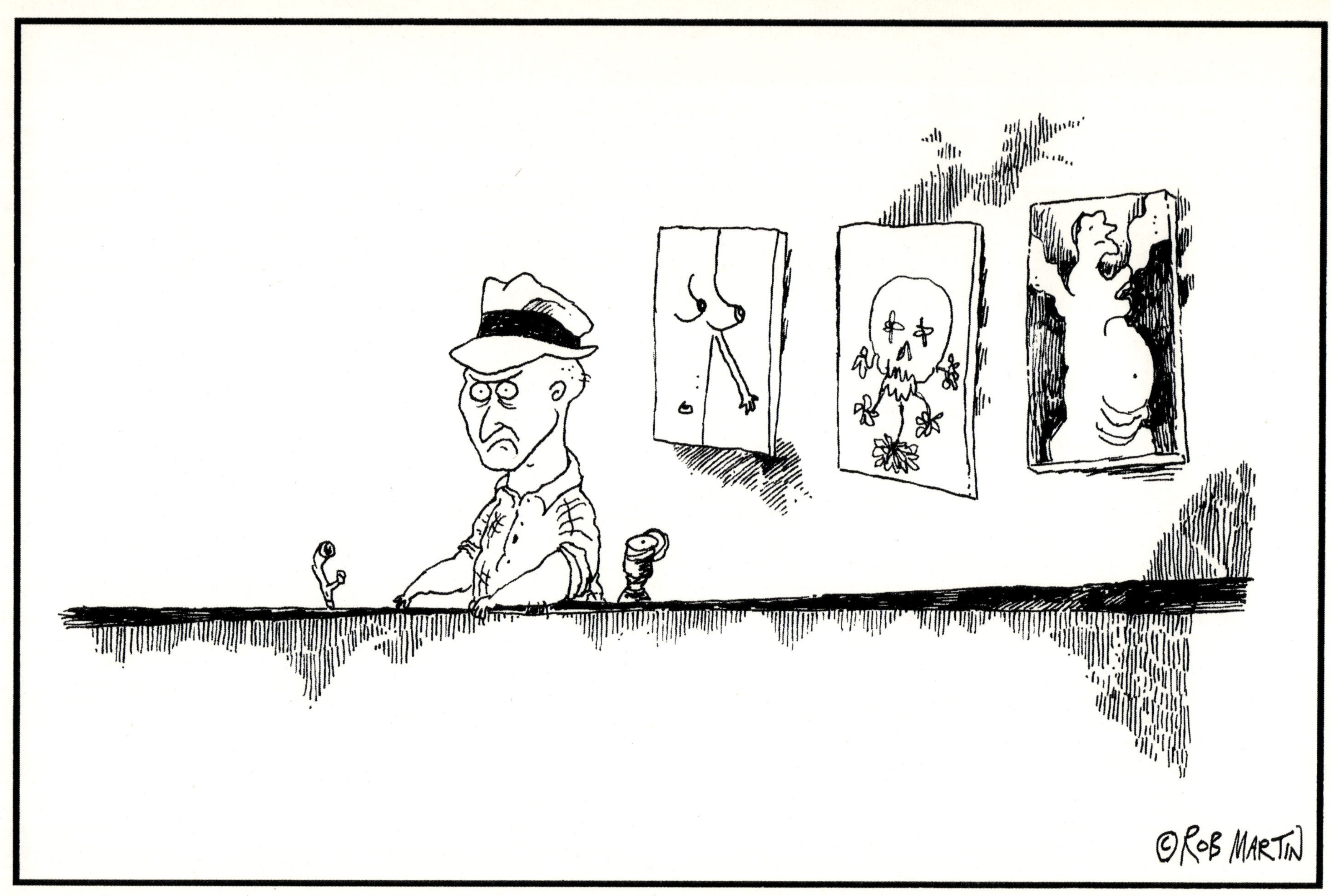

Angry artist Andy becomes disgruntled with his pendulous canvases.

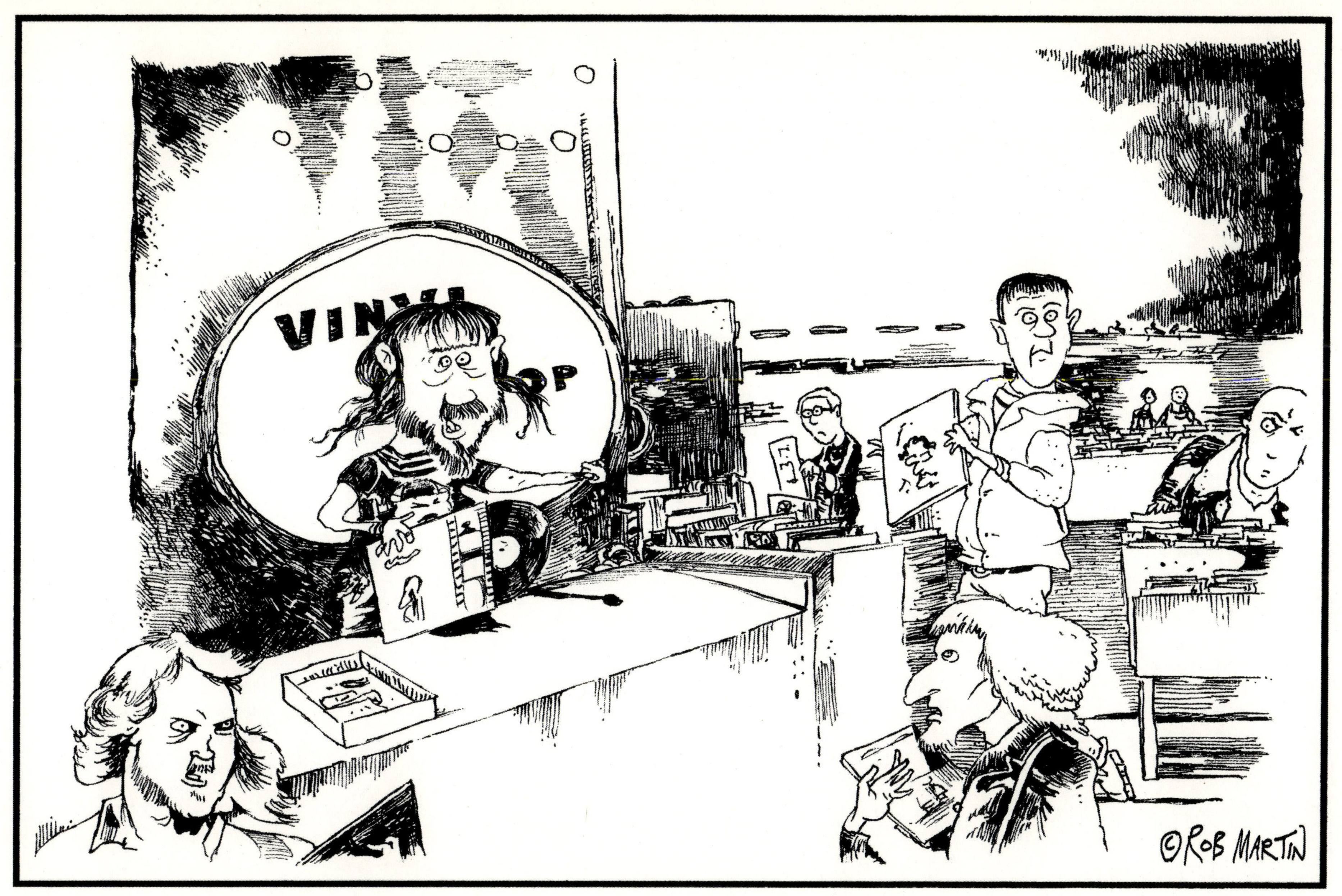

"Can you please not use offensive language!" Says Rodwell, failed rock star working on the vinyl counter.

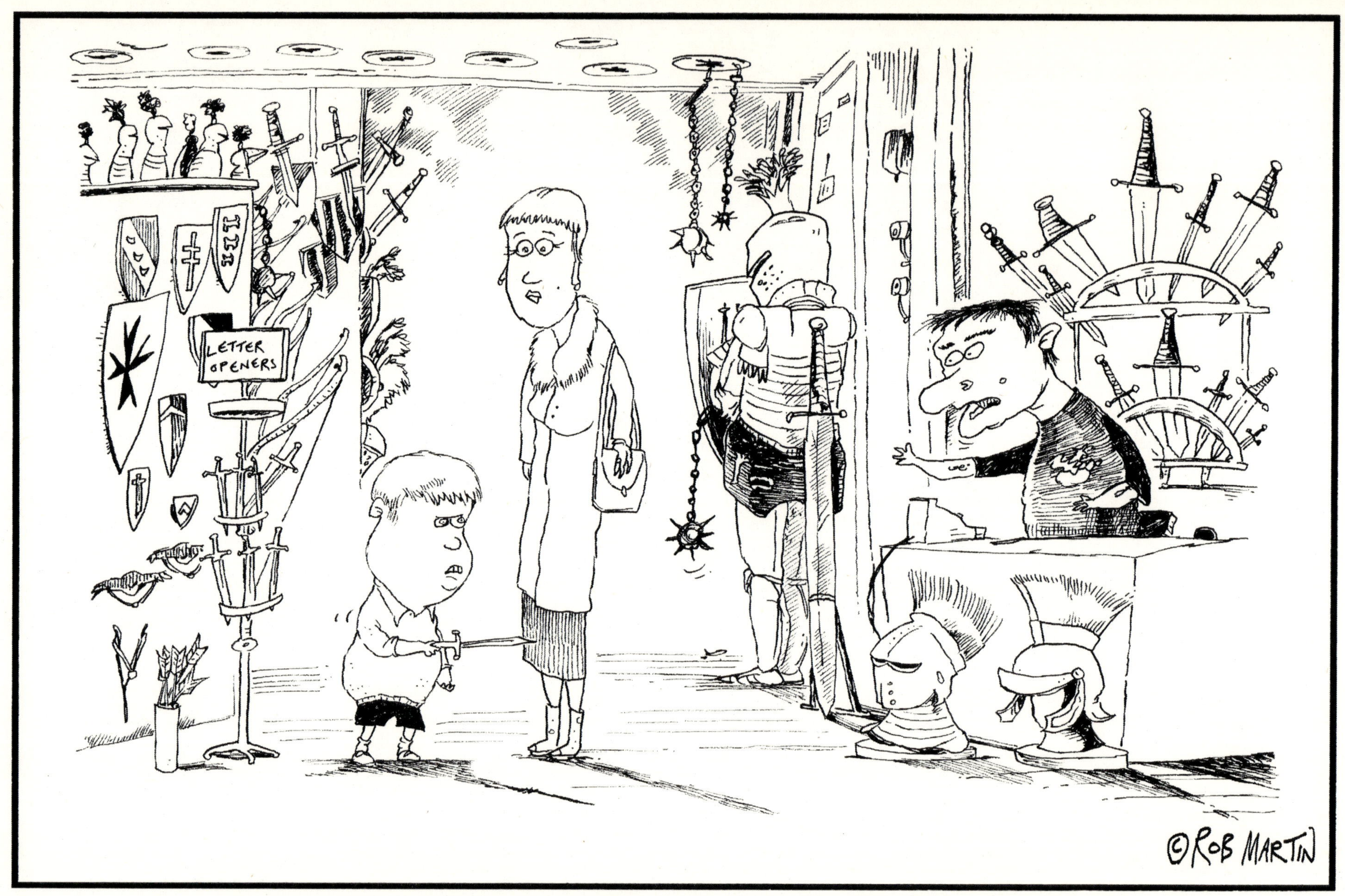

A shop assistant selling medieval items gets worried that he may be disemboweled by a small spoilt boy waving a letter opener.

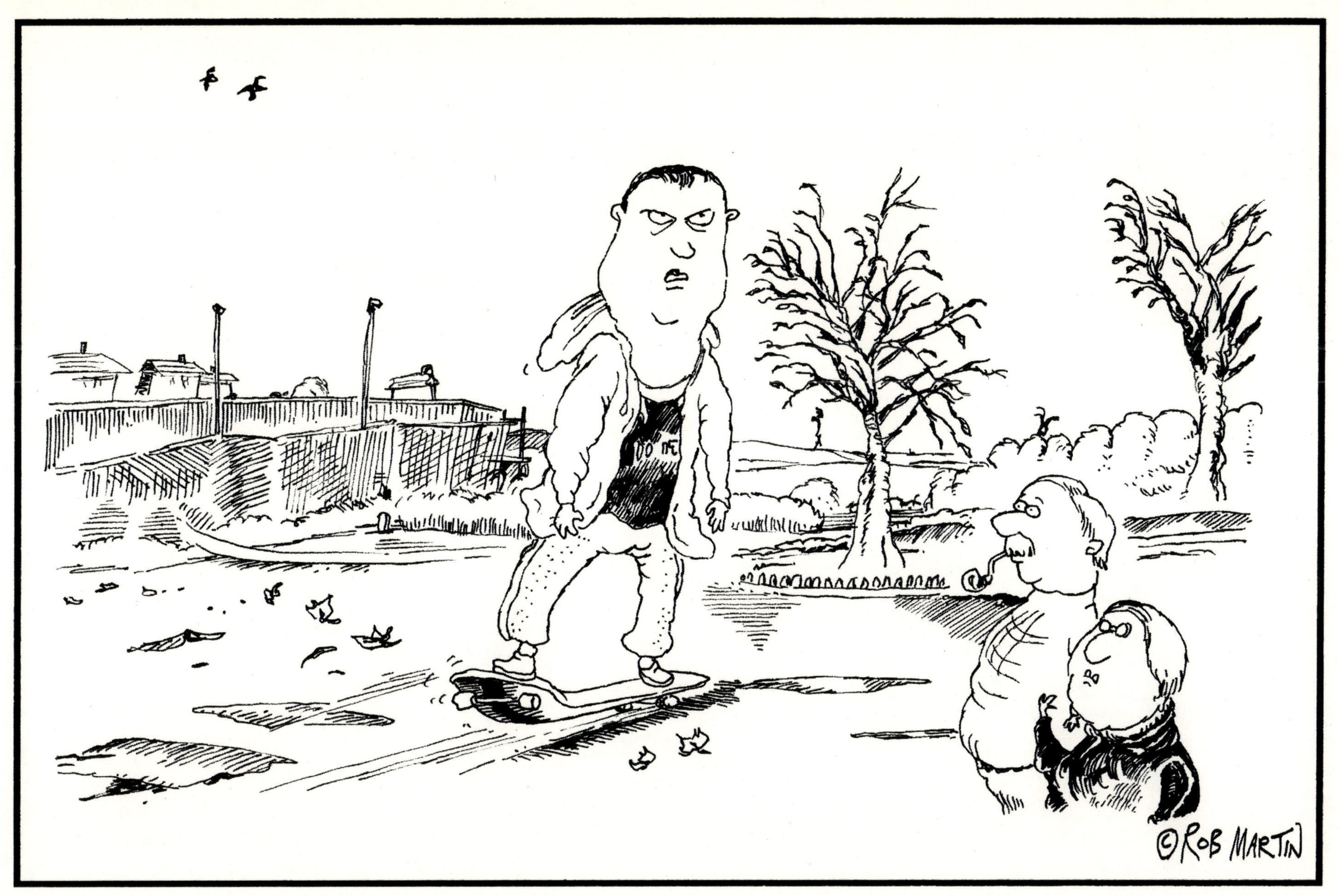

A 31 year old man on a skateboard tries hard to think why the man with the pipe just called him a "Man brat!"

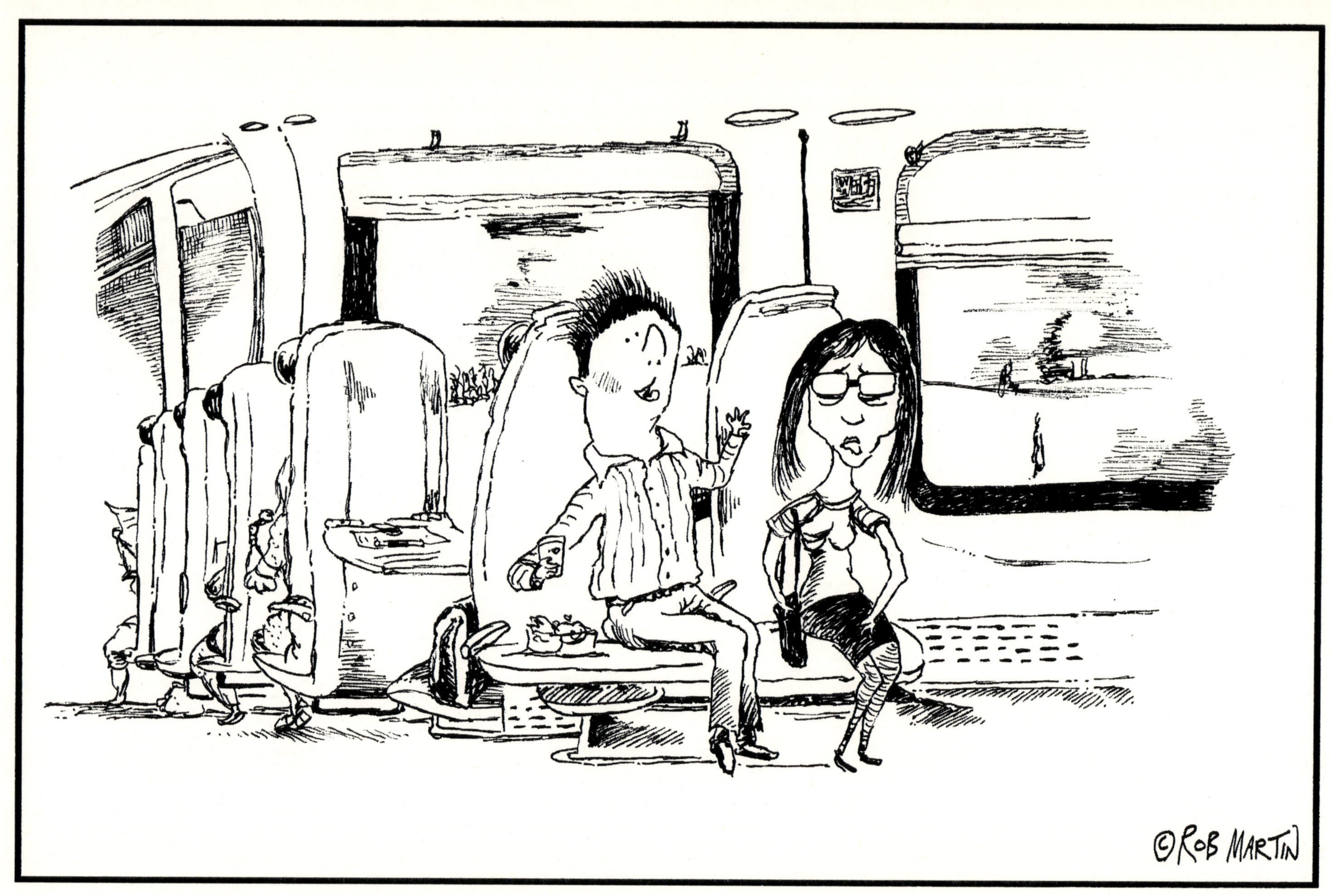

On the train to London, Tarquin tells his P.A. of the miracles of potty training.

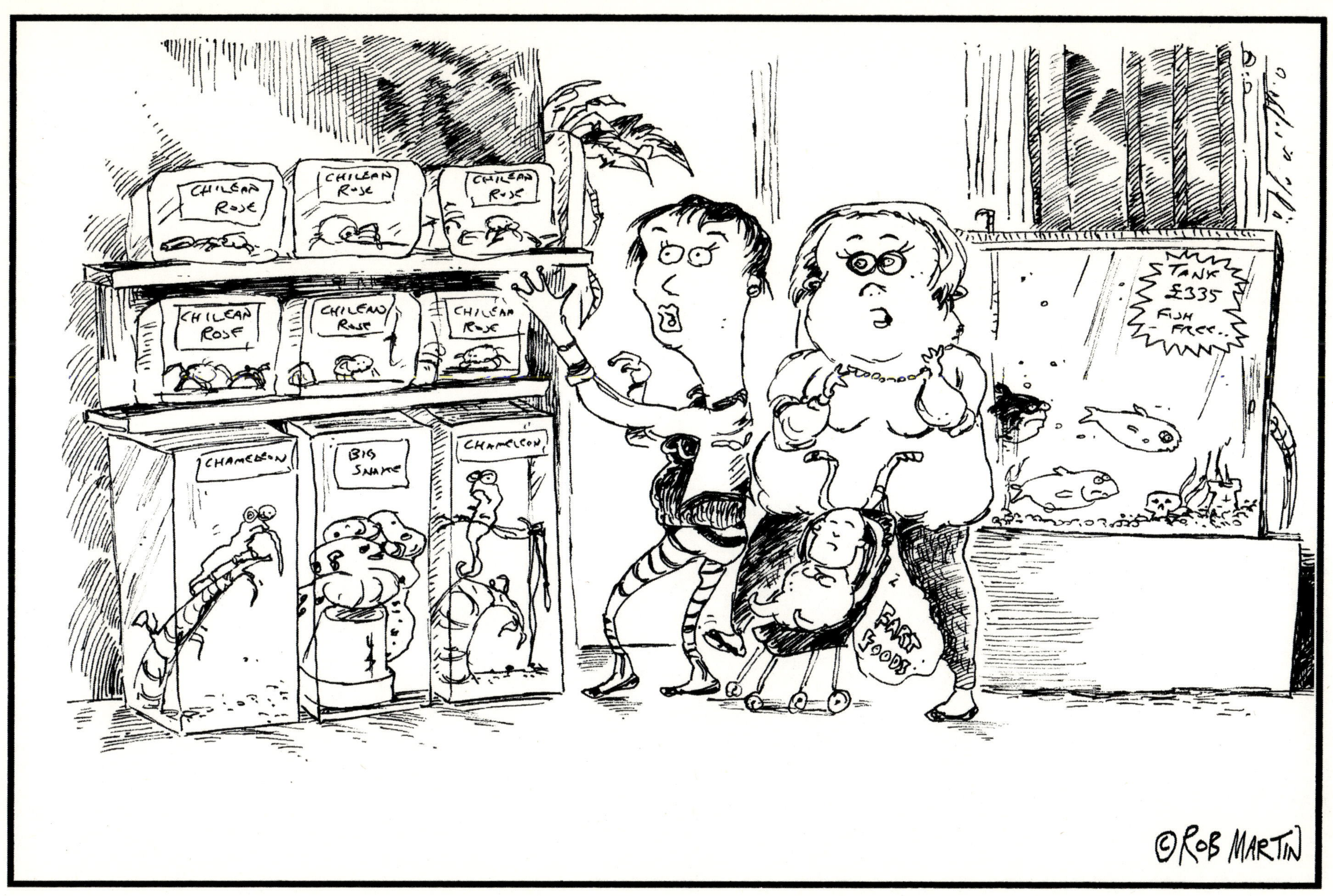

In the pet shop, a woman freaks whilst looking at a Tarantula.
But still rubs her hand on the tank's glass.

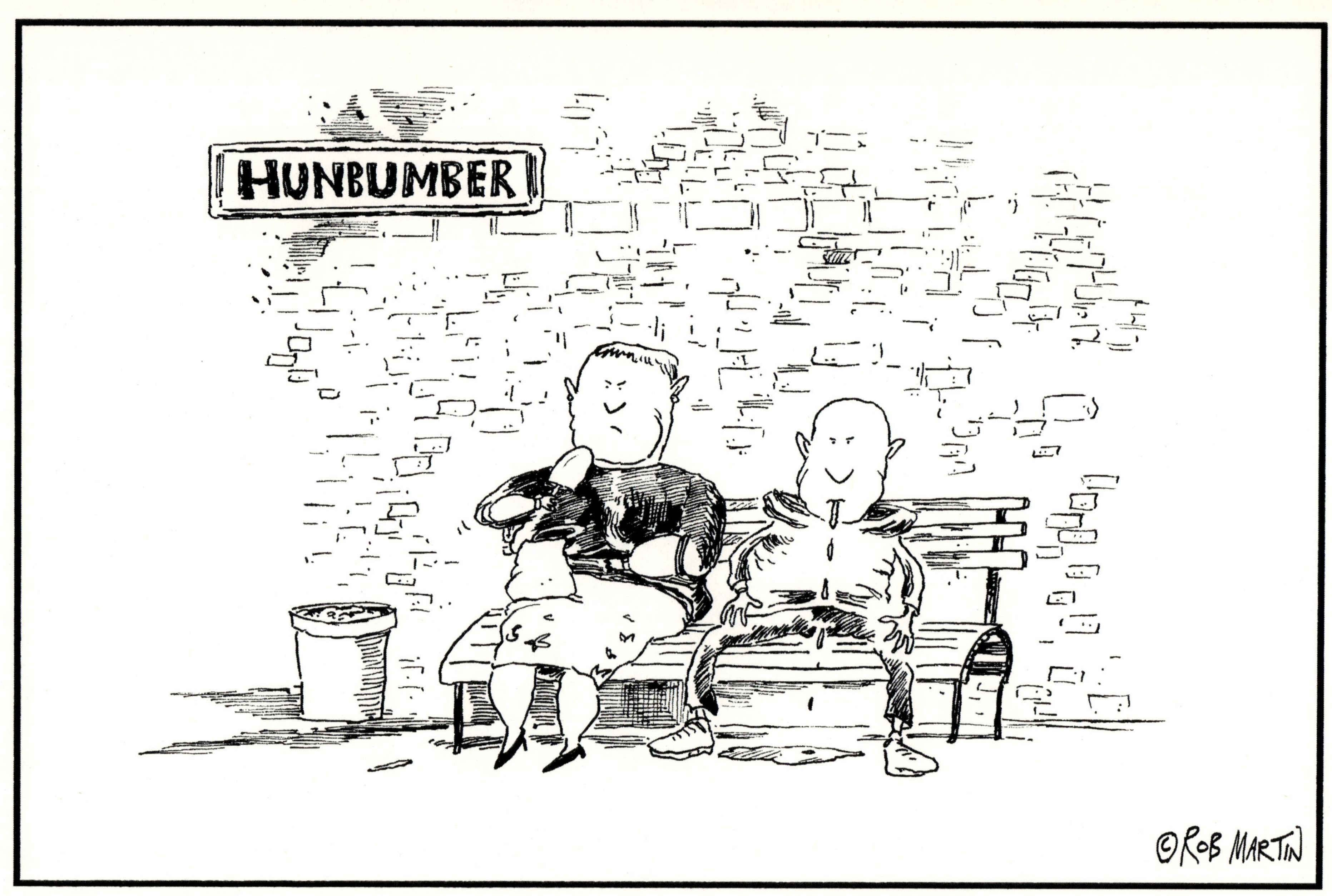

Mother and son wait for a train.

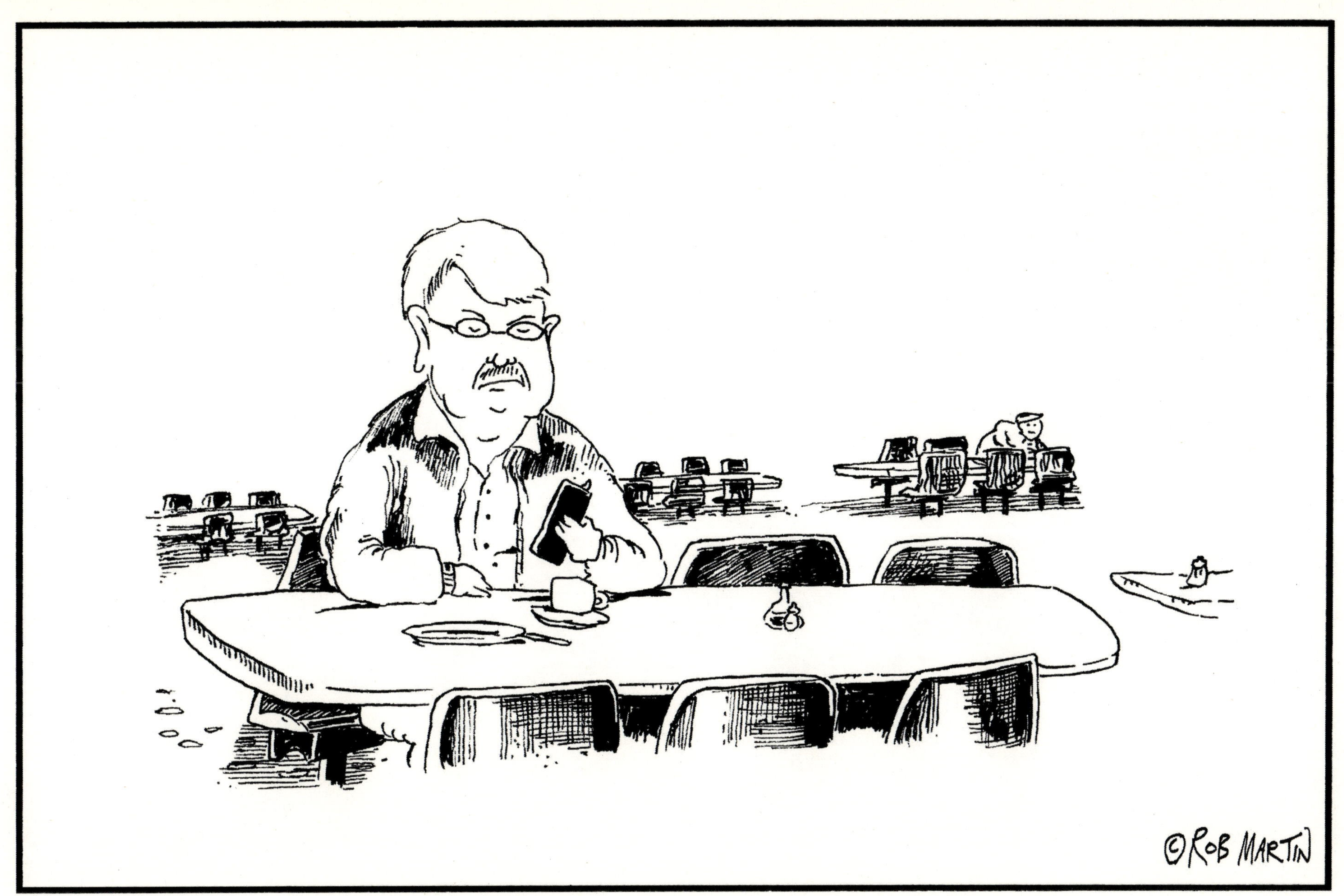

Mr. Finchley reads a random text which asks,
'Are you shrivelled Prawn balls?':)

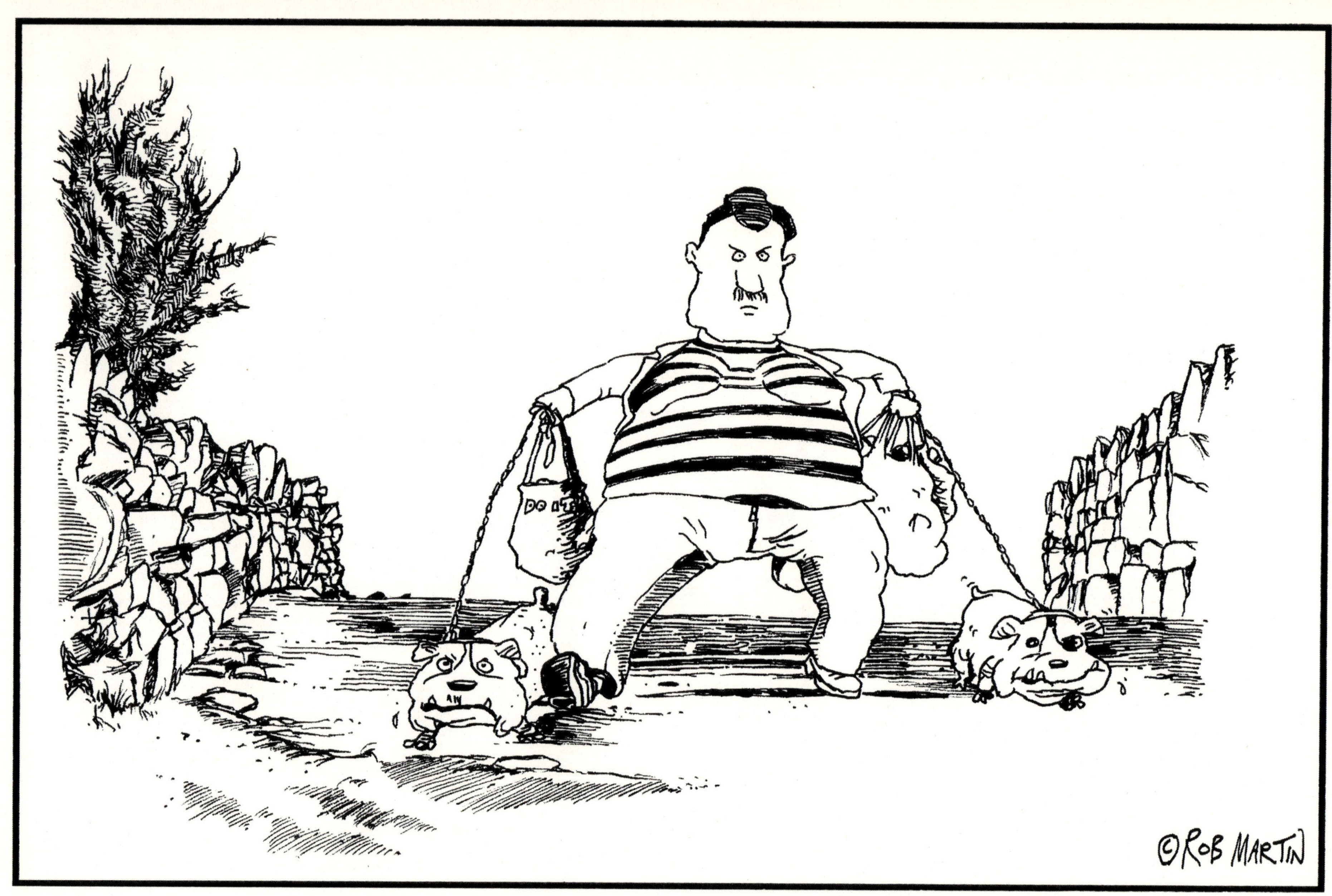

"Don't you think I'm hard?", thinks Alan.

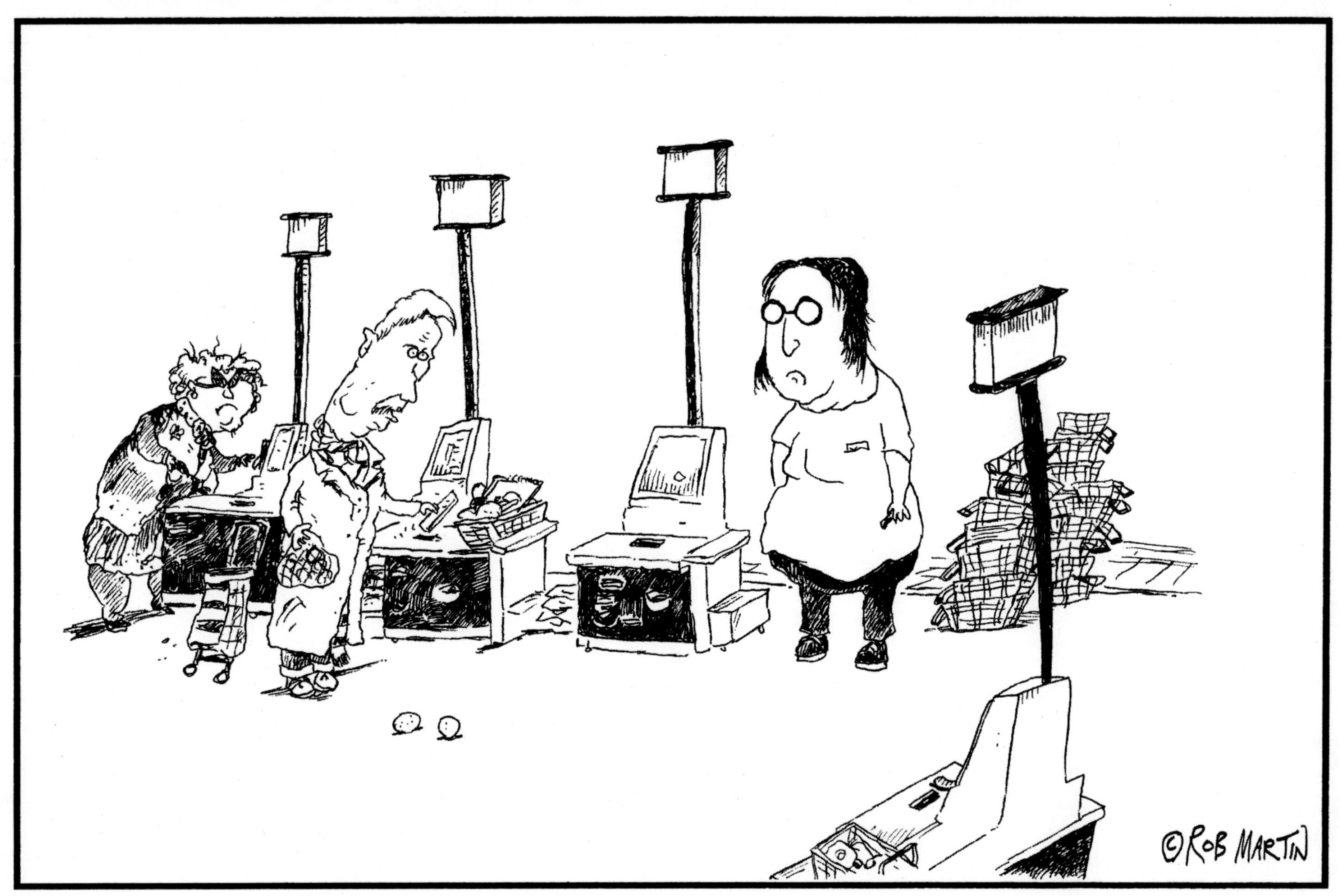

The lone existence of the bagging area operative.

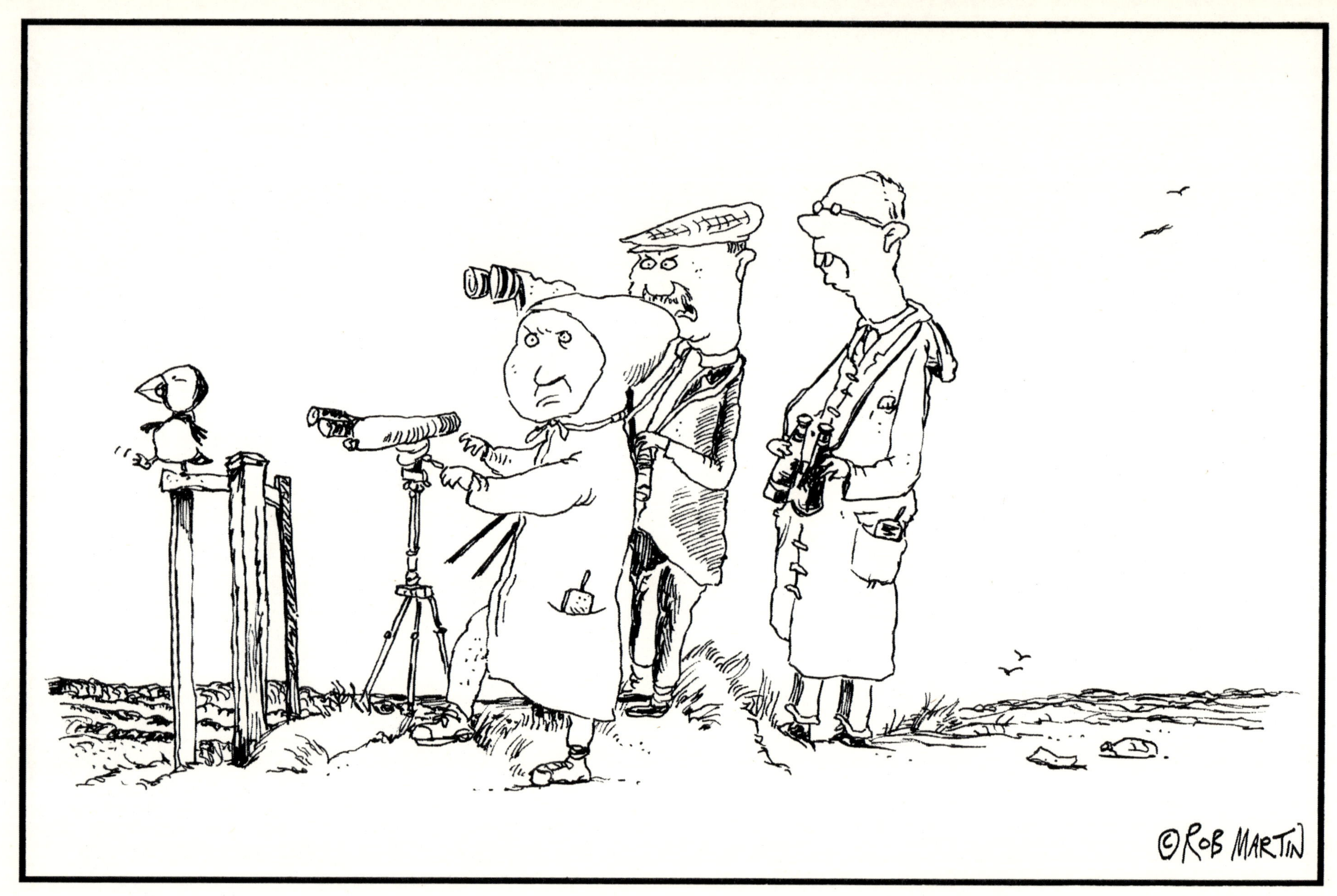

A group of birdspotters get angry trying to spot a rare bird.

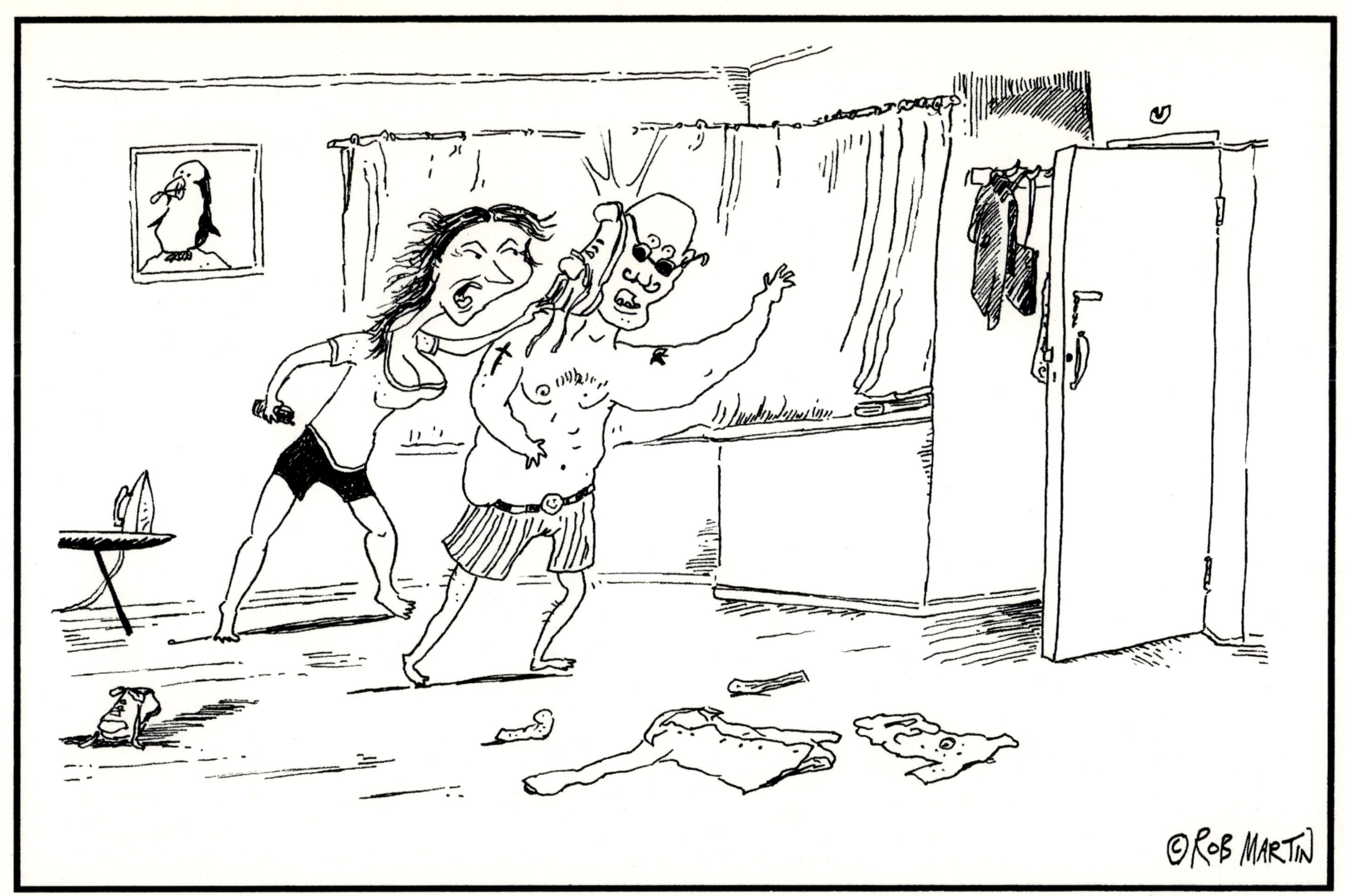

Sally smacks Leo in the head with his size 10 shoe after reading a text from his work colleague Diane. A text which ended in 'Mwah xxx'.

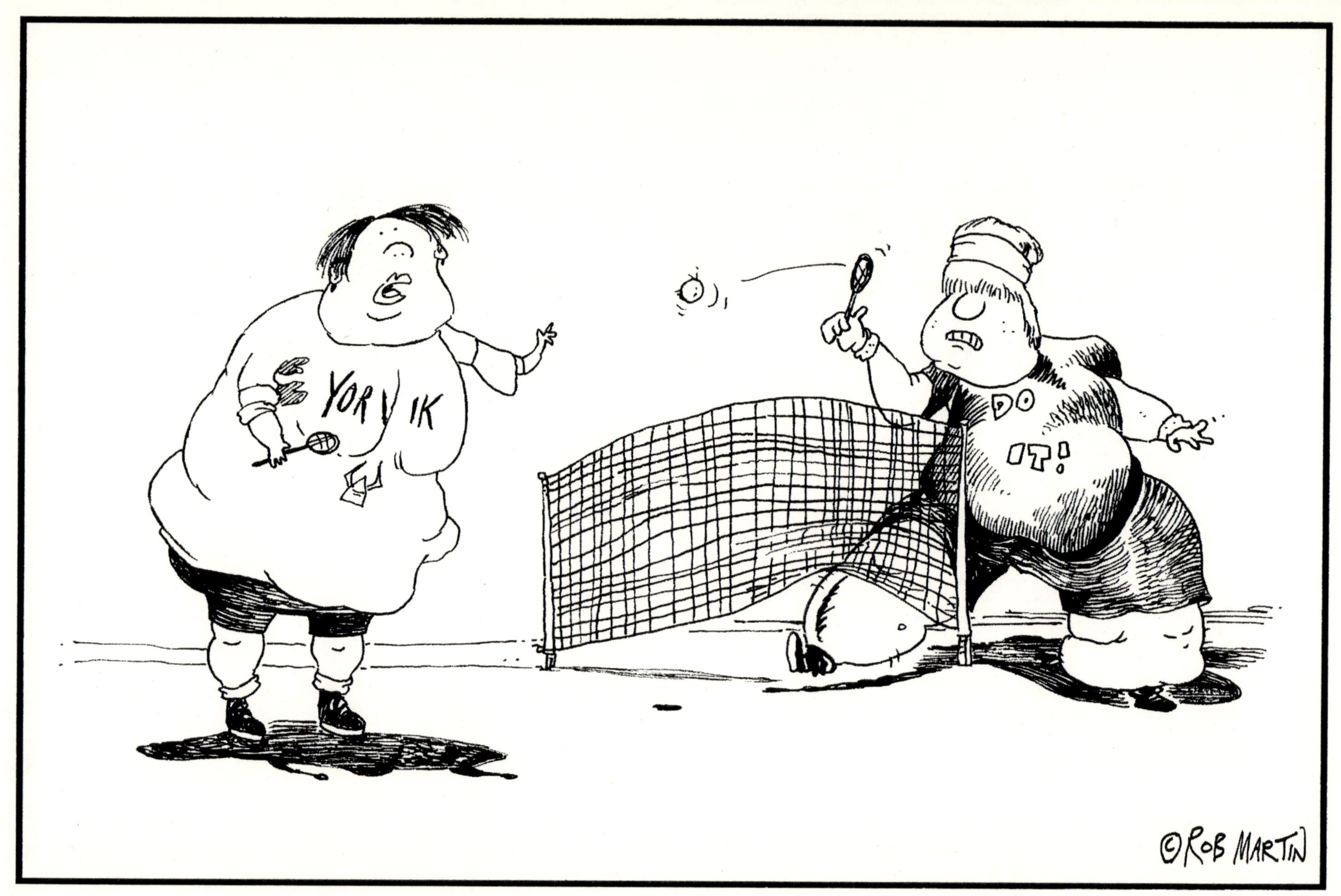

Cardiovascular exercise after eating 15 jam tarts,
4 beefburgers, a chocolate finger and a block of tofu.

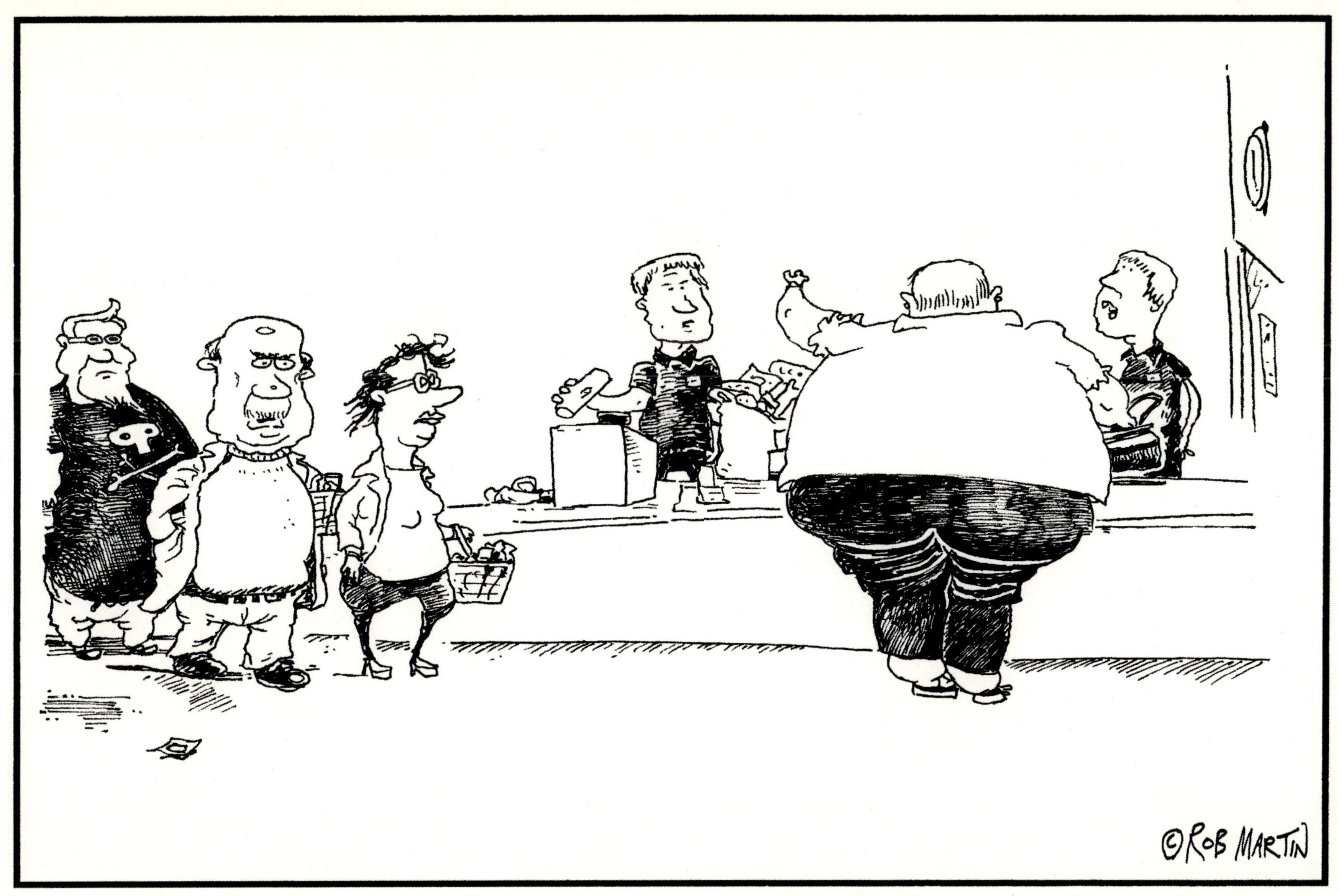

With a morbid fixation, Bill stares and thinks, "Look at that arse!"

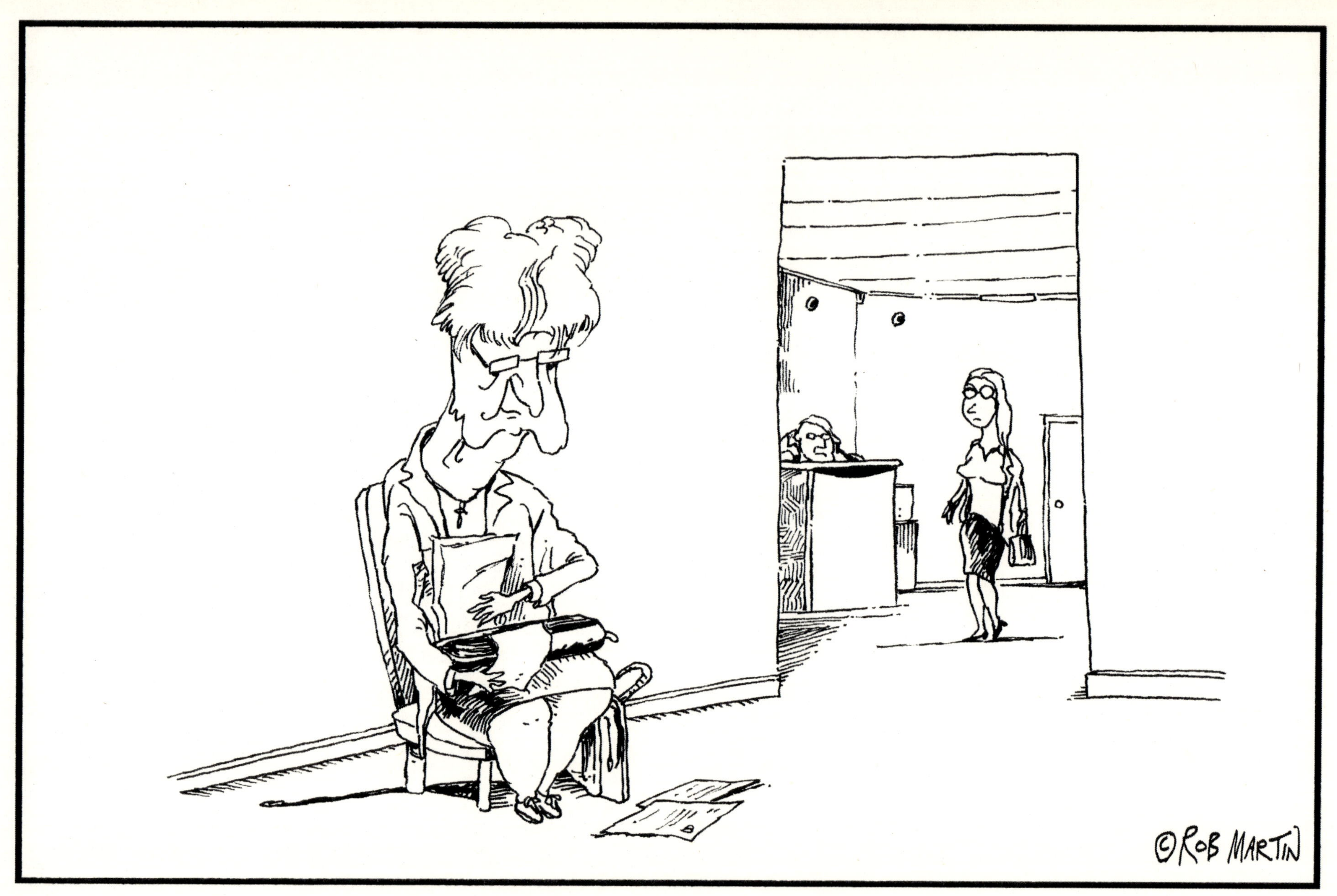

57 year old Agnes Thribblebobble prepares her notes for a job interview at the meat factory.

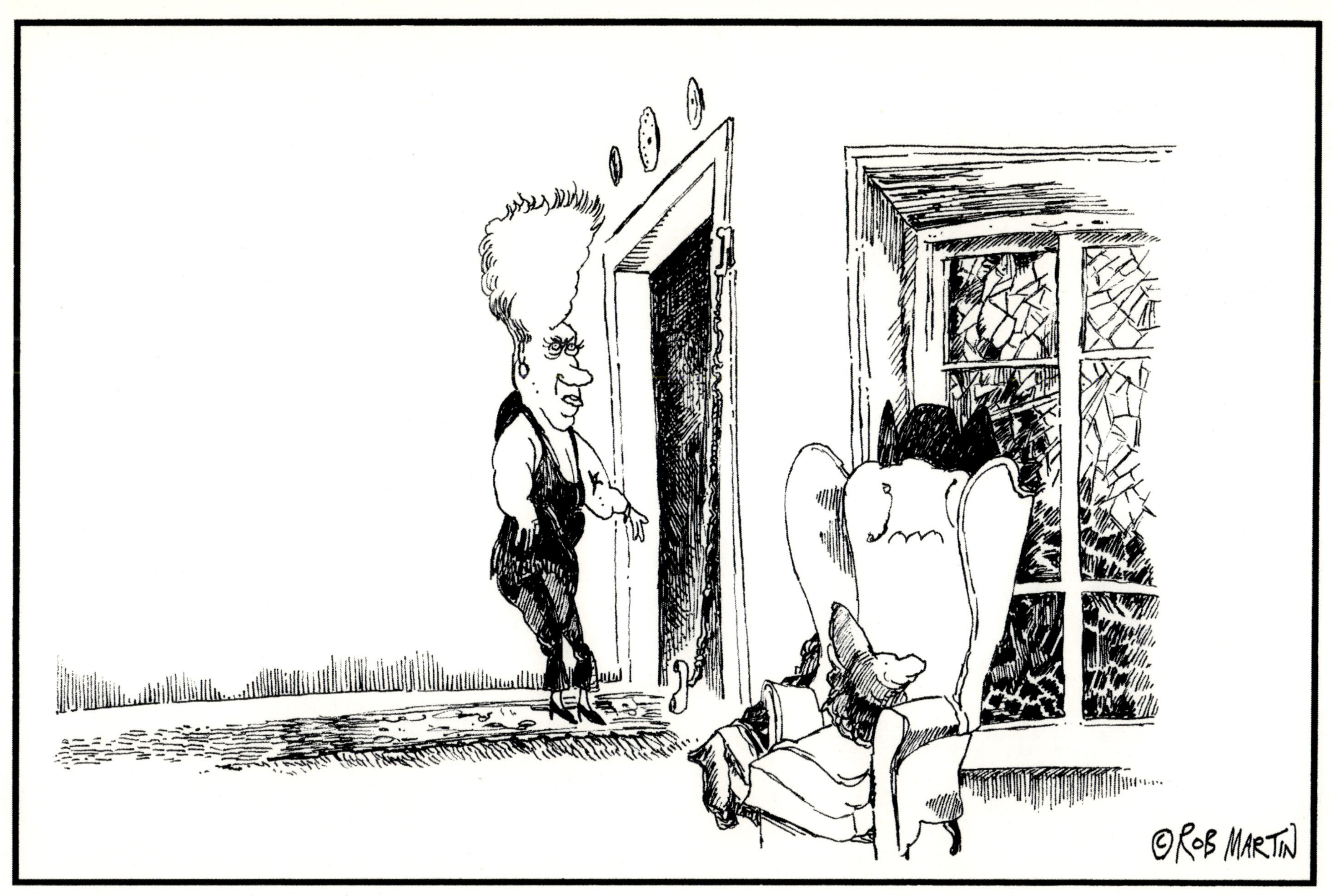

Clementine Jacobs drops the phone as Nigel screams for his dinner.

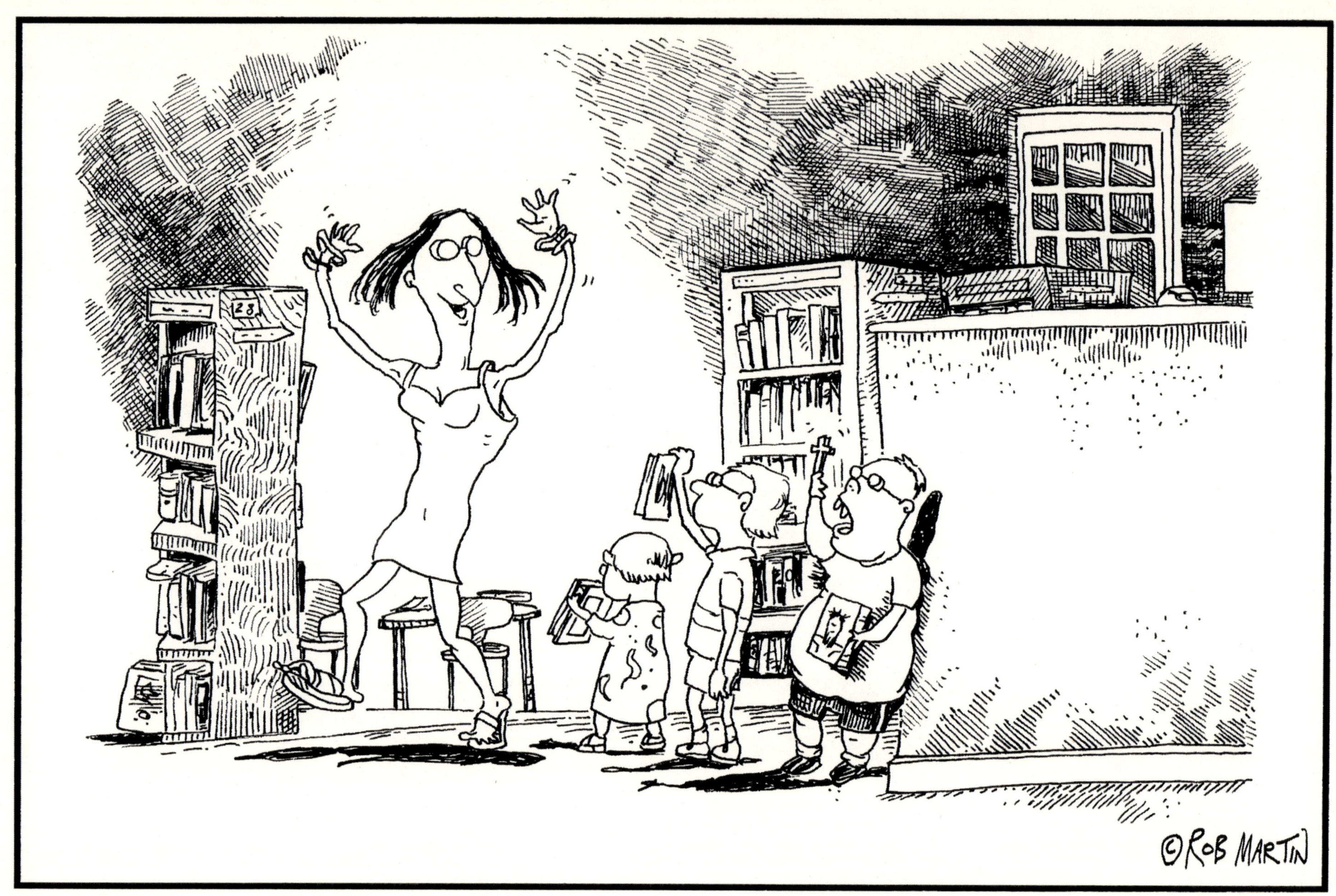

Children decide to perform an exorcism on a free-wheeling whacky librarian.

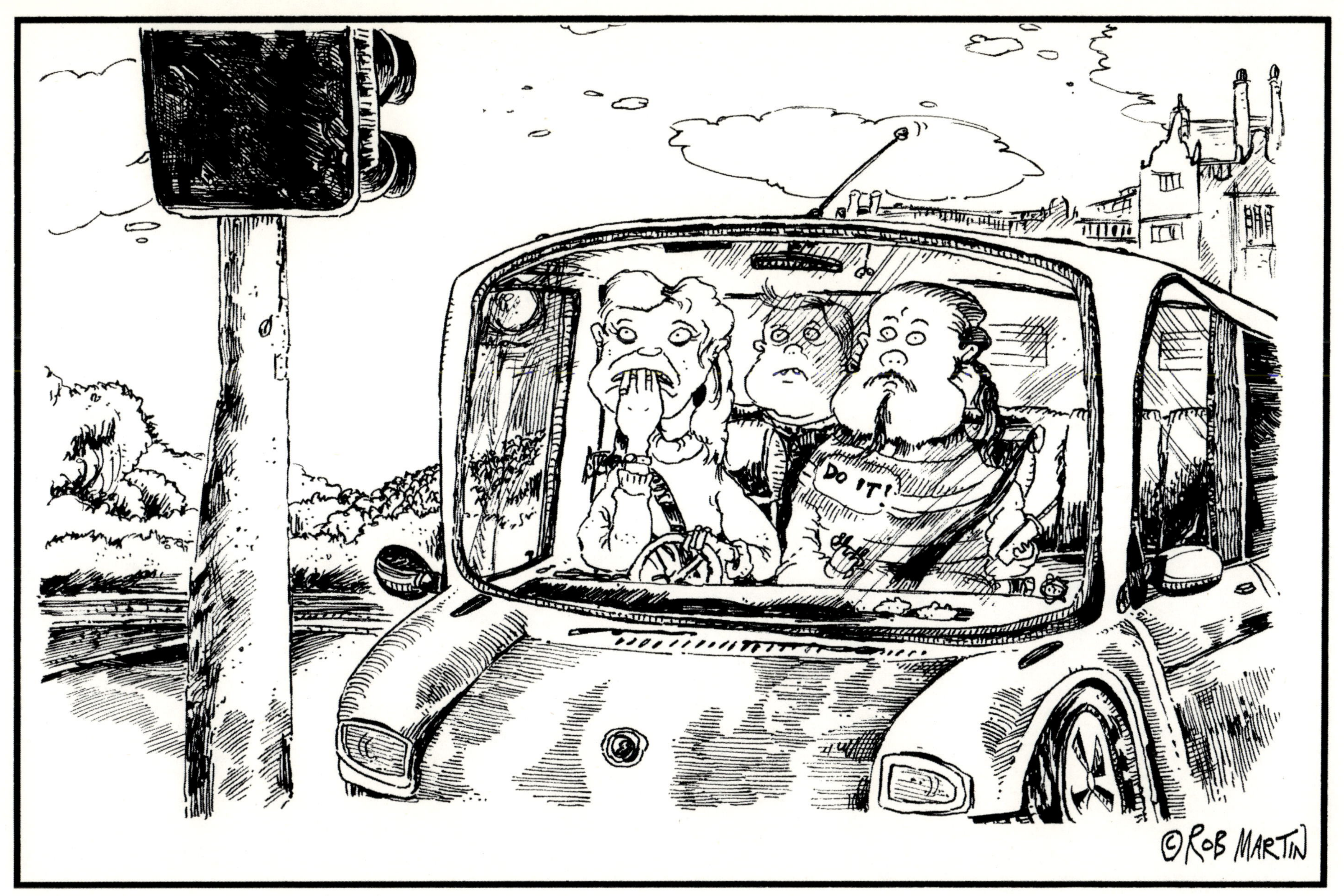

Stuck at traffic lights, Lucy sucks her fingers.

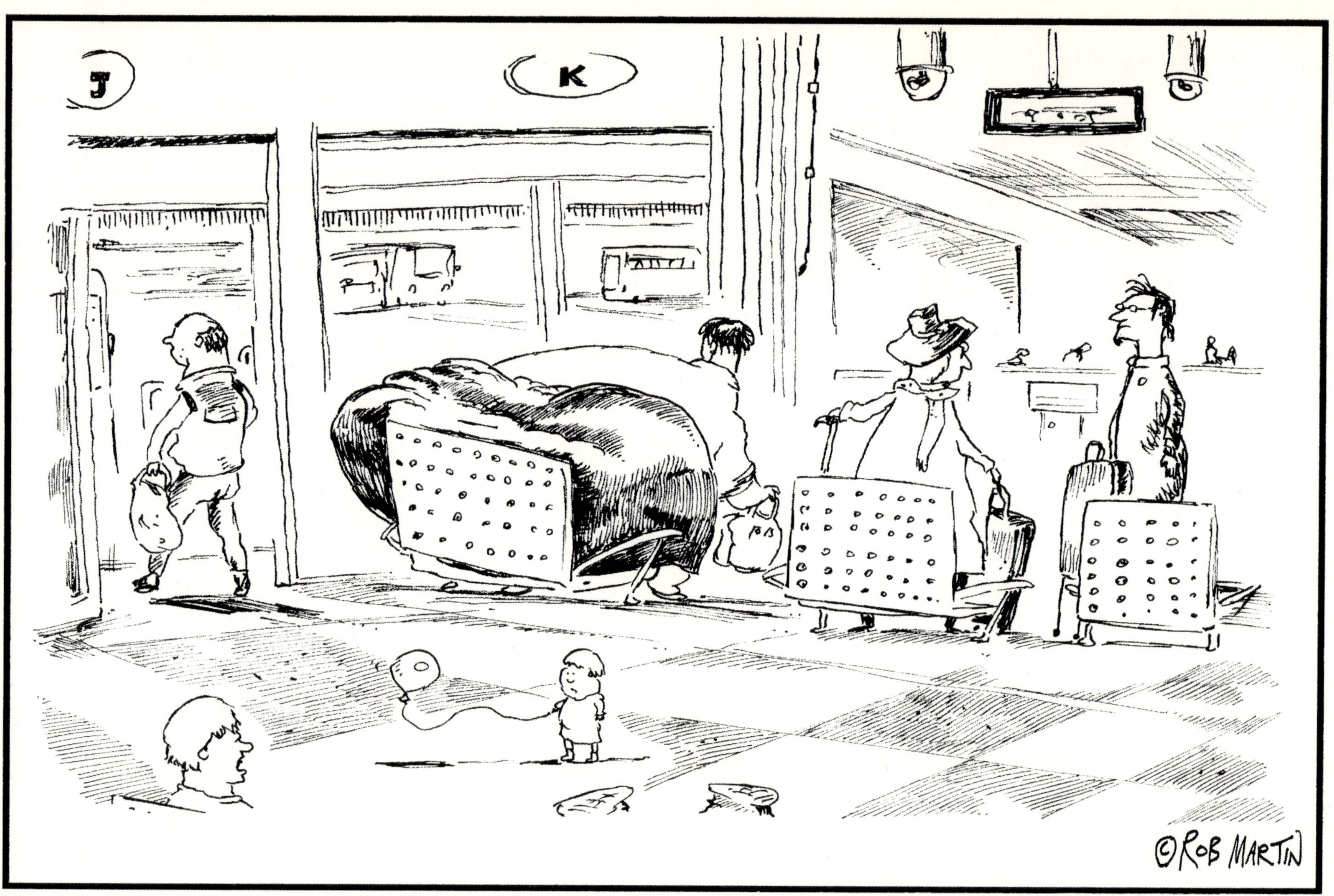
J
K
©ROB MARTIN

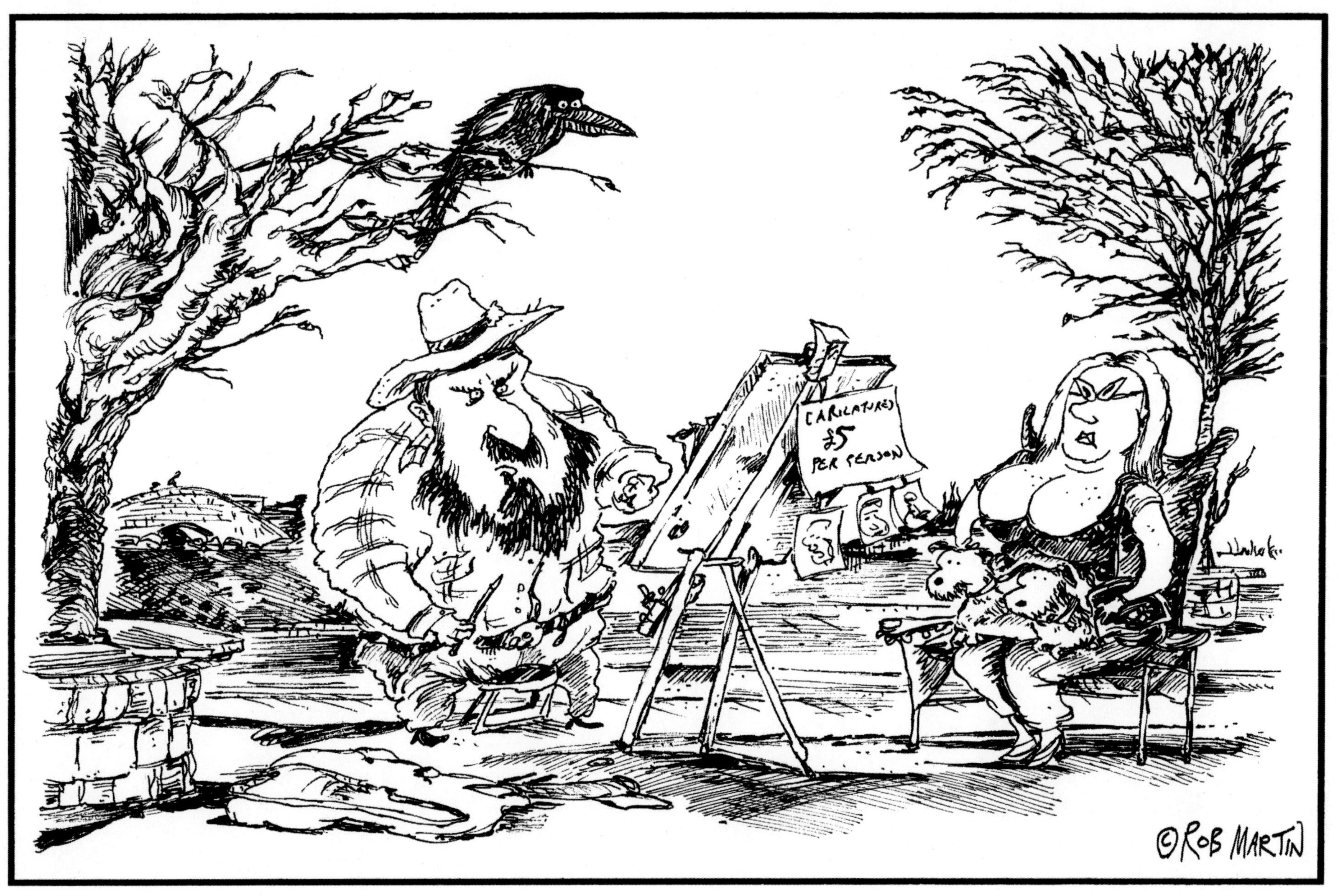

Tom the Crow prepares himself once again to crap on a street artist.

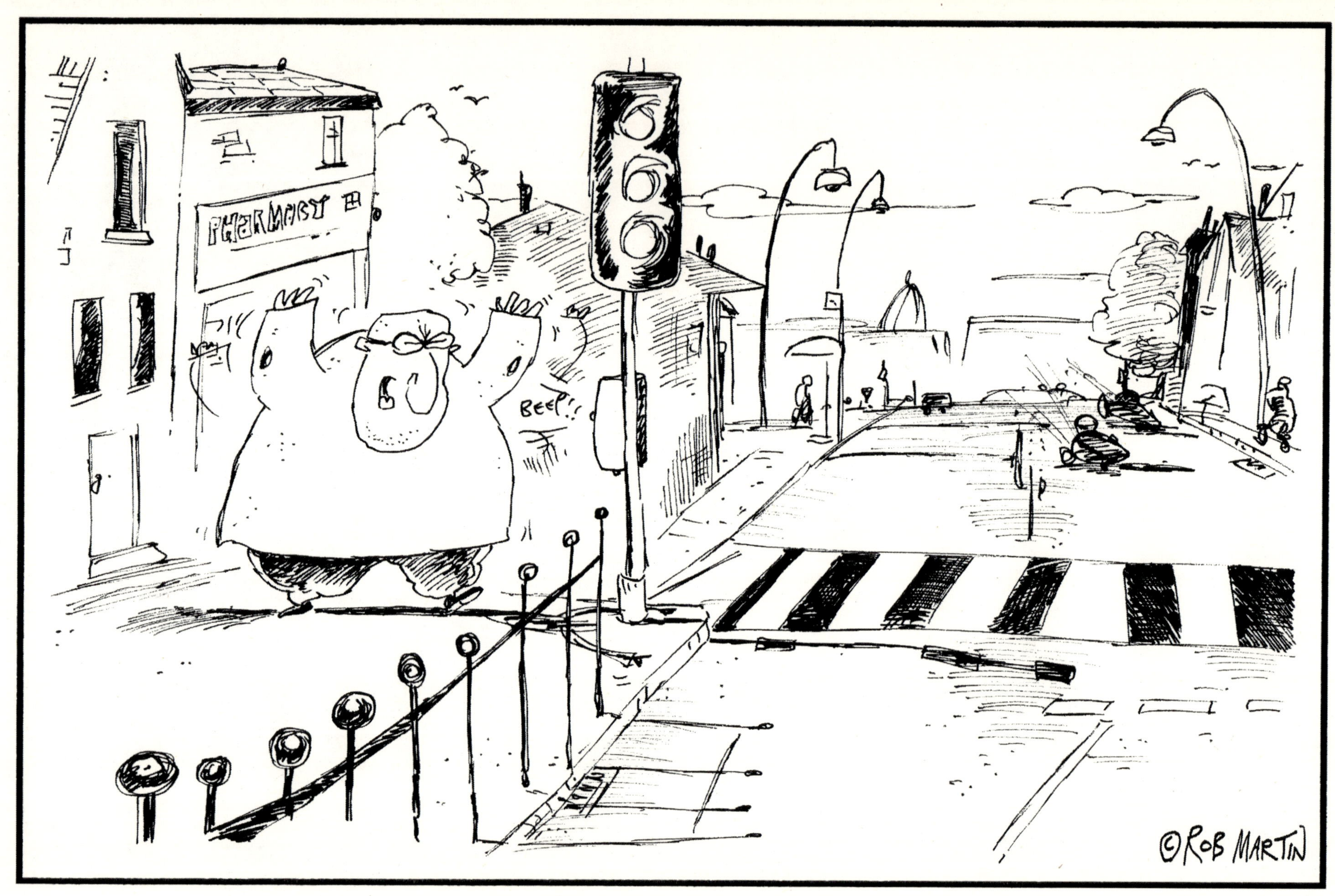

Man with high blood pressure has no patience
waiting for a crossing signal.

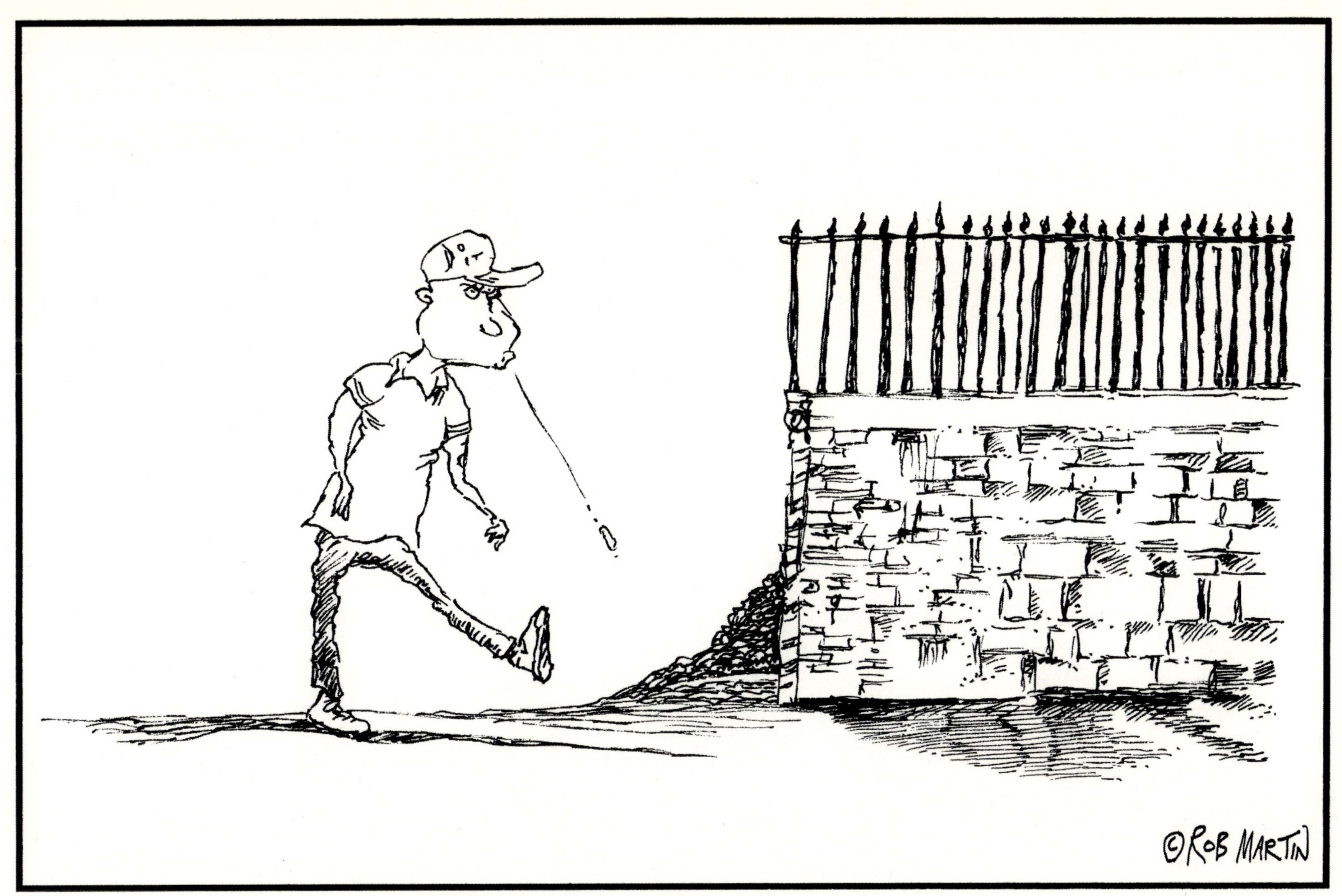

After leaving the Job Centre, Philip Knackersley decides to kick his own spit.

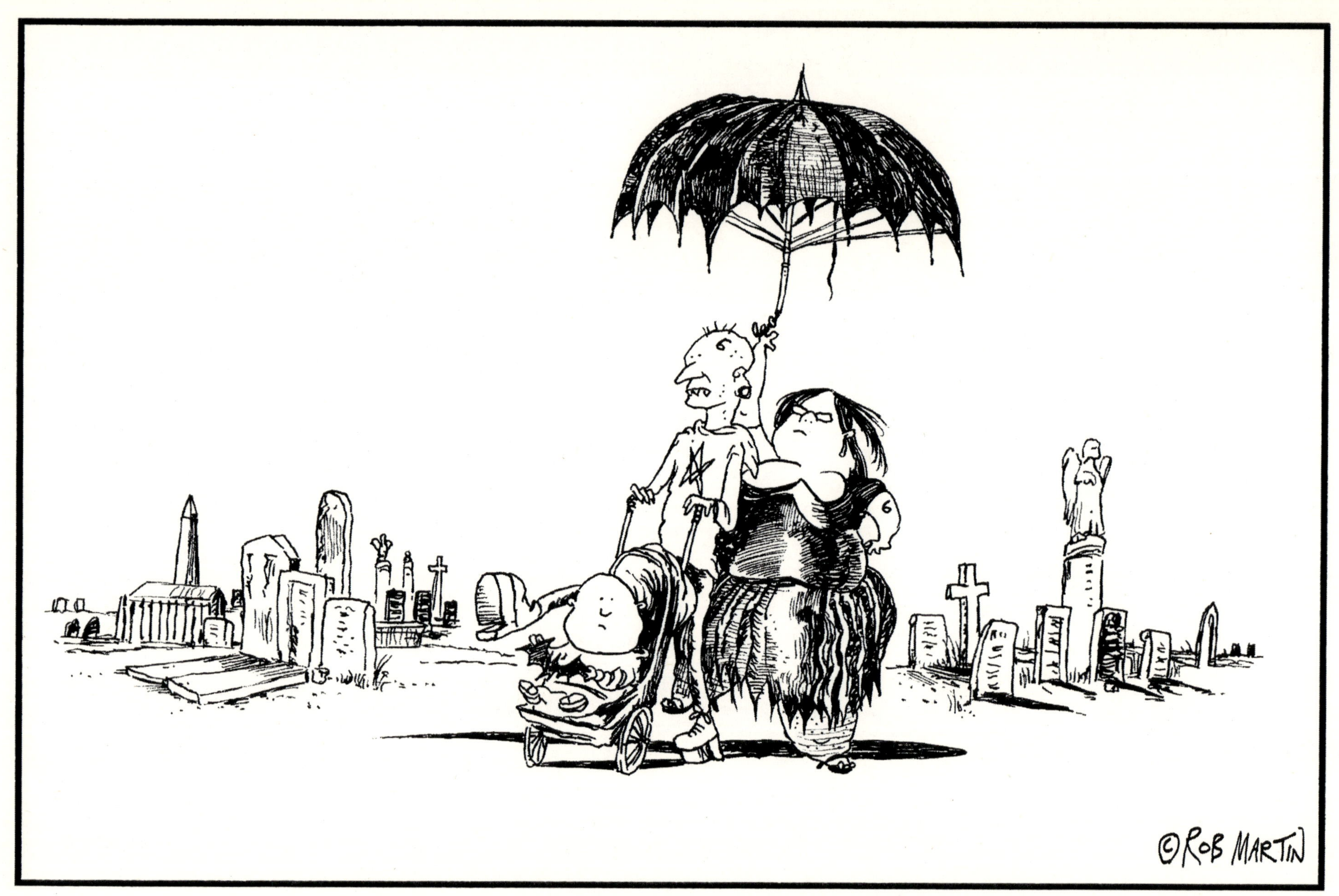

Goths go for a walk on a sunny day.

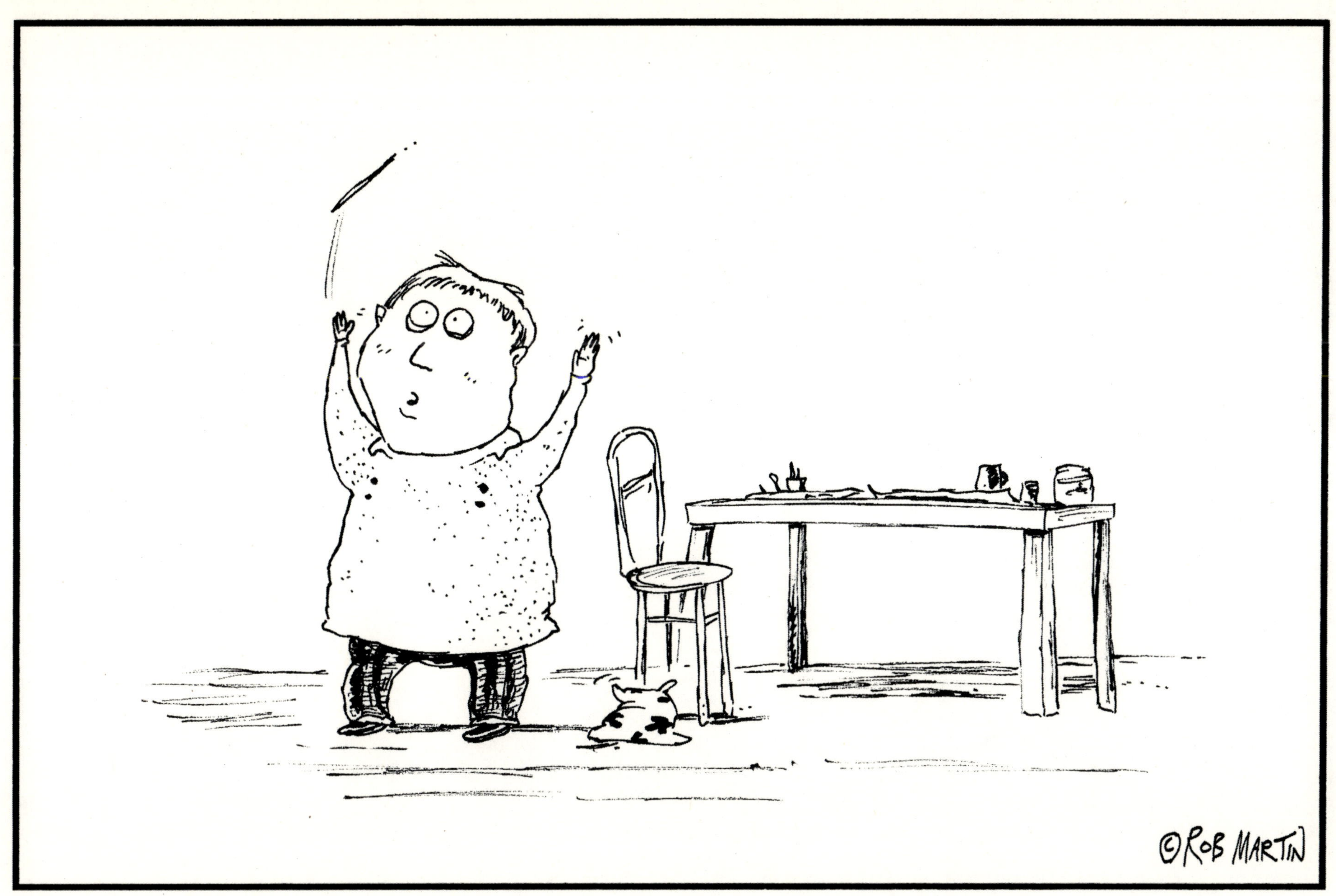

In his study, the nervous man gets angry with the hammering coming from next door.

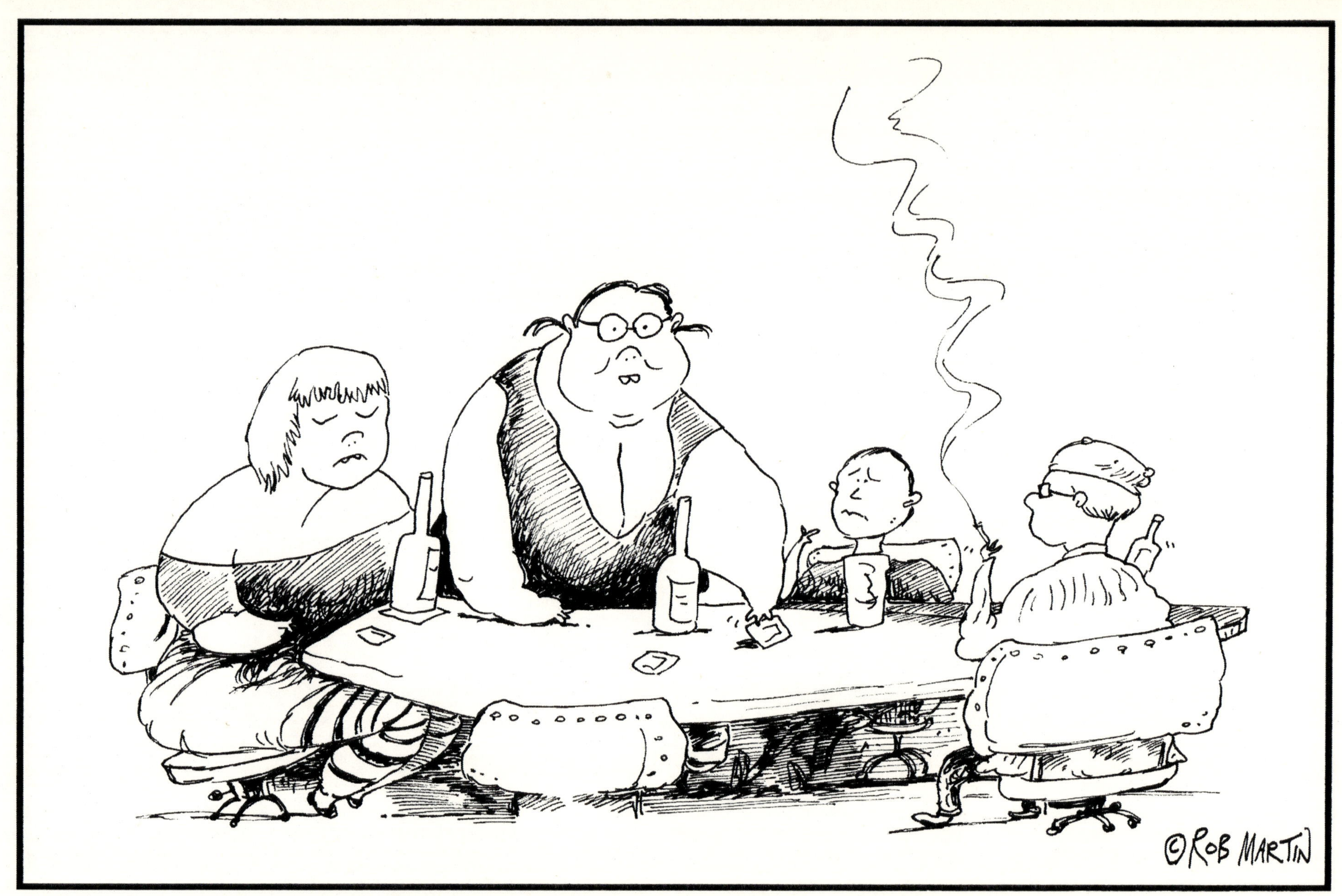

Goth chicks and geek boys.

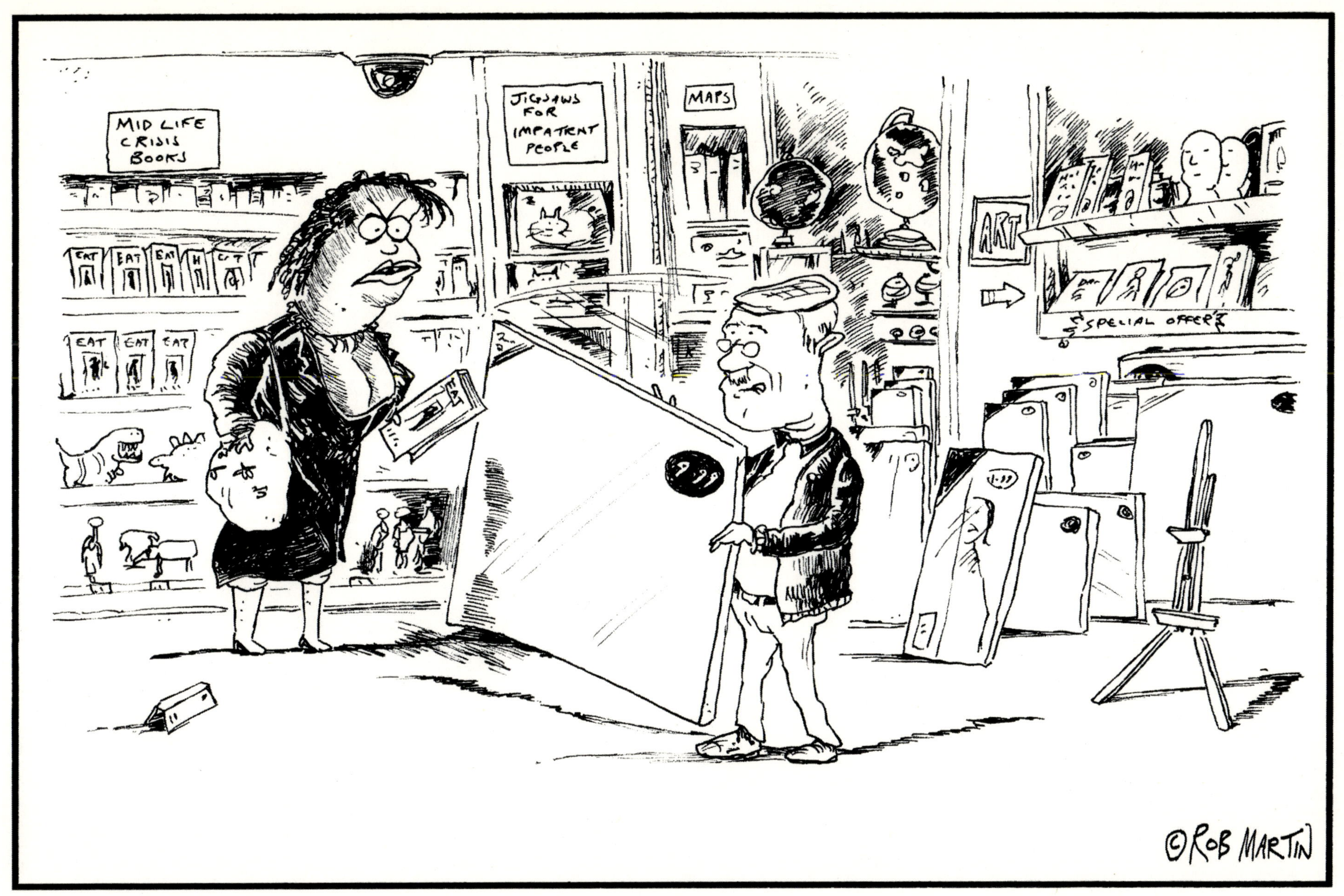

"That almost slapped me in the face! Hey you in the green coat...
Do you apologize or what?"

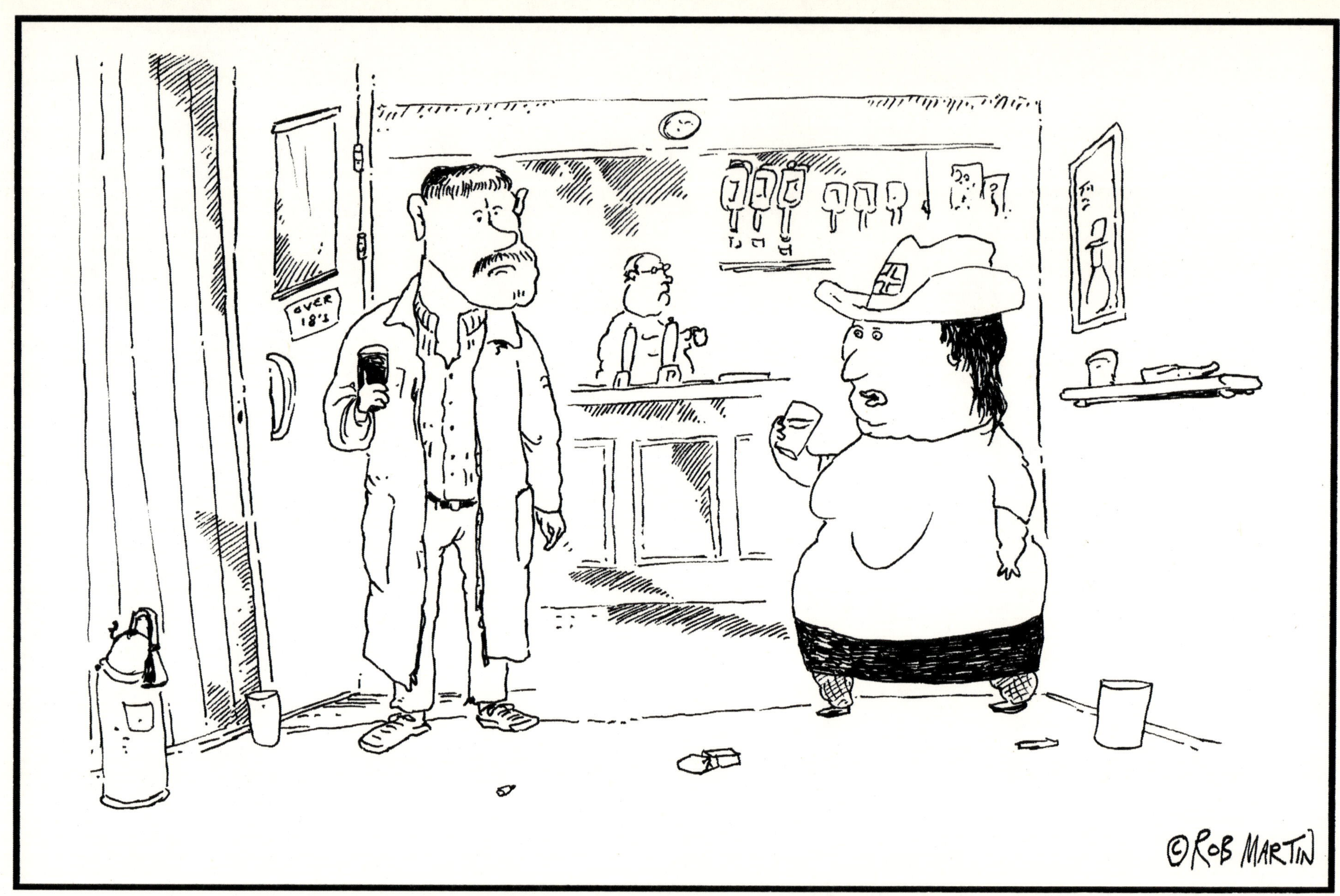

In a pub doorway, a man is asked why he doesn't look happy.

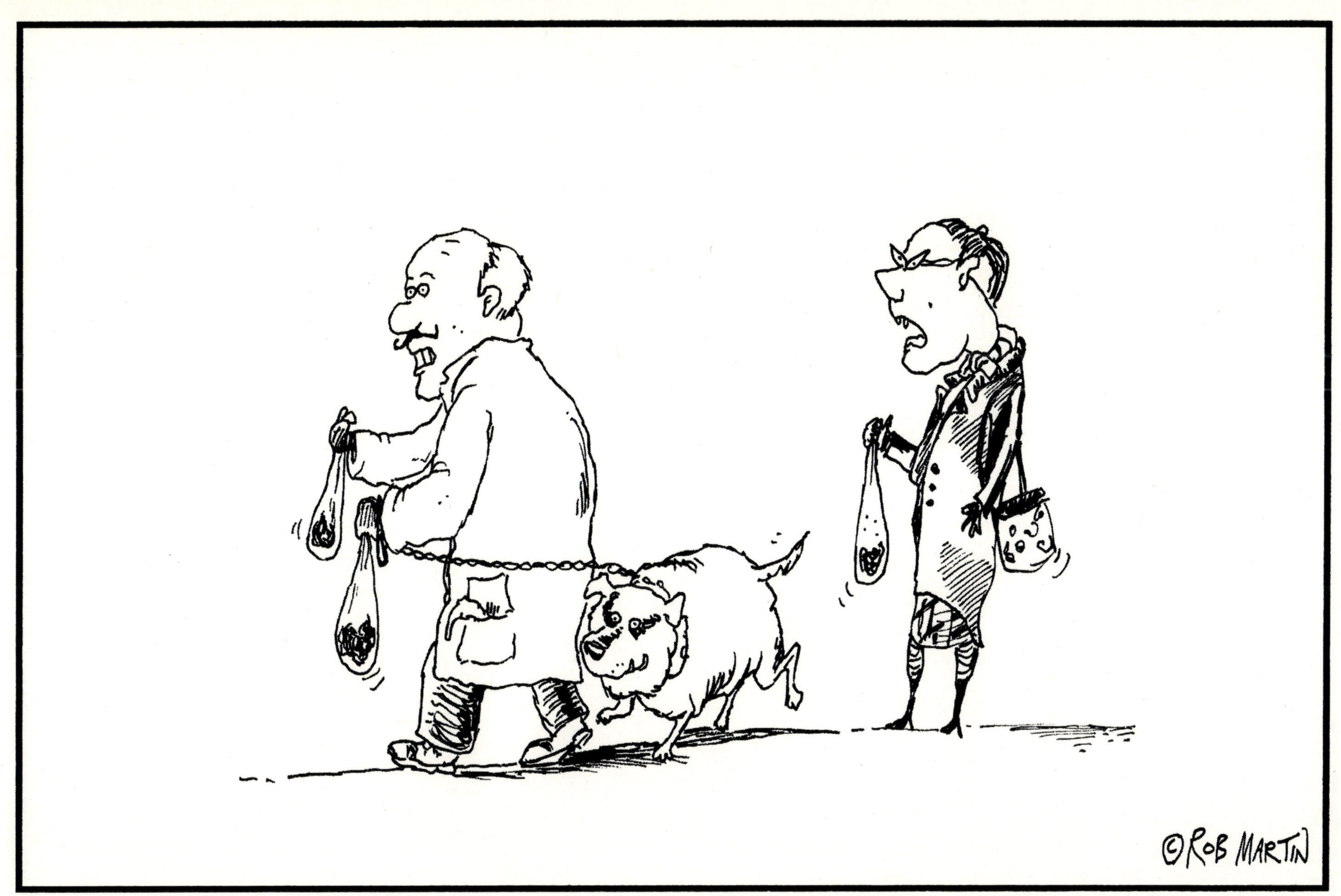

A couple try to find a bin to discard the dog's poo in.

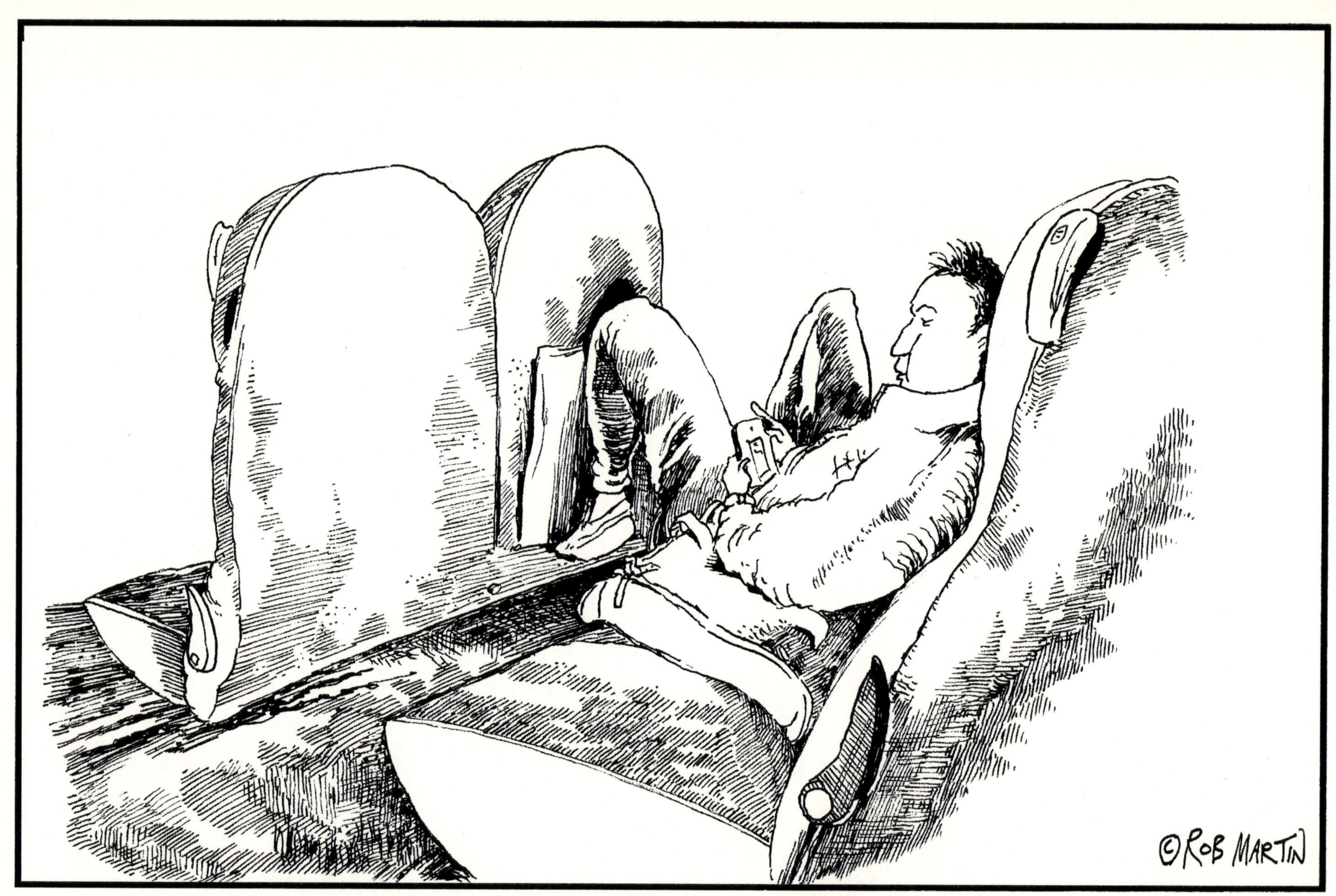

Sartorial Stephen sardonically texts 'LOL LOL LOL PMSL LOL ROFL LOL :) :-0)) LOL WTF FFS LOL... I am on the train now. No, Saturady..'

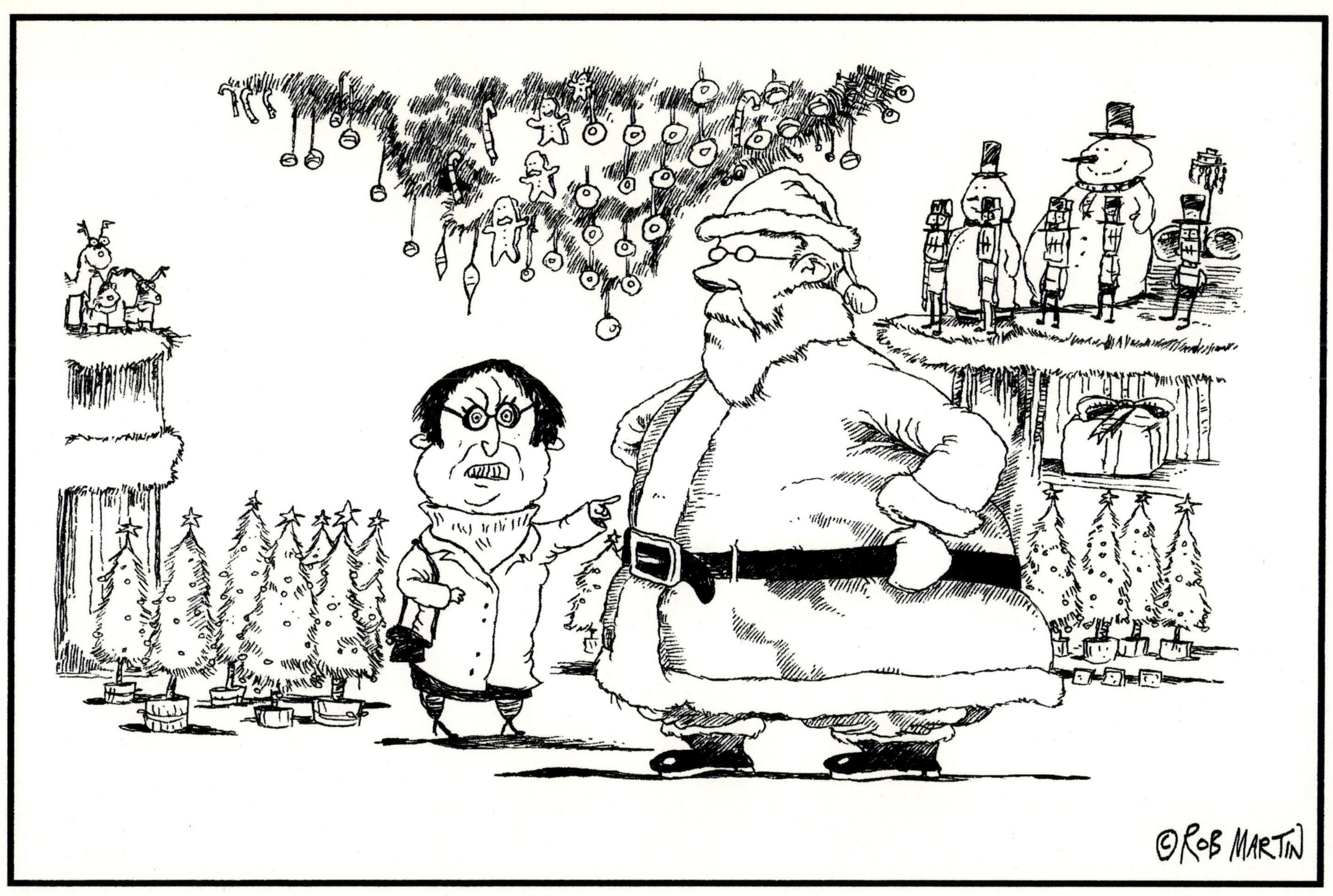

Angry impatient woman in a Christmas decoration shop calls the Santa, "a sad little man!"

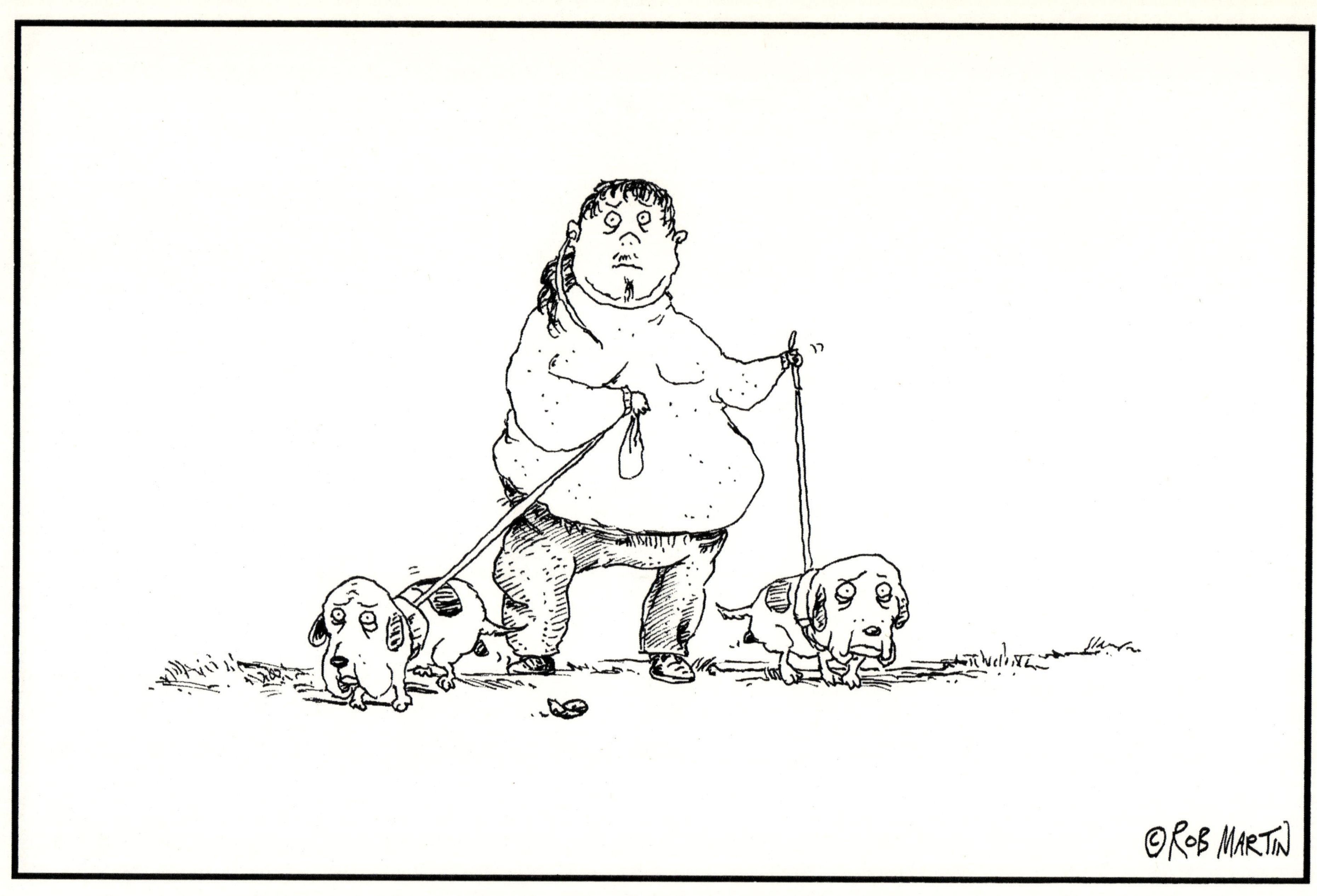

A man doesn't know what to do, when his dogs synchronize poo onto the stately home lawn.

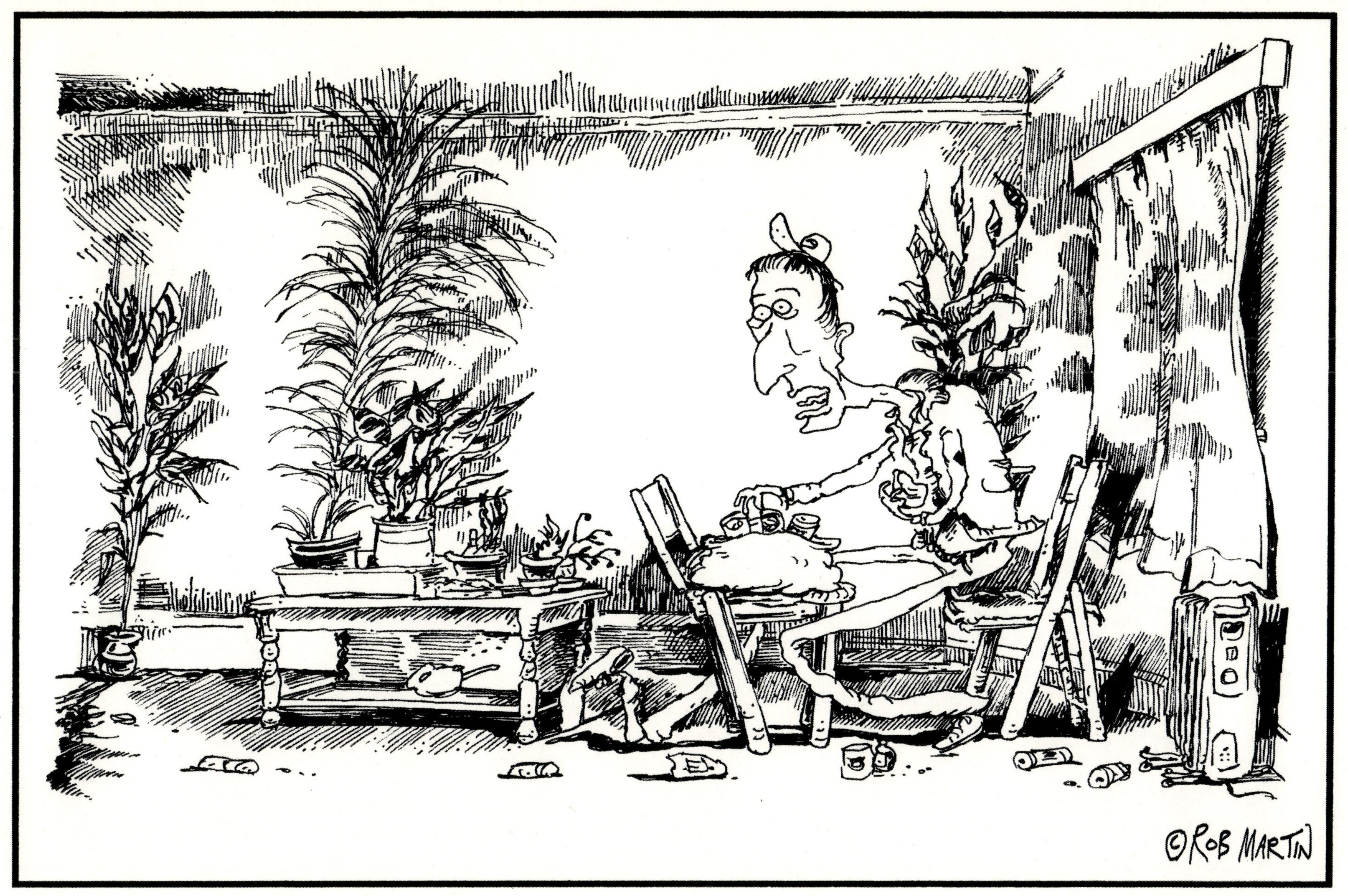

Sugar addicted Hedley, reaches for his fifth can of fizzy lemonade.

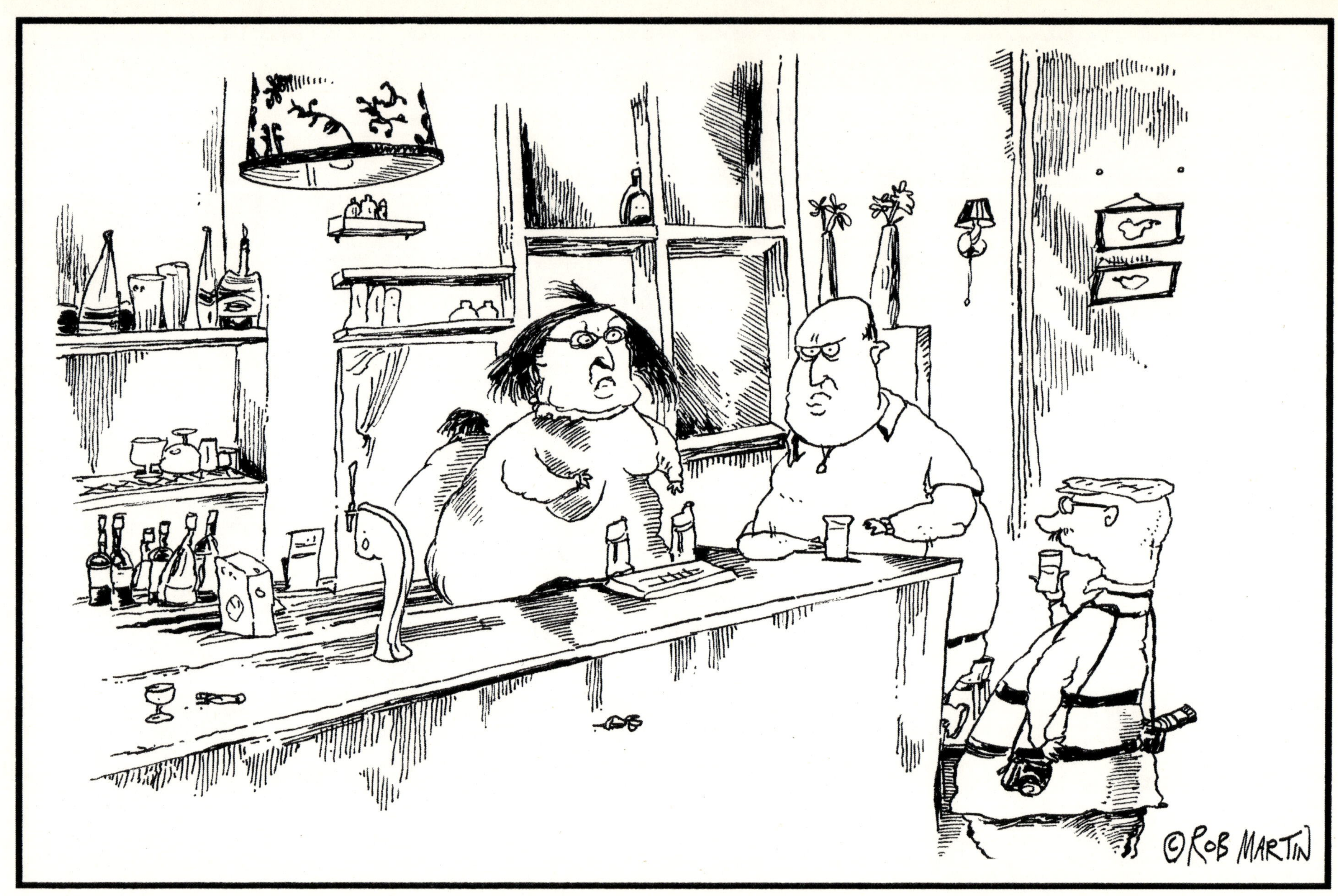

Man drinking bitter lemon is ignored because he talks about trams rather than bowling.

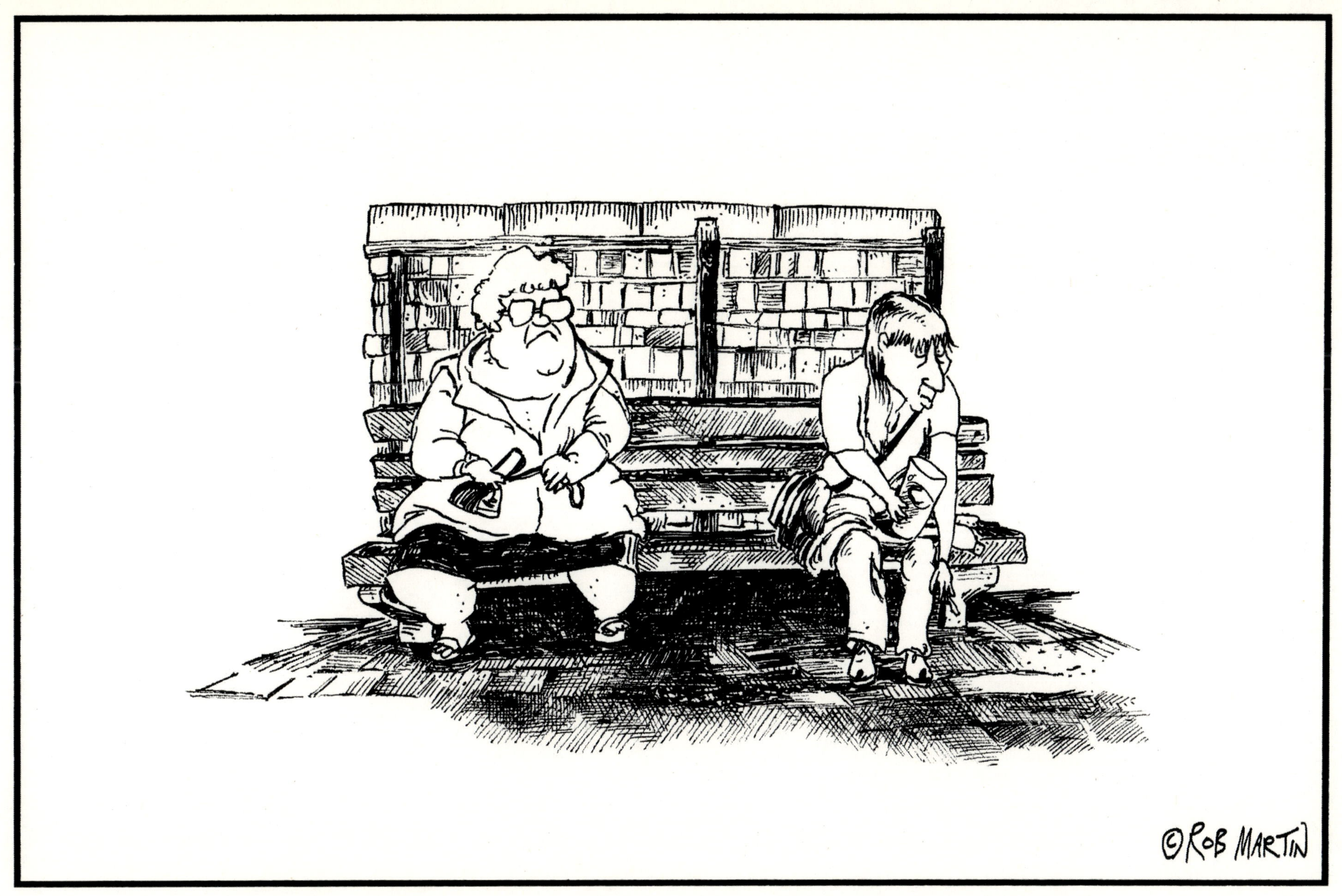

Mable tightens her fingers on her handbag strap.
Whilst Linda, tries hard to remember if a Crystal Bear
had really visited her at twilight.

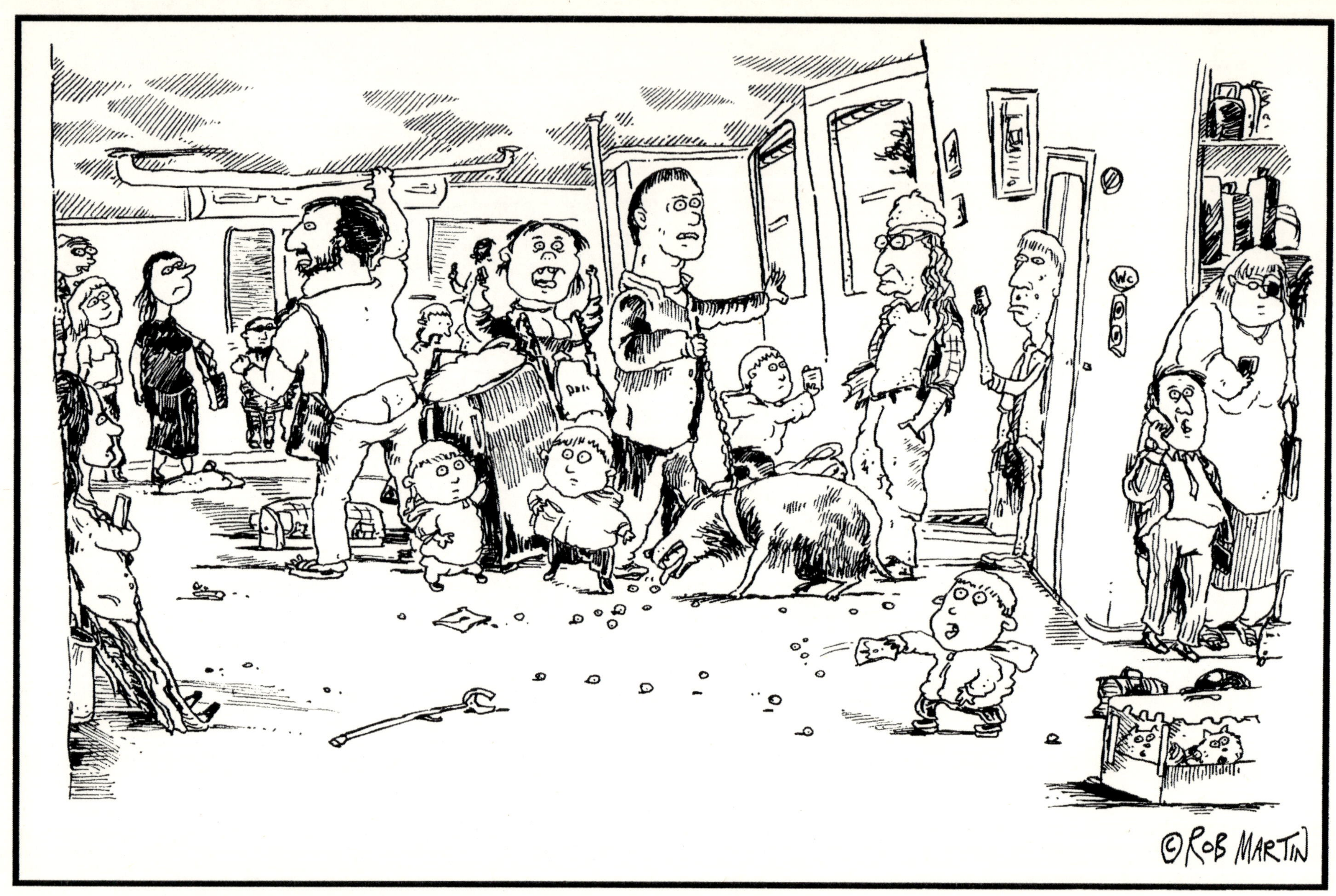

Catching the afternoon Friday train is a new experience for Mr. Spootloot.

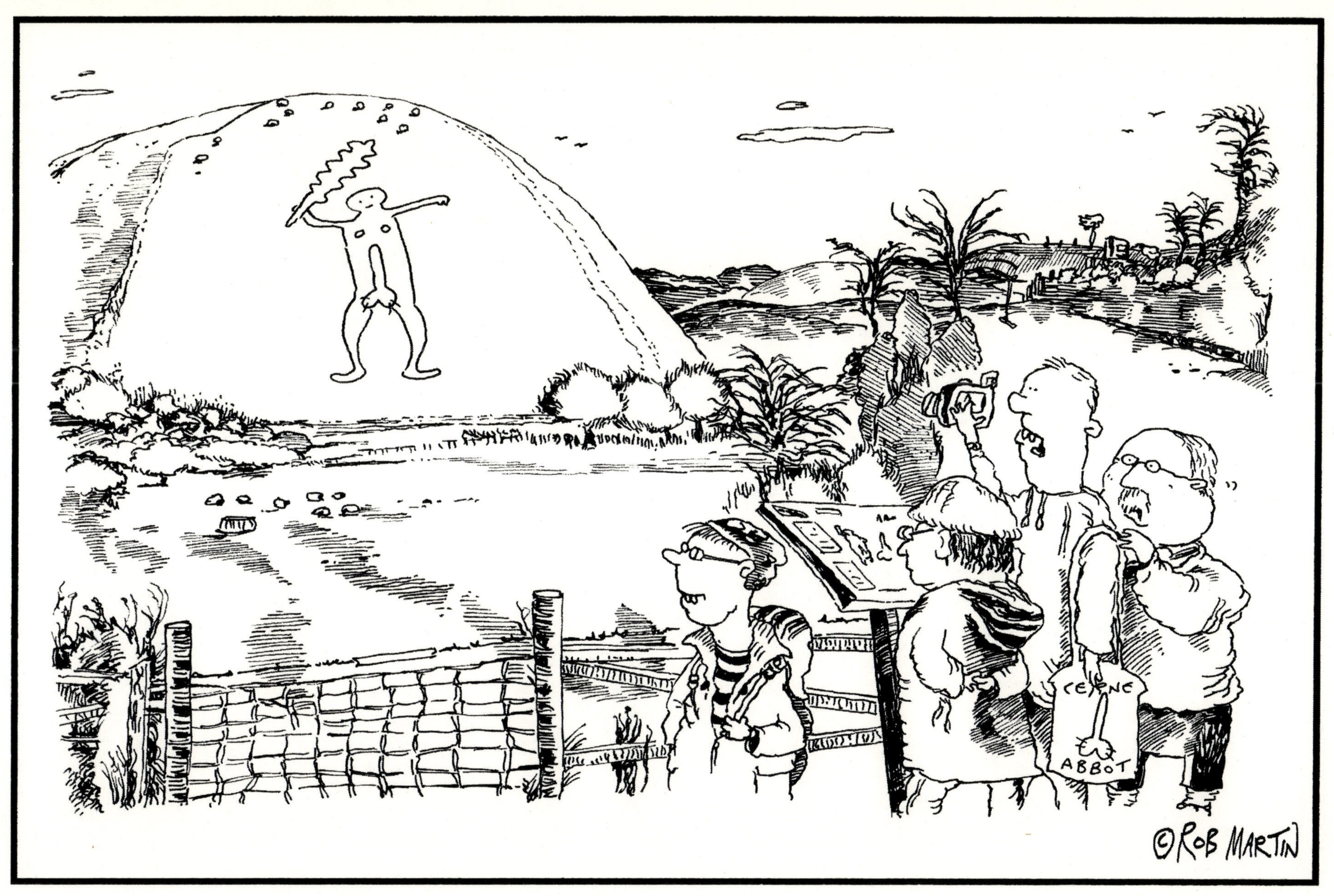

Randy Cockburn is suddenly struck by a fear of Giants.

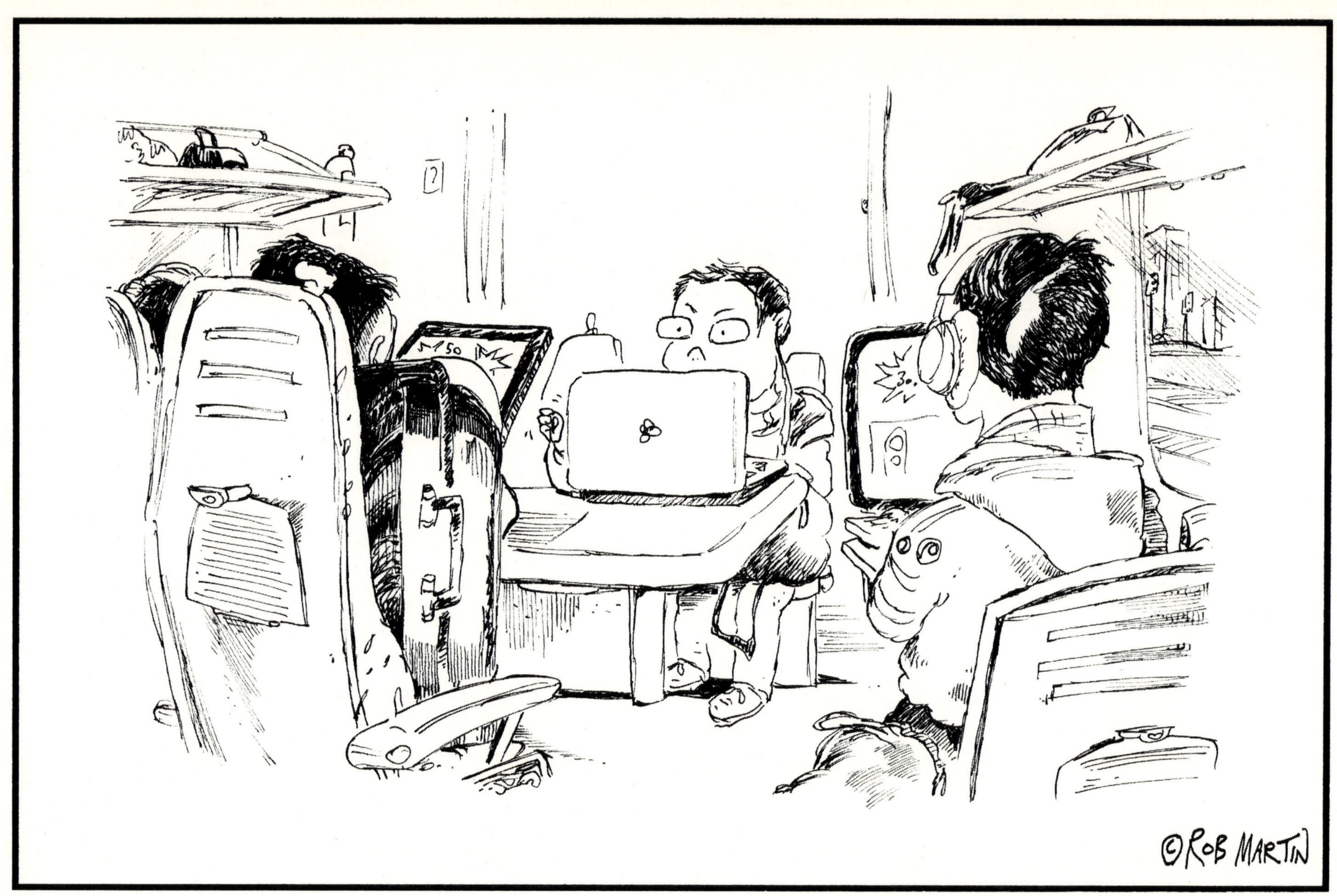

Shoot em up gamers with laptops at noon.

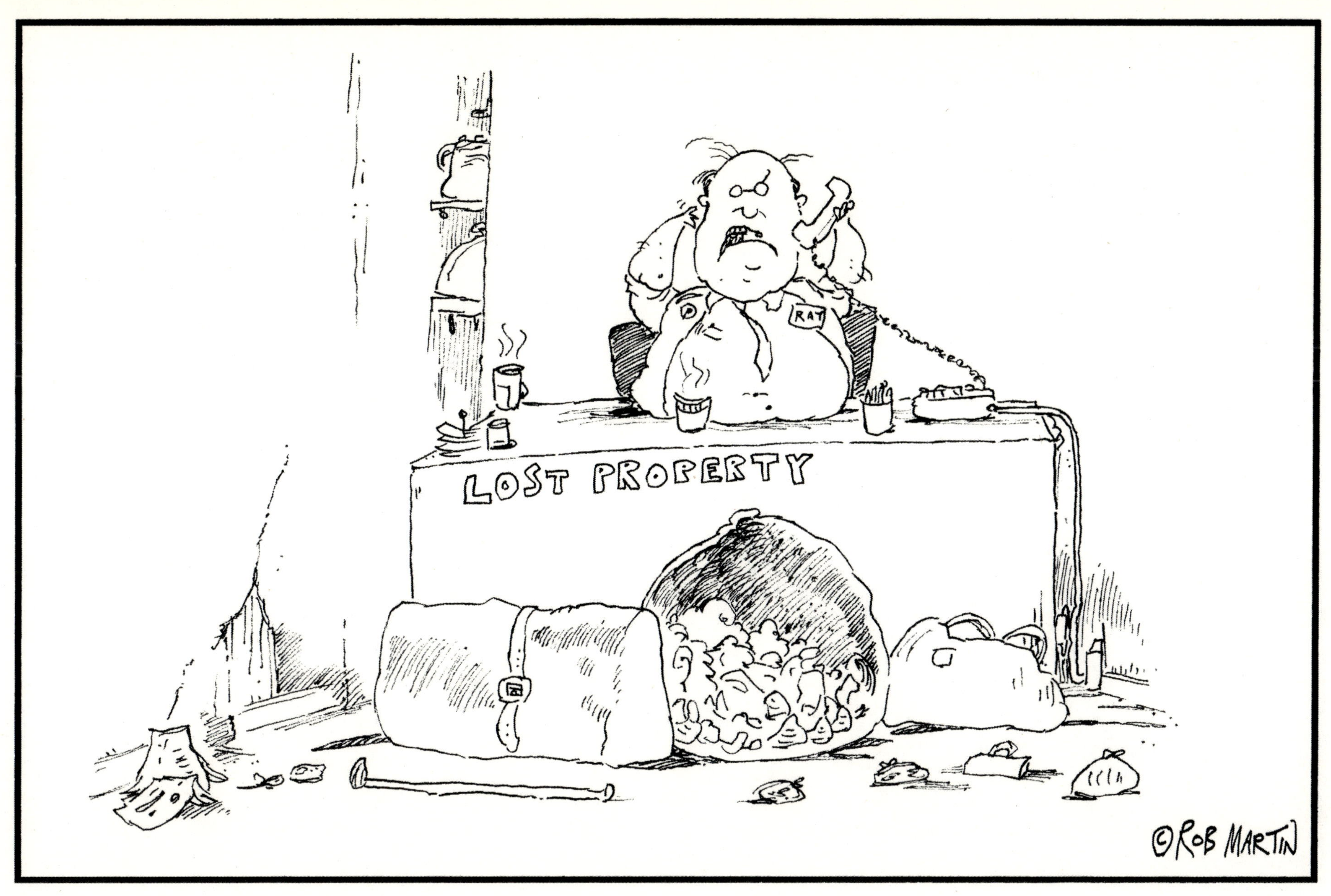

"It's highly unlikely you'll find it!"

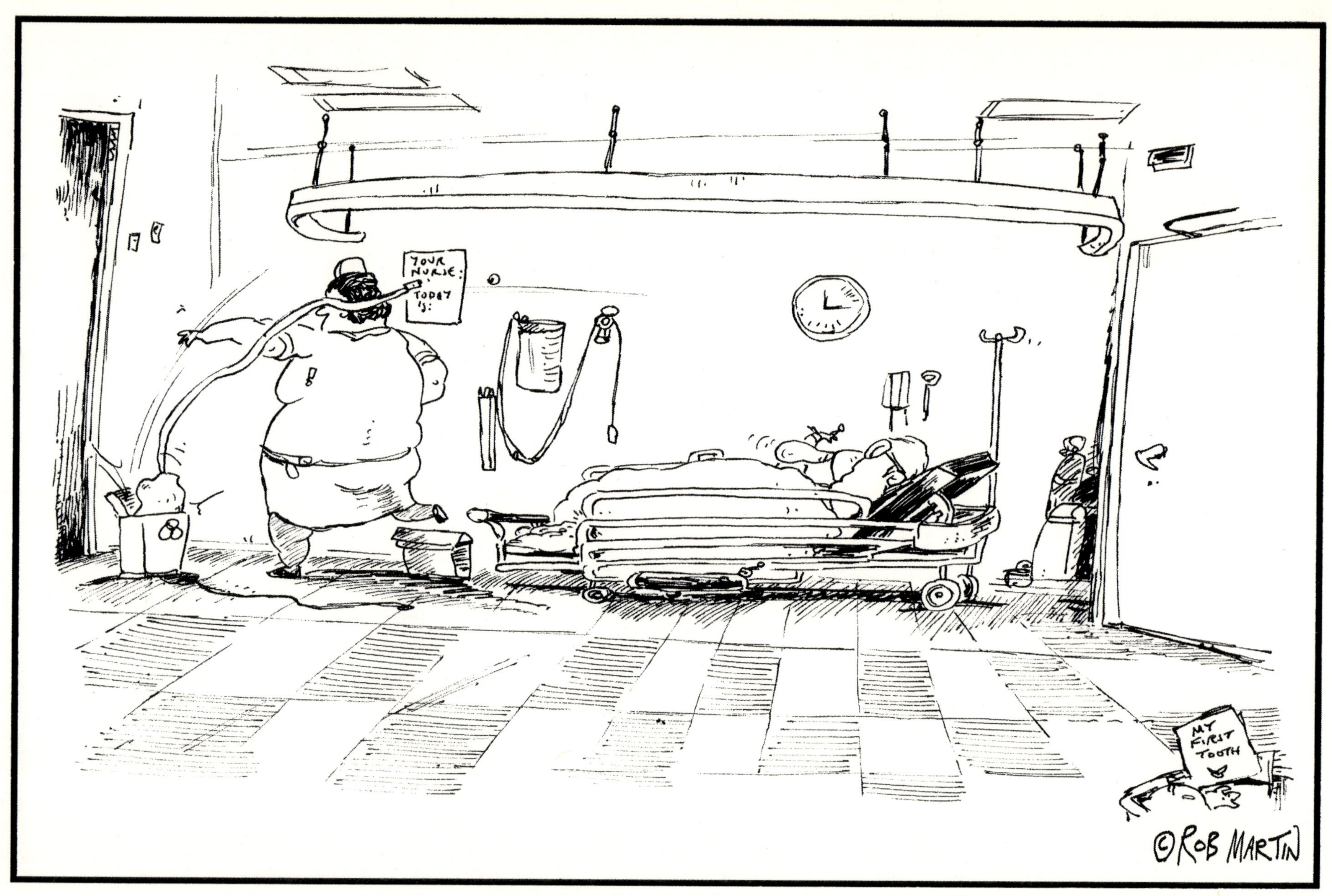

The saline solution pipe gets blocked again, leaving the nurse to slam dunk it into the biohazard bin.

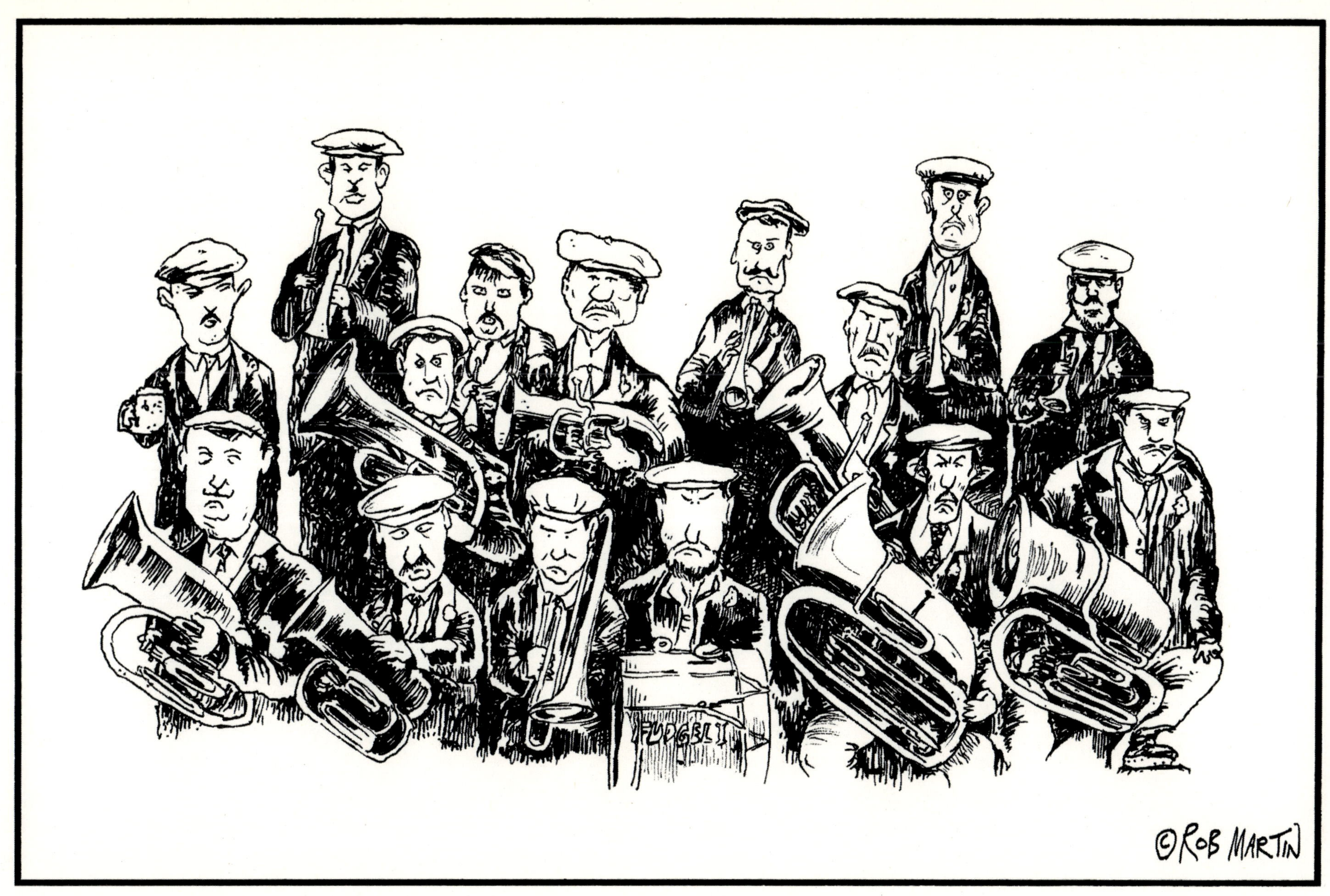

Haworth Brass Band prepare to play a rendition of 'Wuthering Heights'.

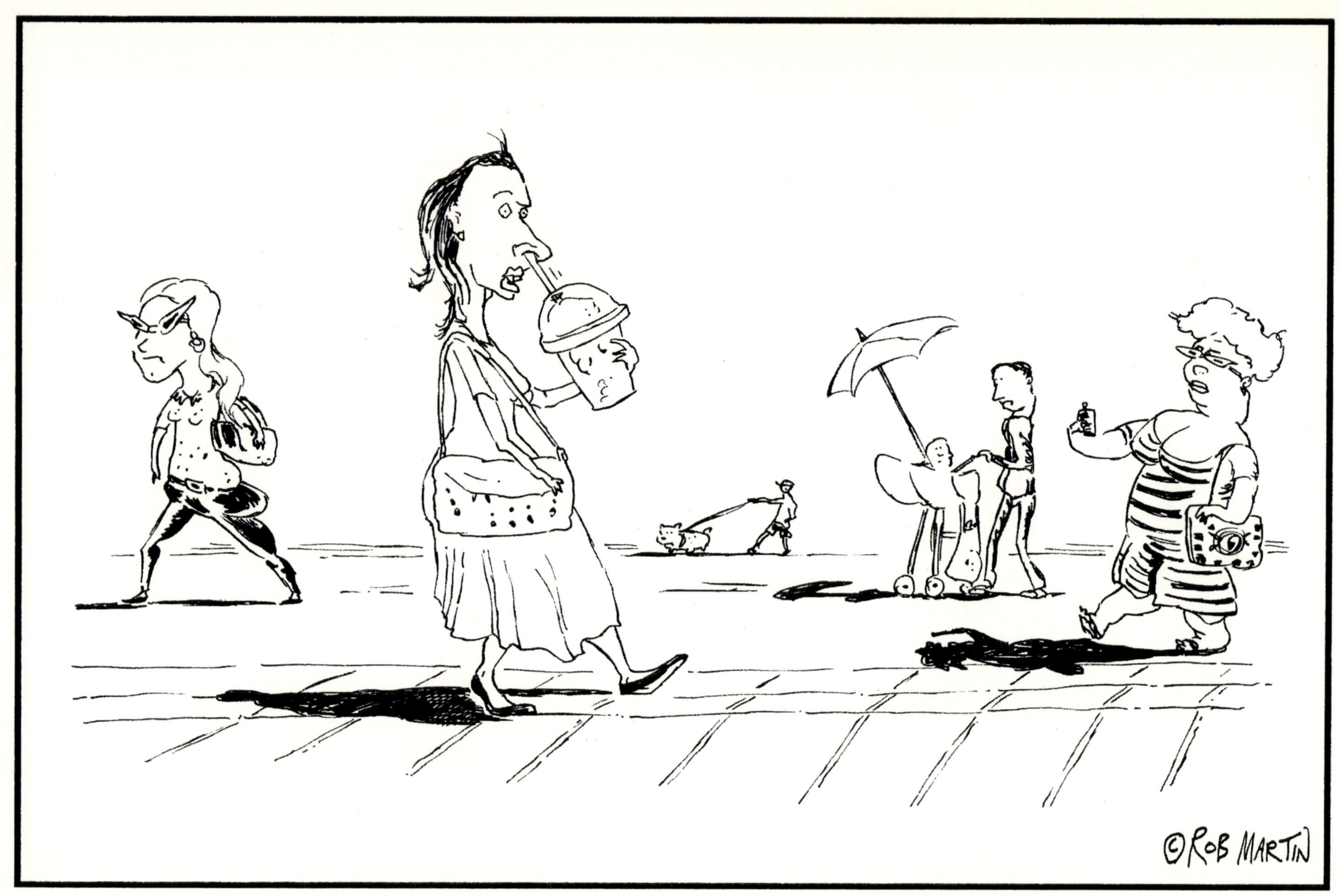

A woman sucking on a slushy, accidentally misses her mouth.

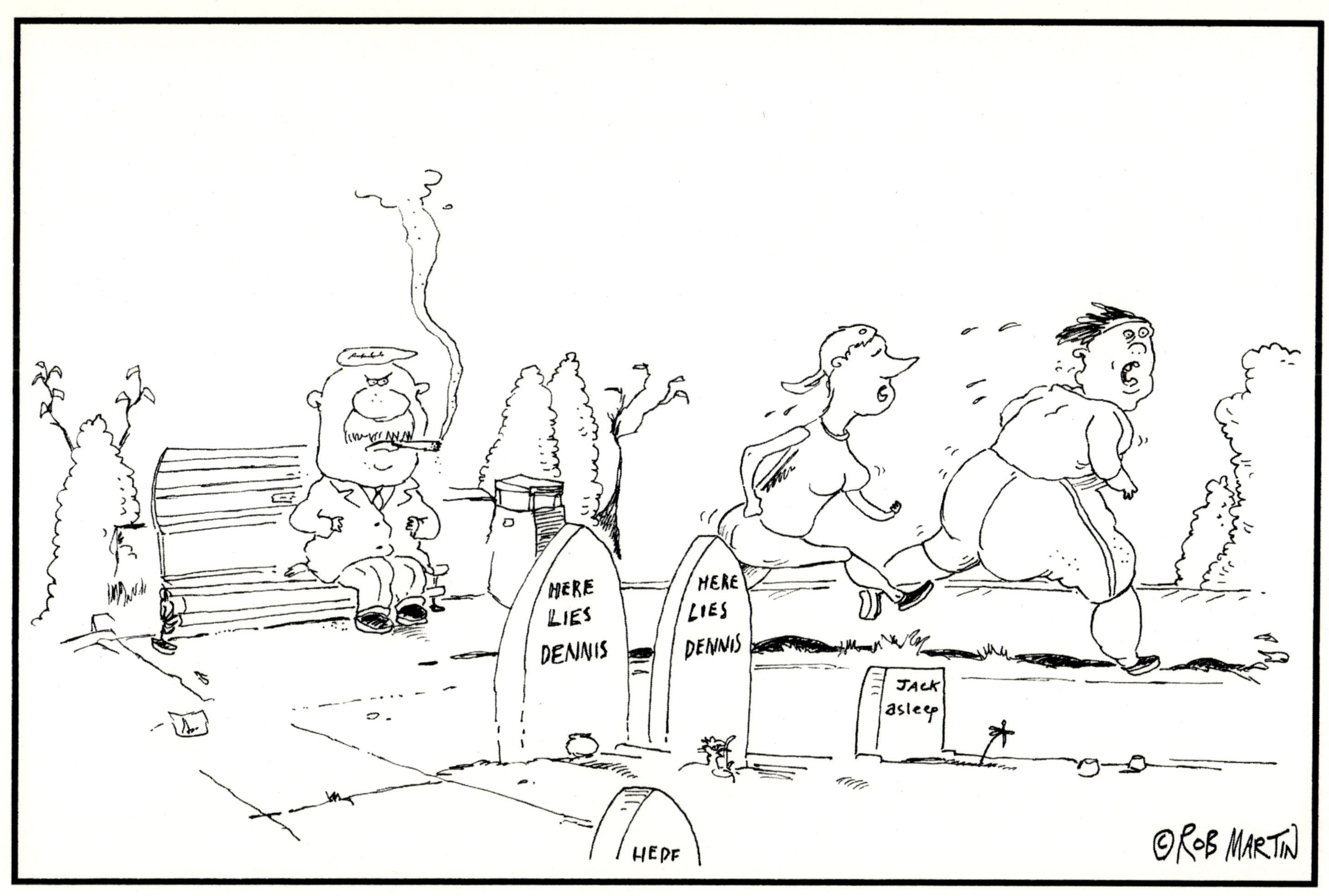

In the cemetery, an old man starts to become grumpy.

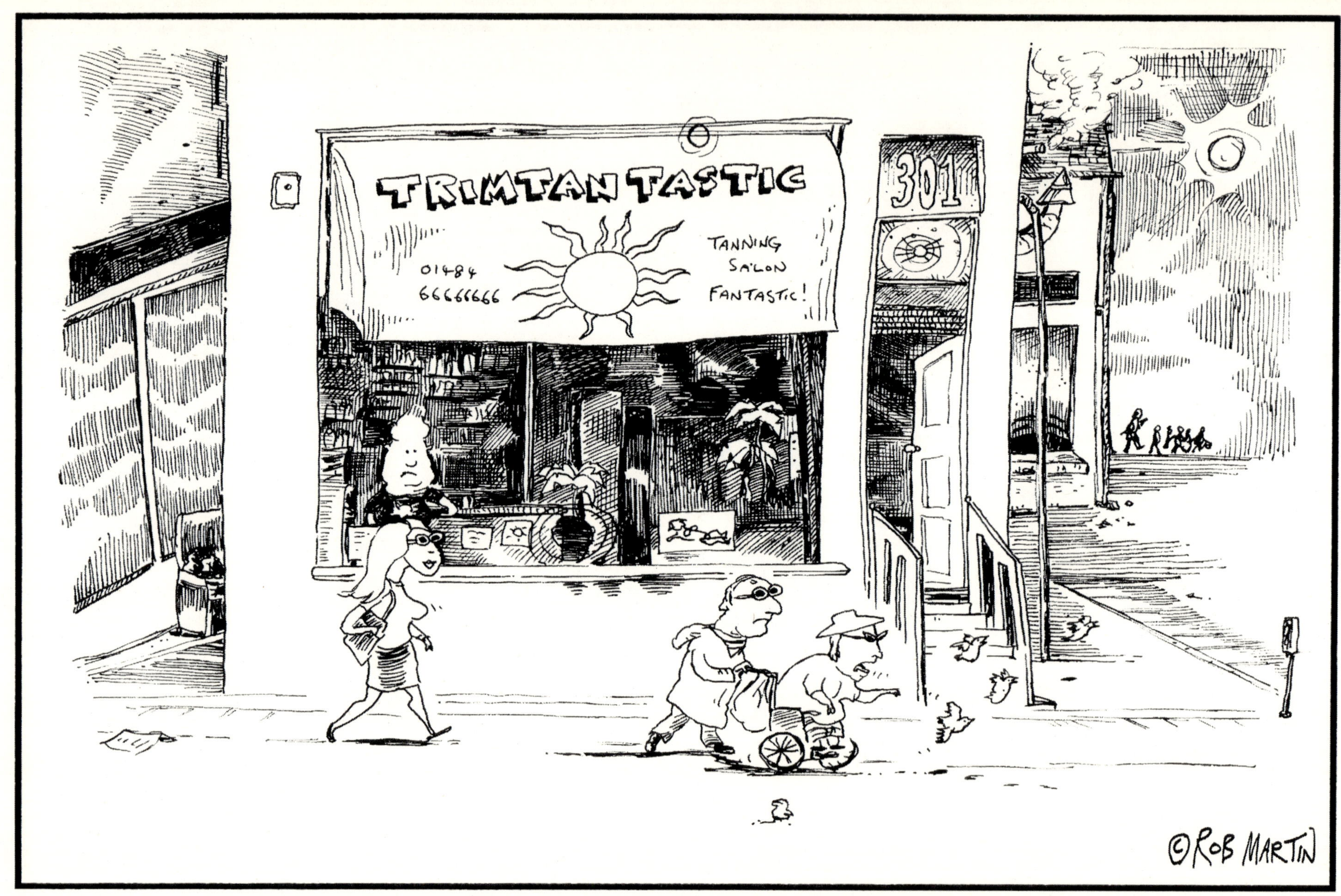

The tanning centre manager looks out onto the second week of hot blistering sunshine.

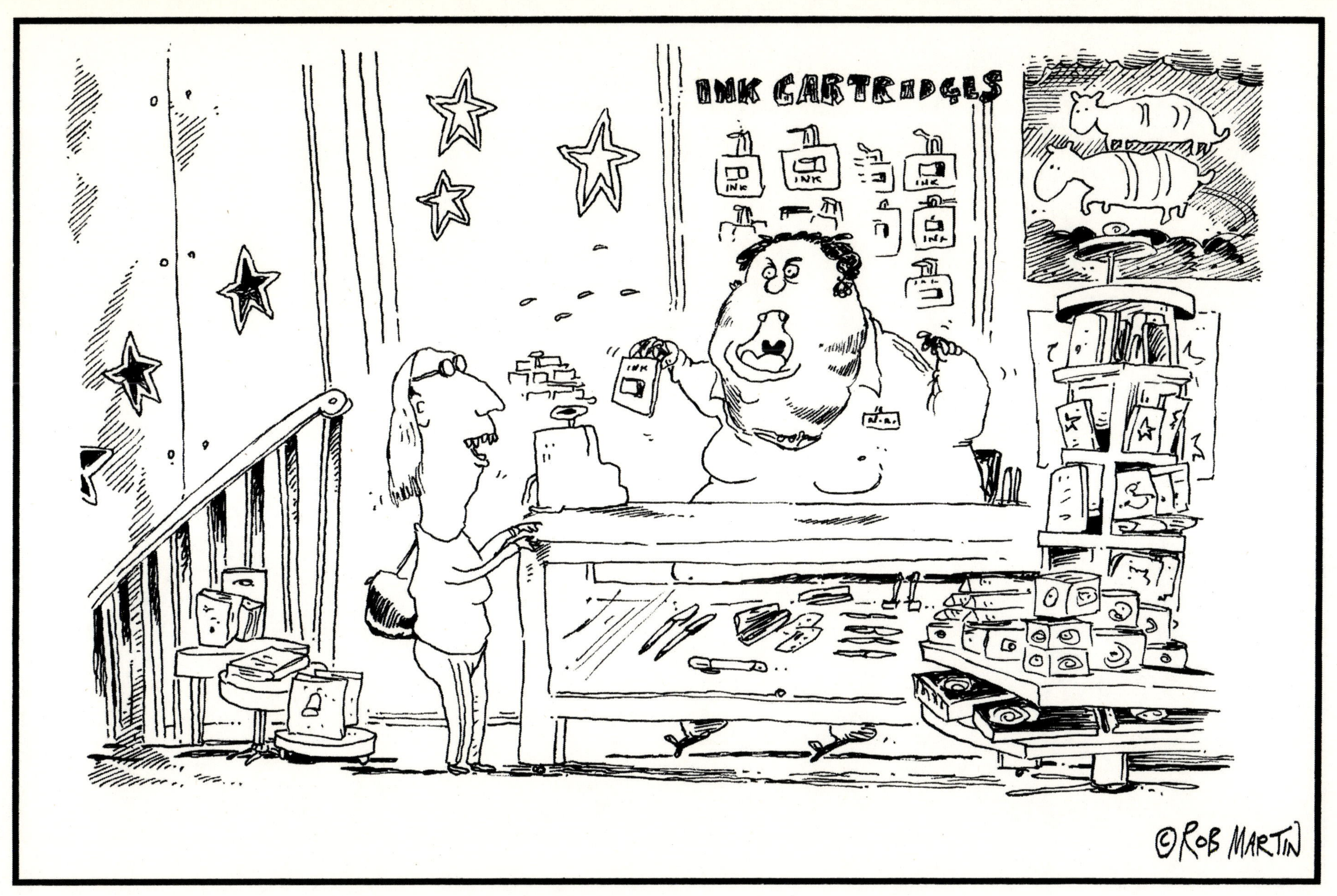

For the 14th time Bernice asks, "ink cartridge sold out?"
Causing Margaret to yell, "Aaaaaaaaargh!!"

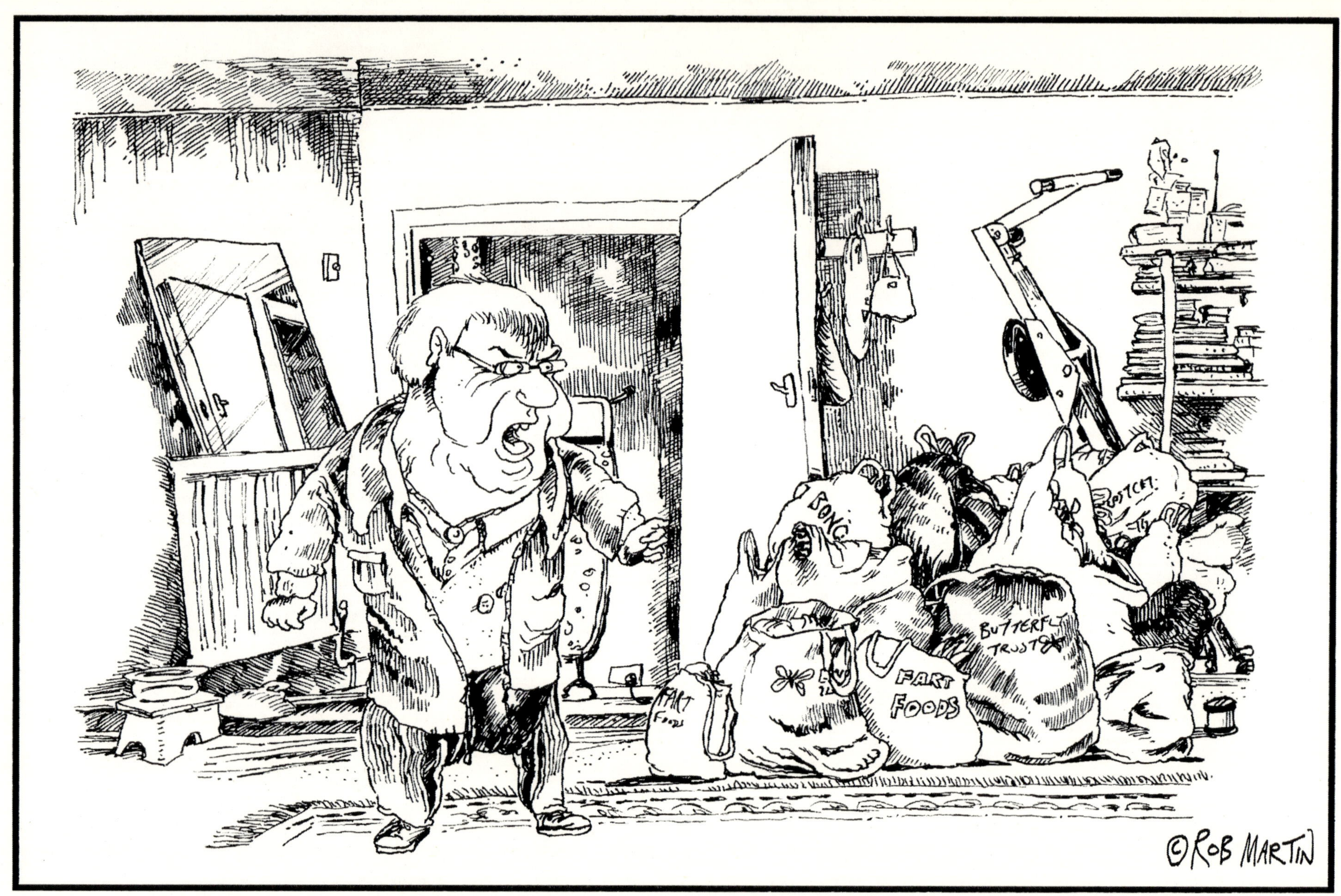

Mr. Robin with a morbid hate of scarves. Shouts insults at all the plastic bags containing his ex wife's knitting patterns.

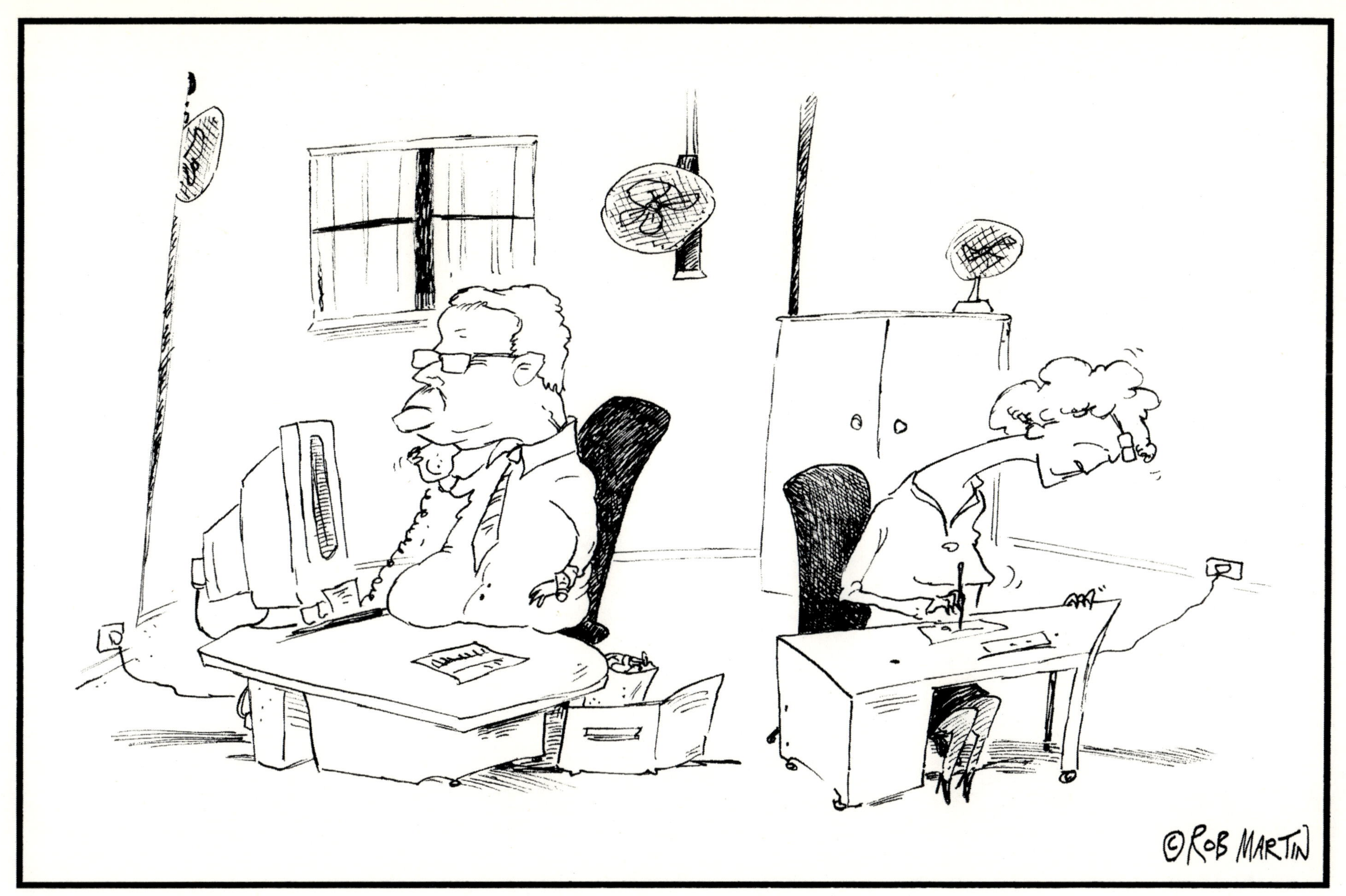

Office workers have no eyes. - PART 1

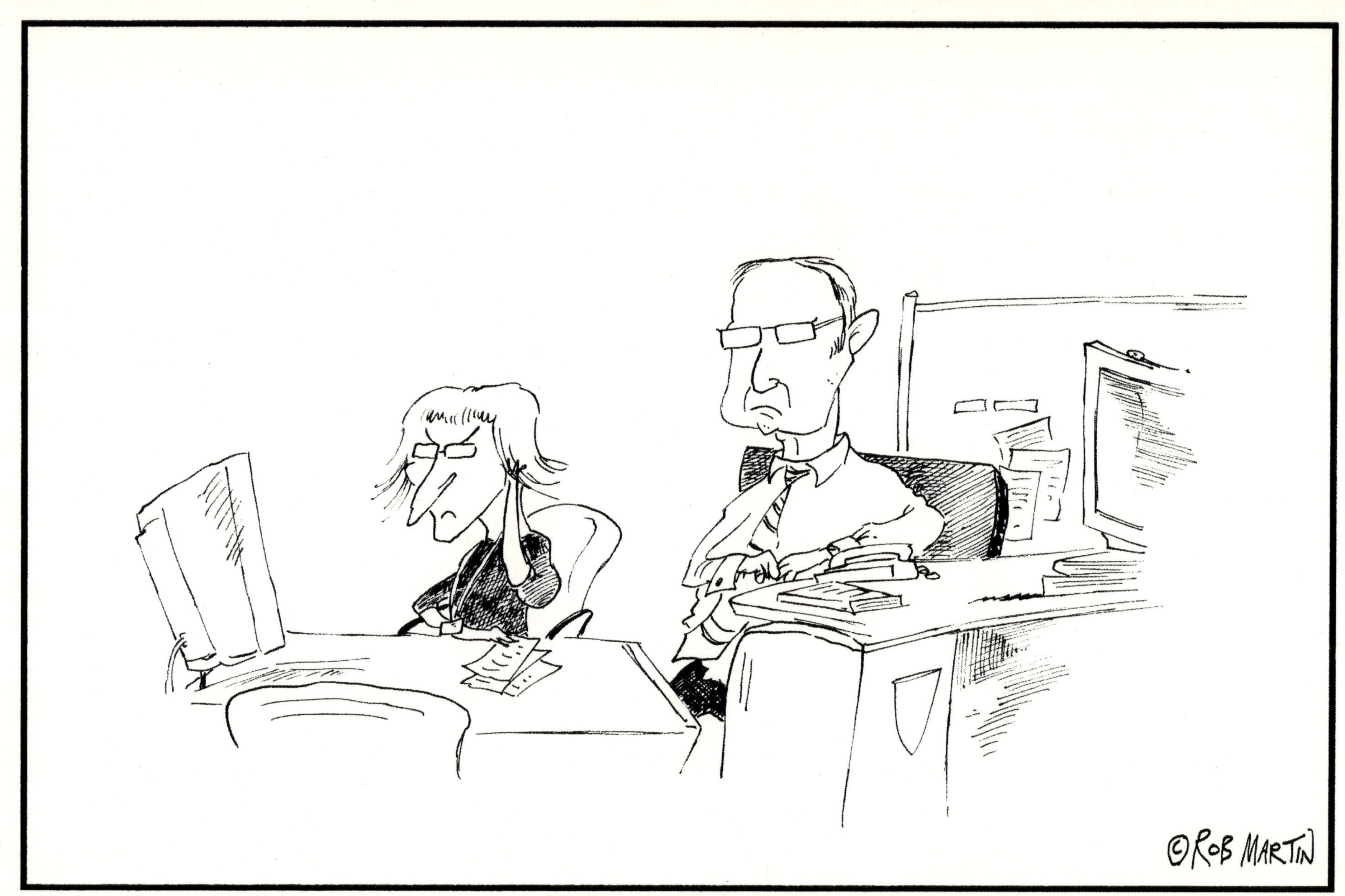

Office workers have no eyes. - PART 2

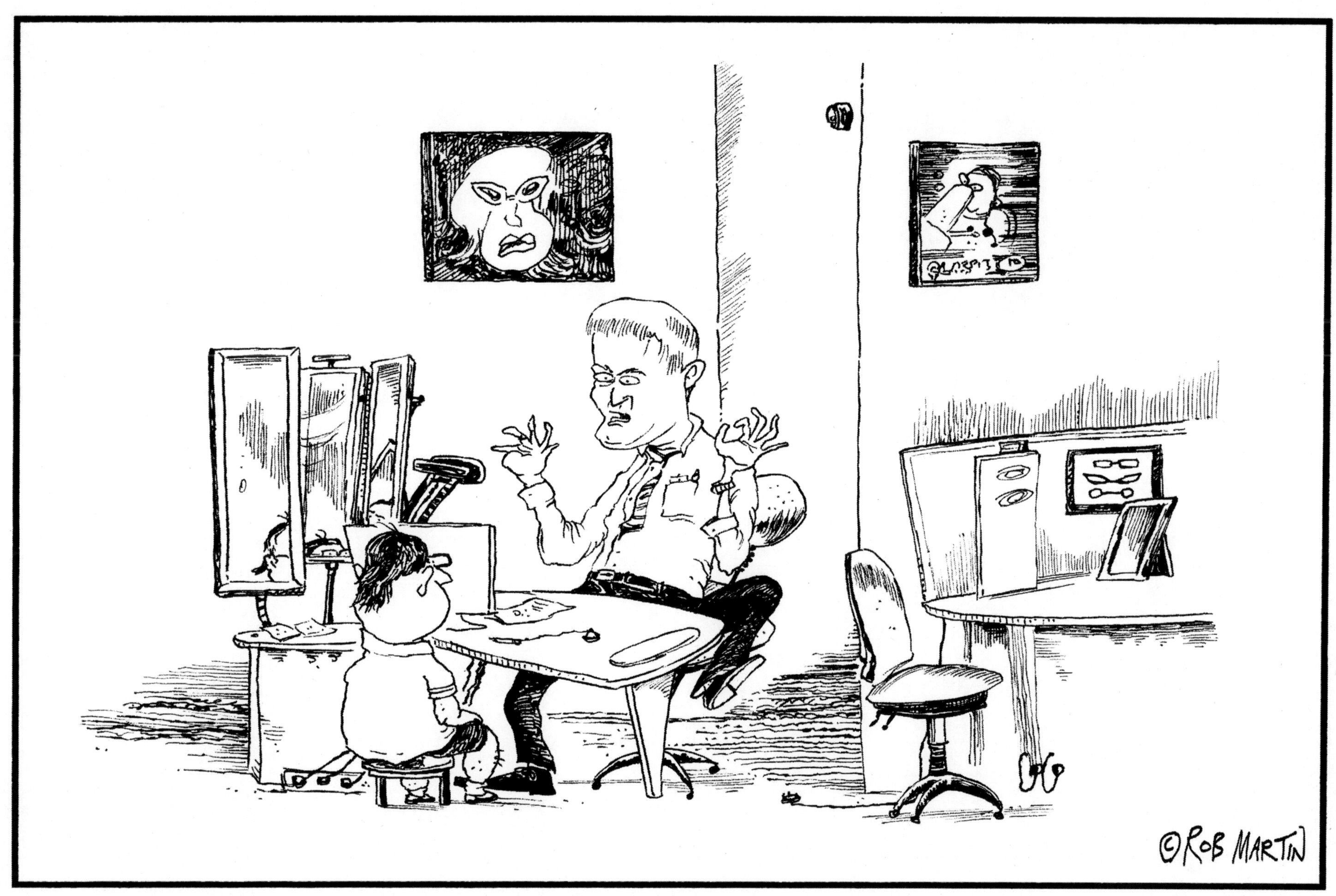

An optician warns about weakening eye muscles, hoping to make a sell on some clear plastic lenses for £147.

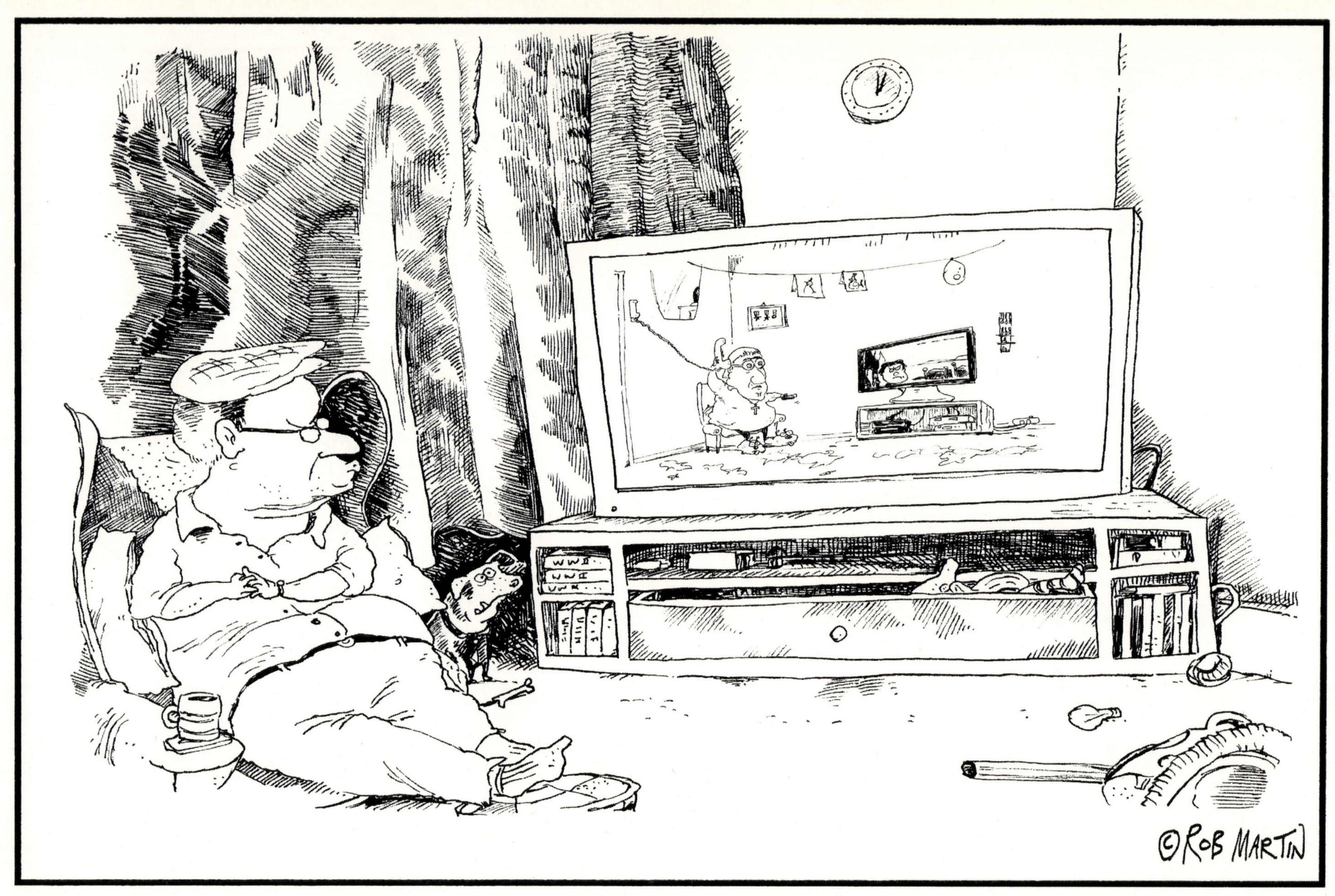

A man watches a T.V. show about someone watching T.V.

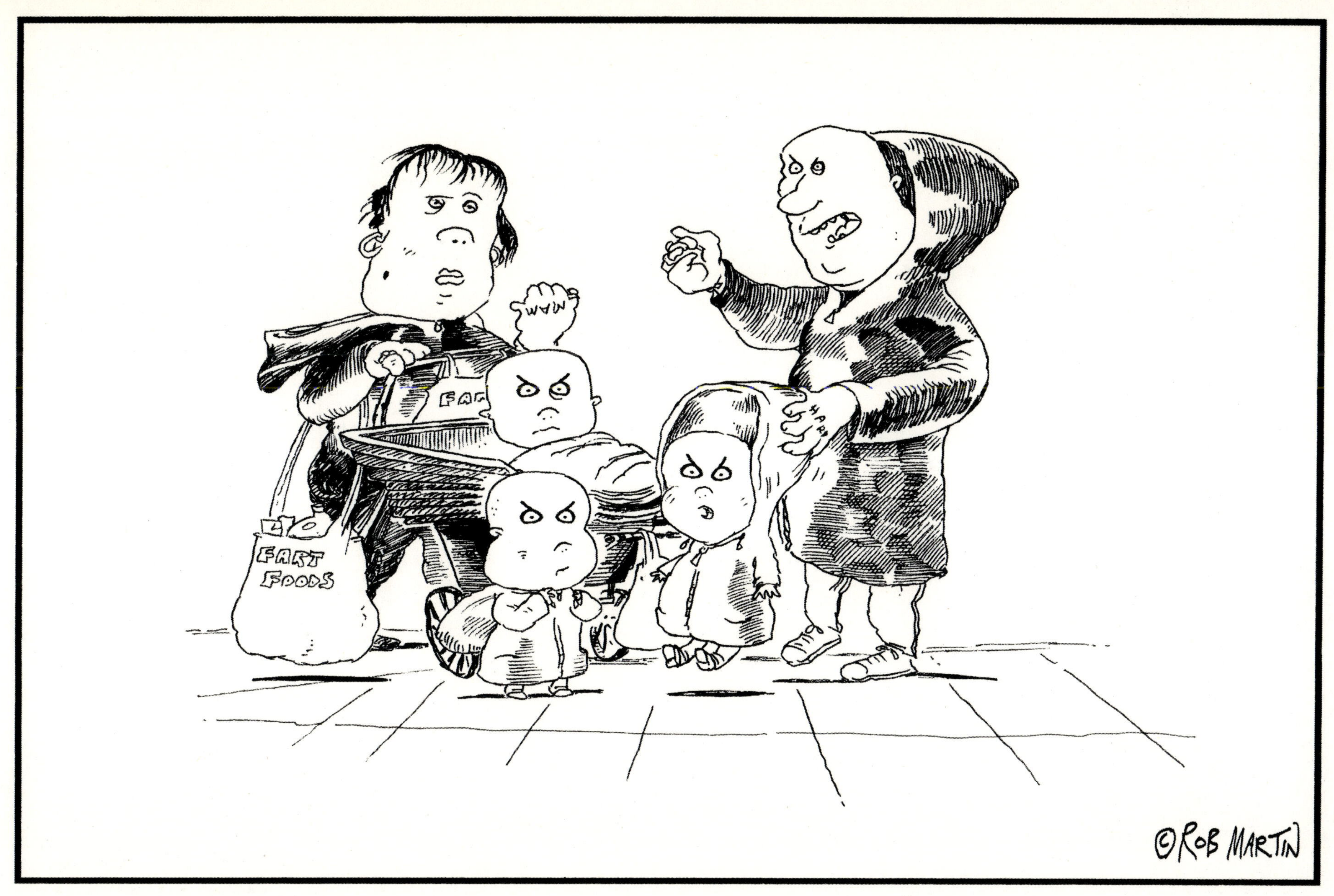

The angry family block a doorway in the supermarket.

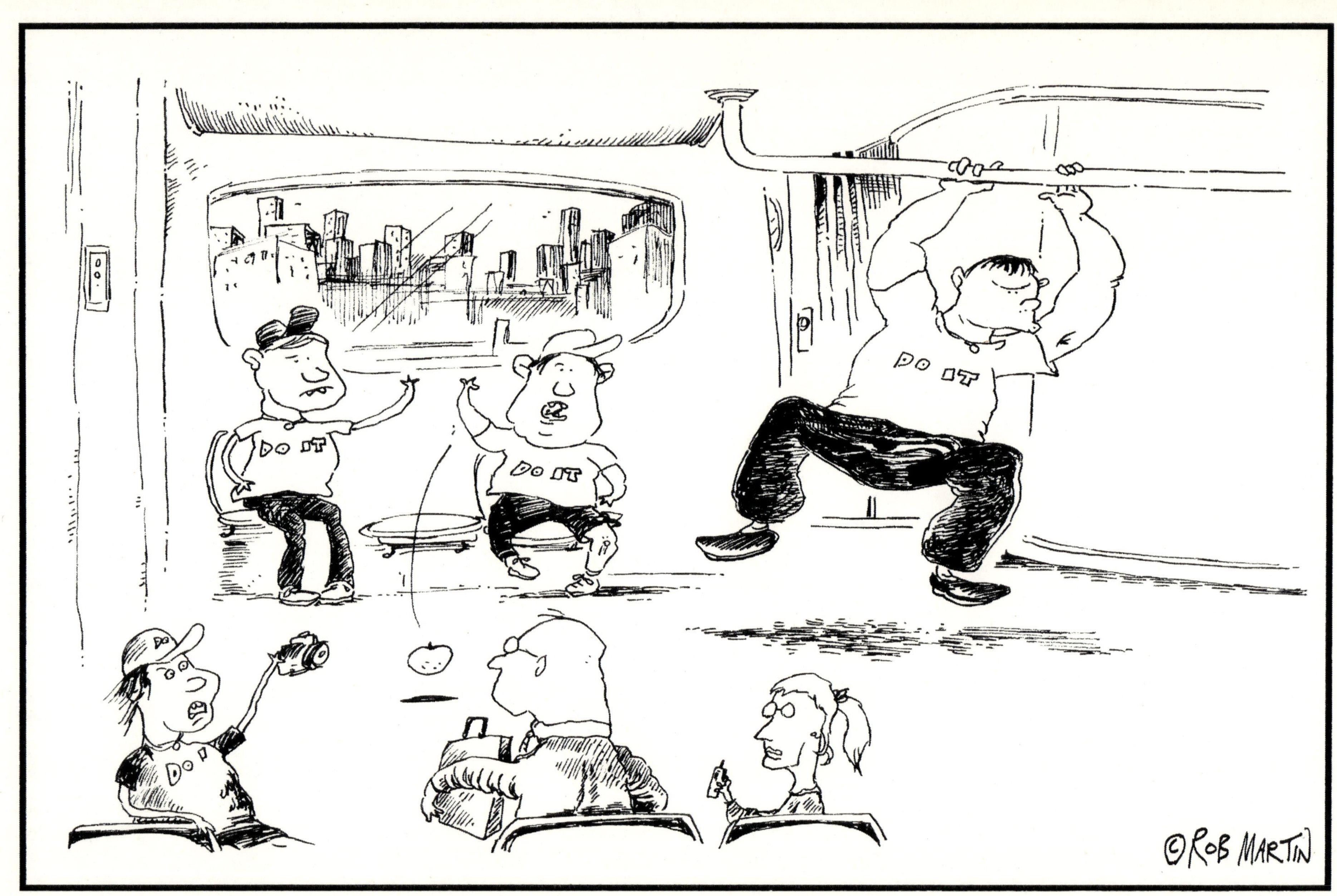

Dangling acrobats harass office workers.

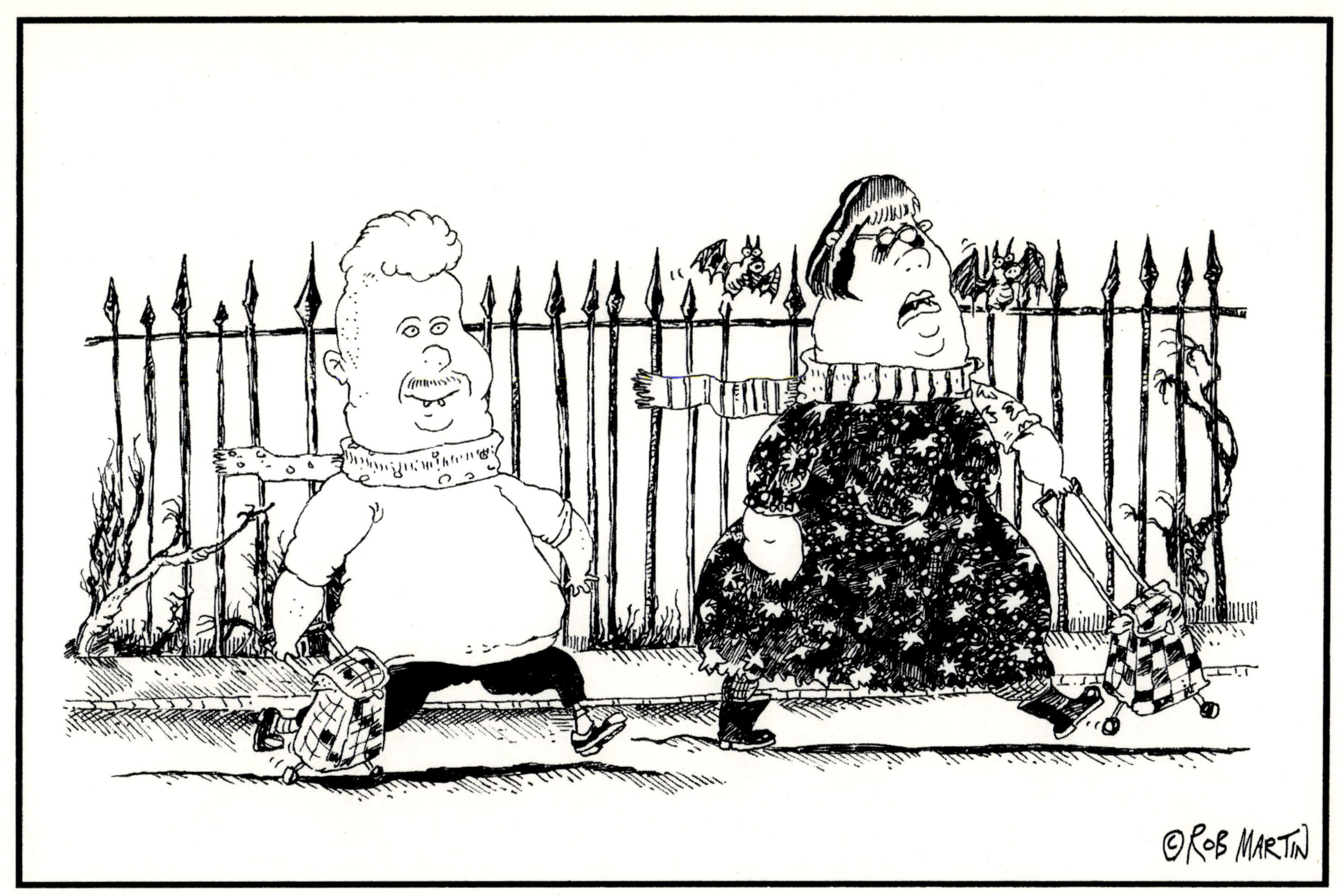

Besotted Barry follows bounding Belinda
unaware he is about to be dumped, due to the way he brushes his teeth.

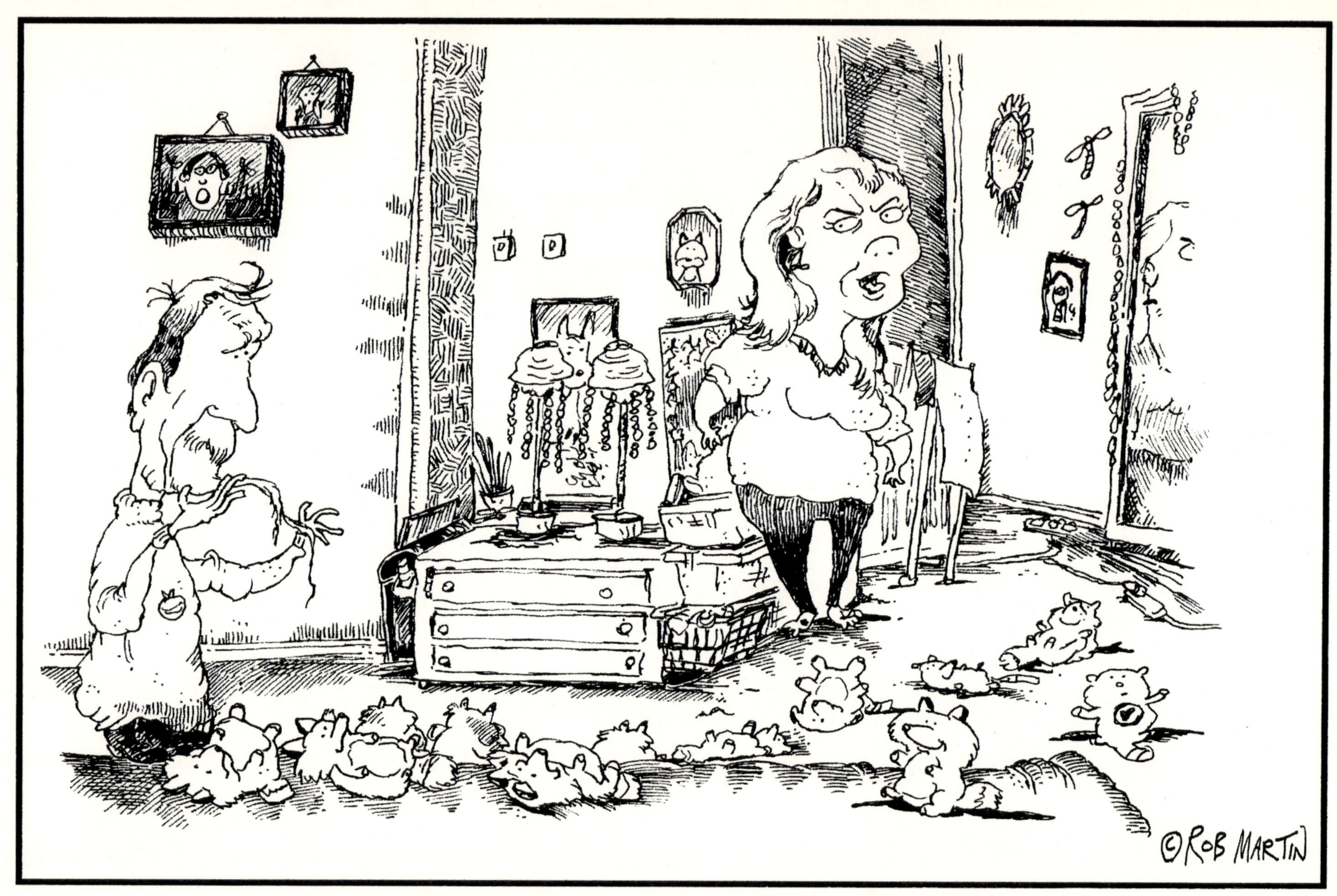

Having knocked over Mr. Squibbles, Mrs. Sniffly and countless other toys, Herbert is told that he is a daggy faced pratt.

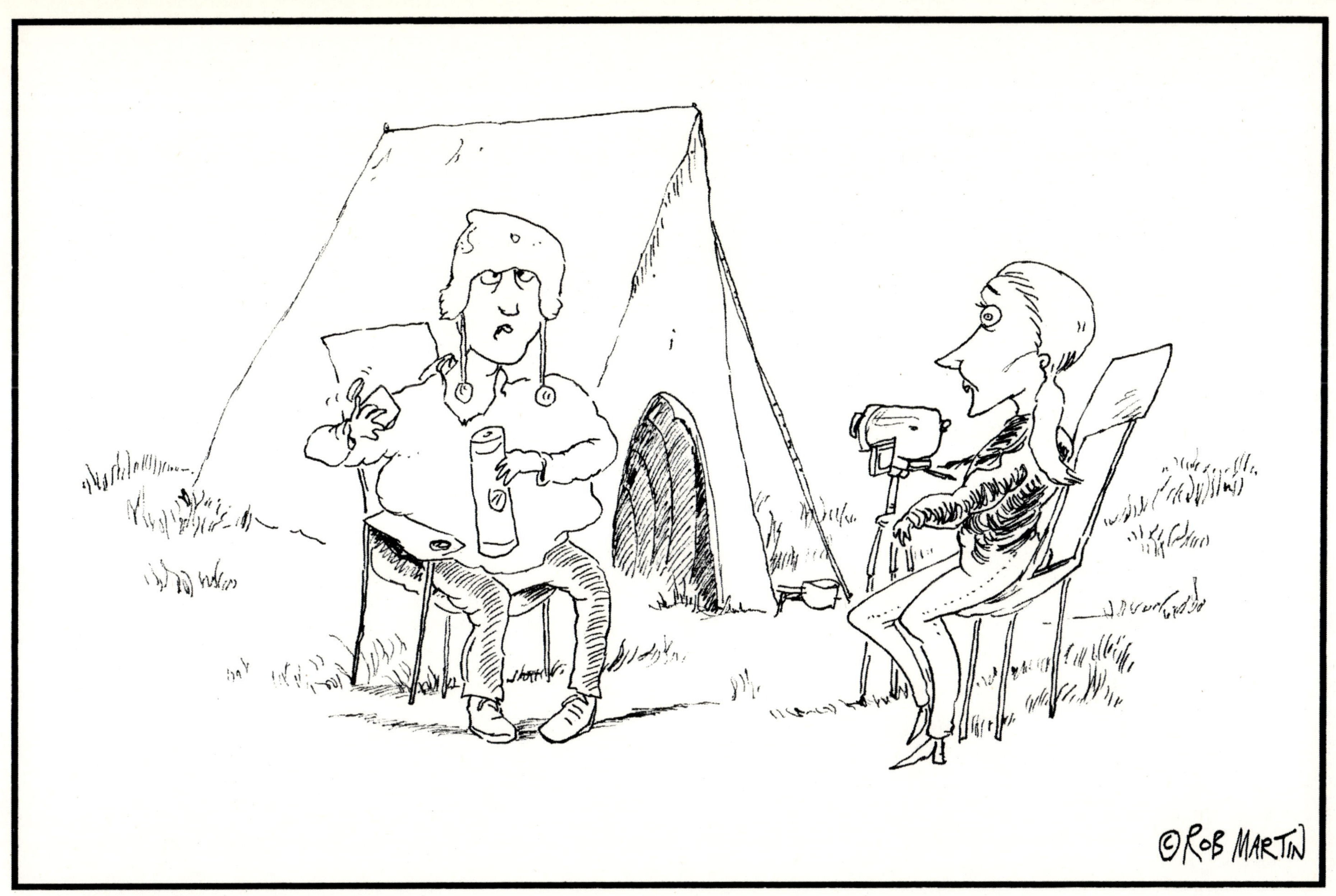

Stephen gets his thoughts into a tangle, as he thinks about an ever expanding Universe and how un-insignificant his graffiti is.

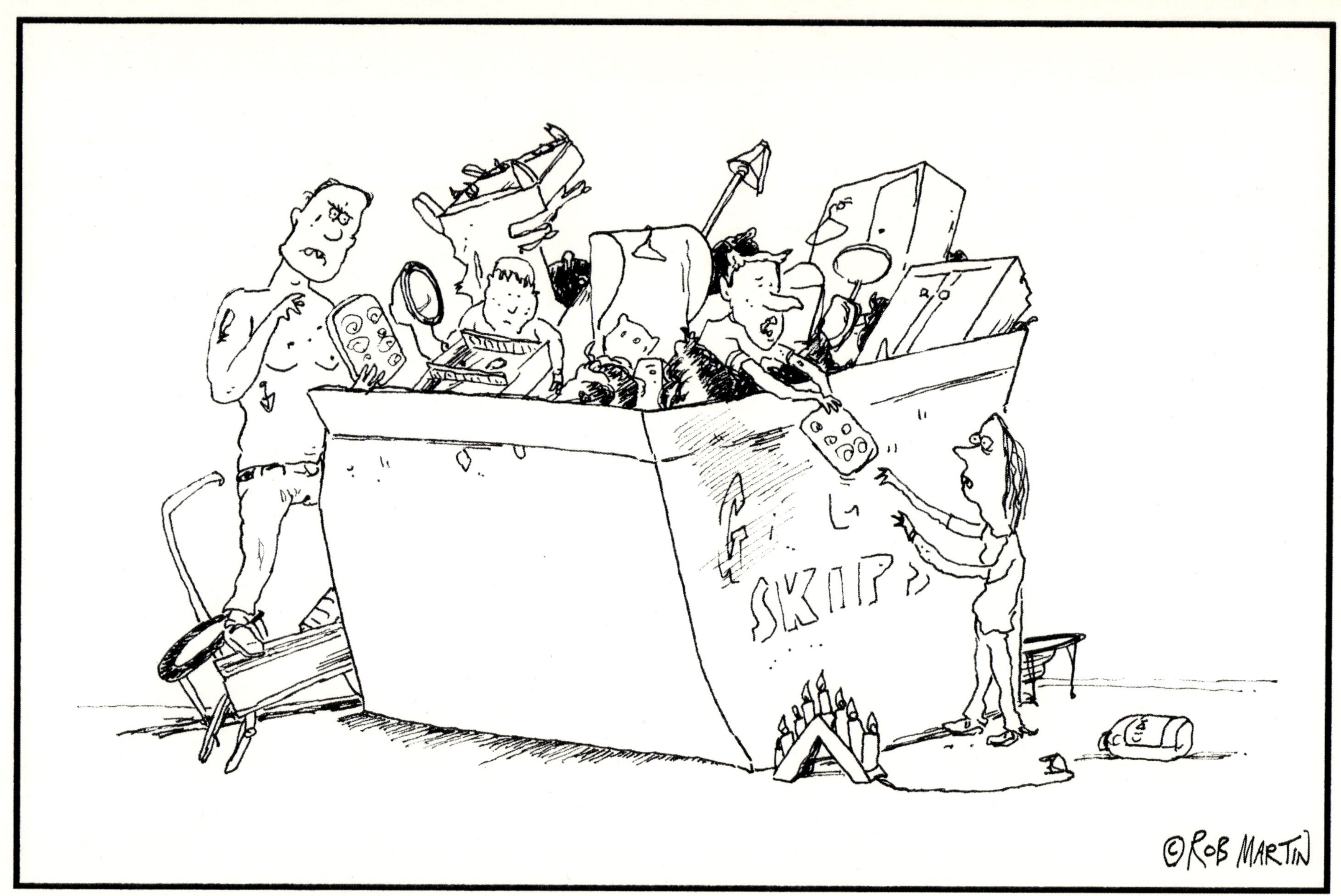

Bums raid care home skip looking for placemats.

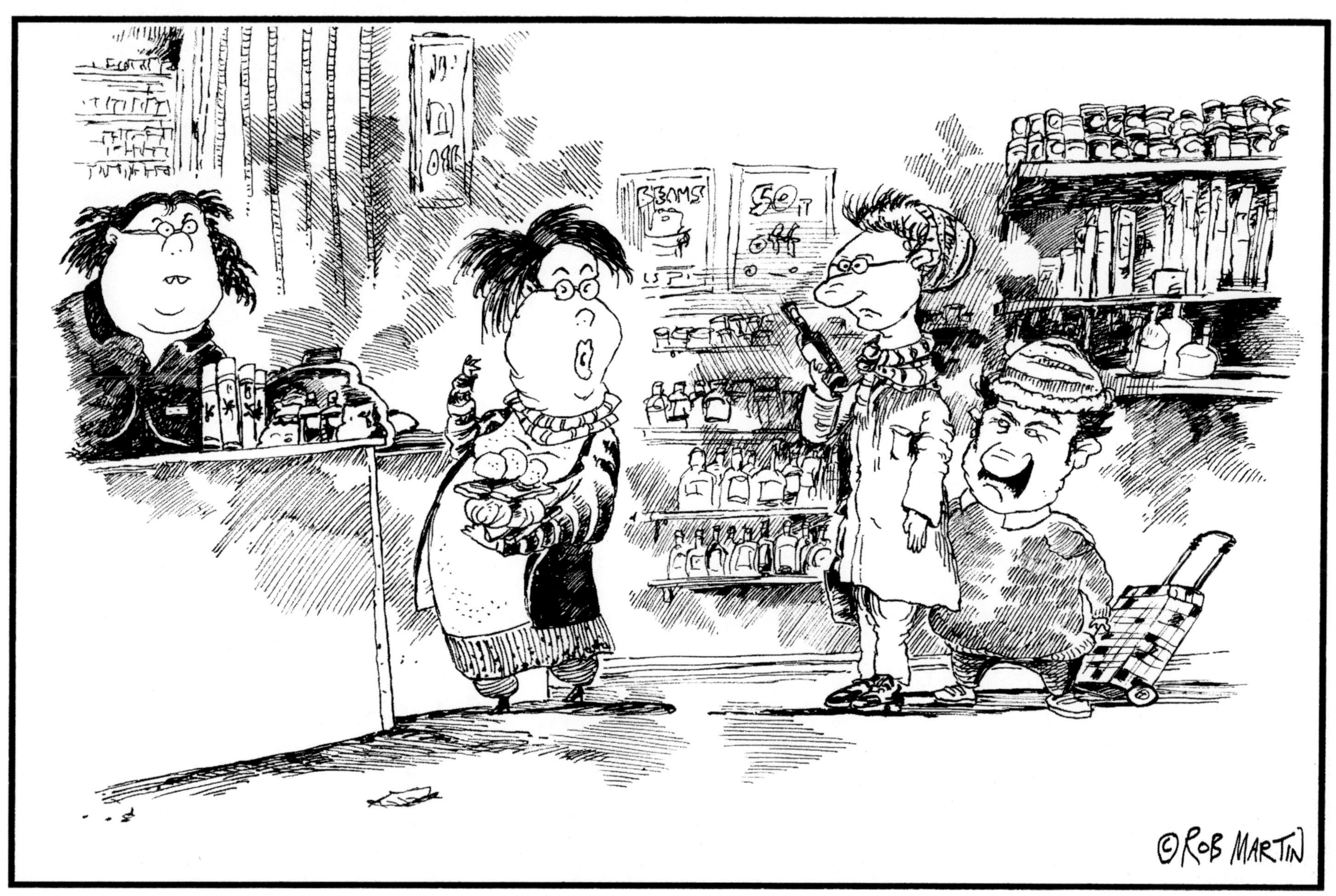

"Oy!! I will headbutt you!" Shrieks Gill the Physics teacher, miss-hearing the man behind reading, "tasty full body".

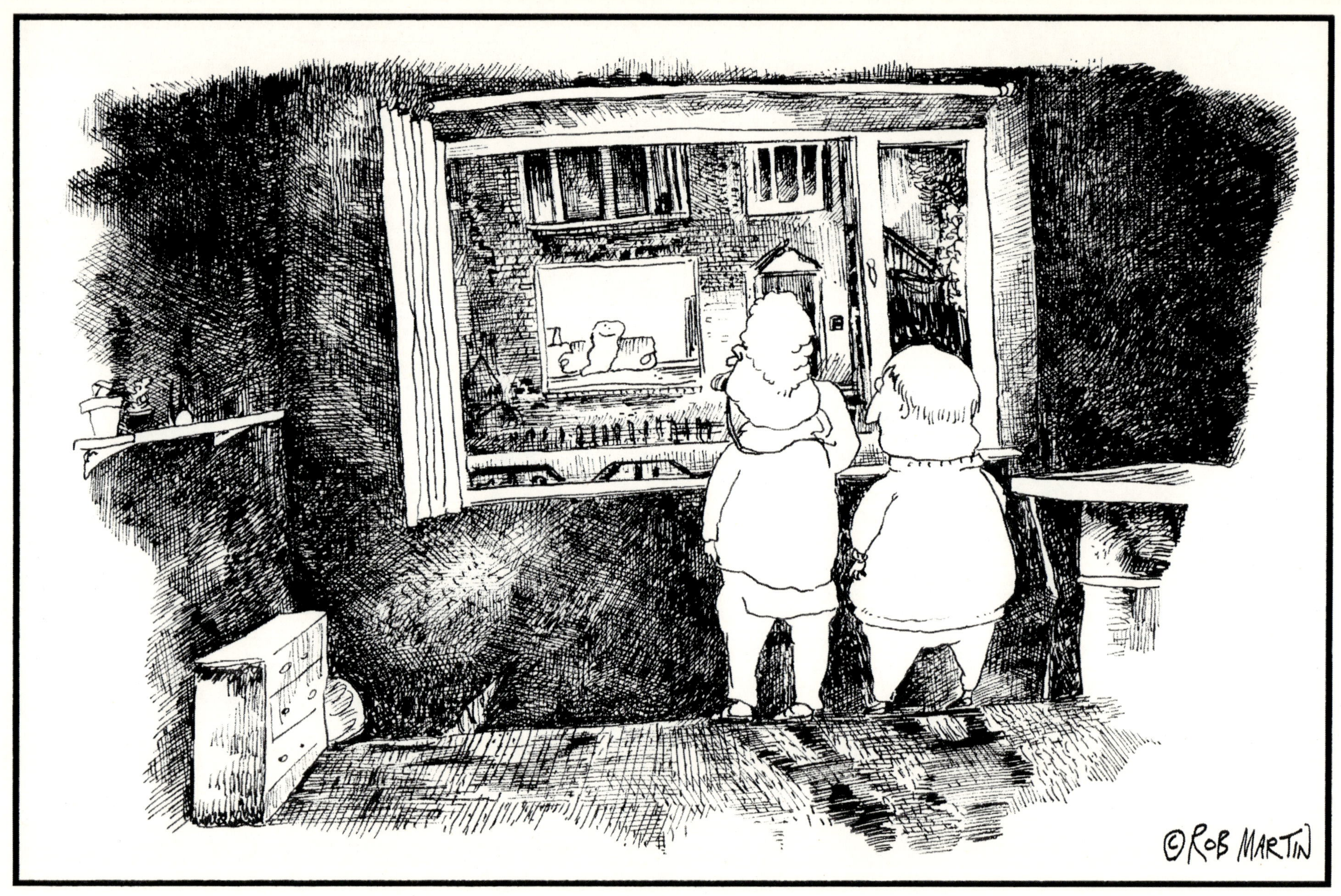

An old couple stare out at the house across the road, unsure at what is sat in the front room.

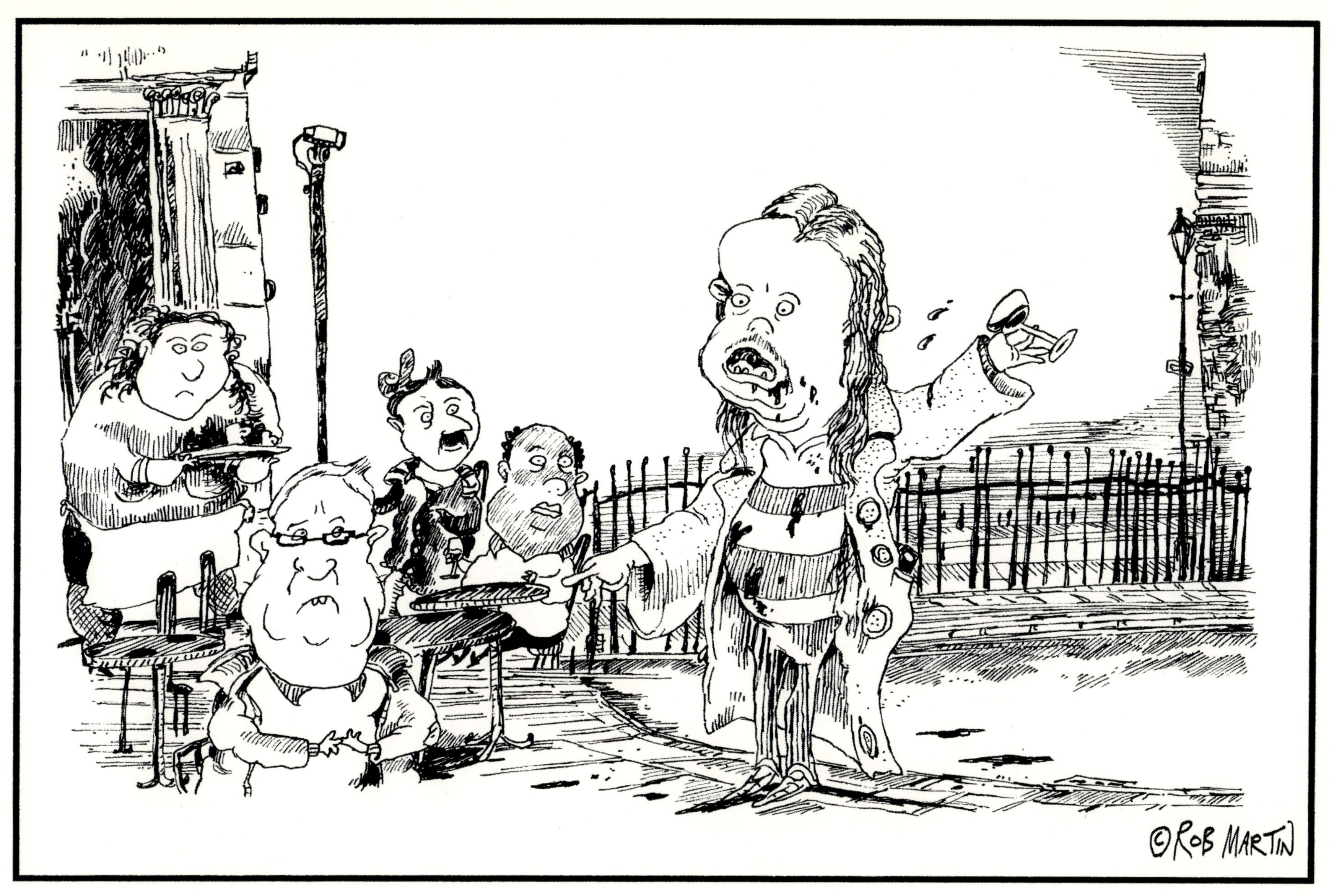

"All I hear is waffle!" Slurs Mr. Horius in a defiant tone.

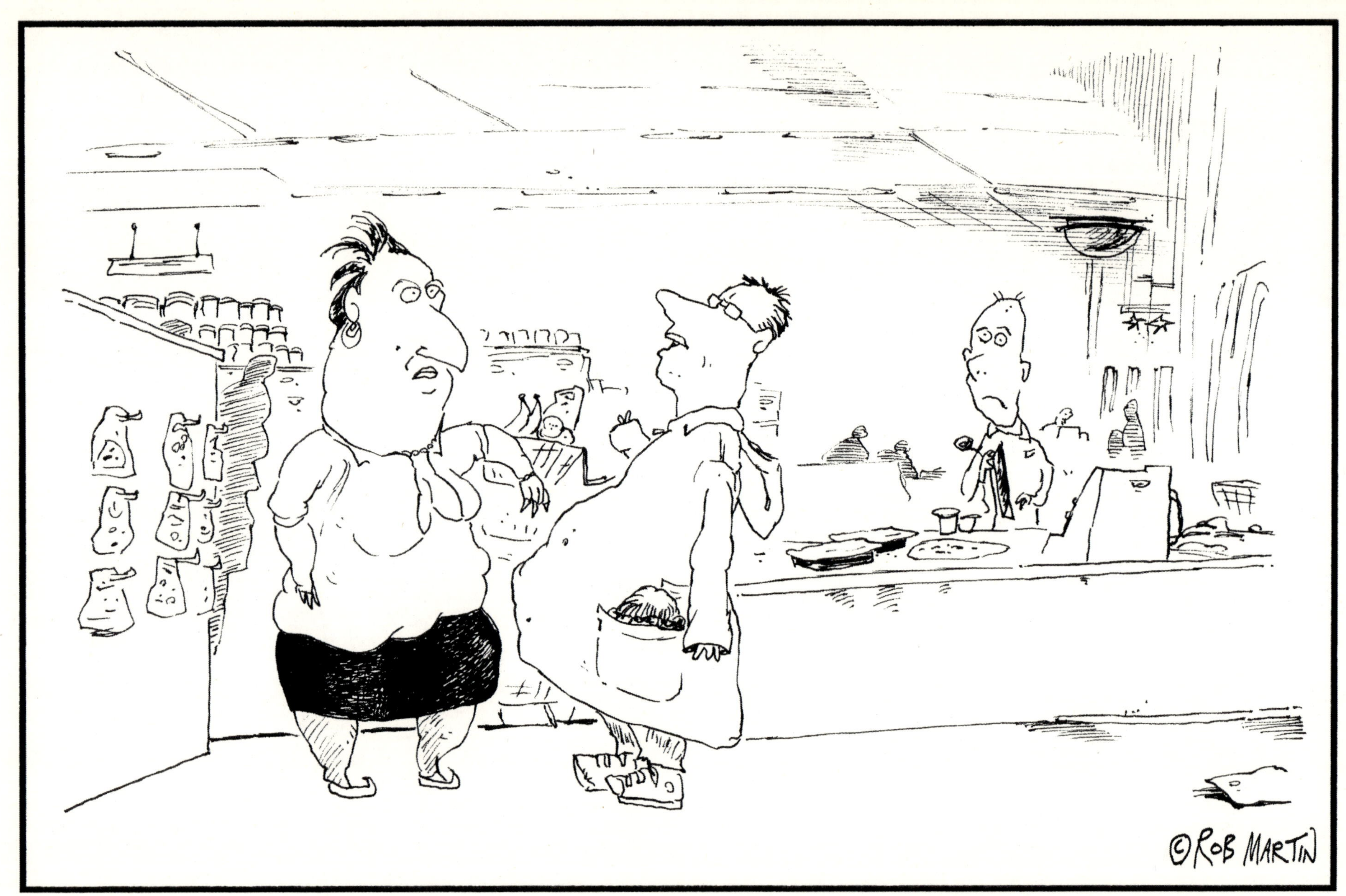

A customer at a supermarket checkout is unhappy with the closeness of the woman behind him.

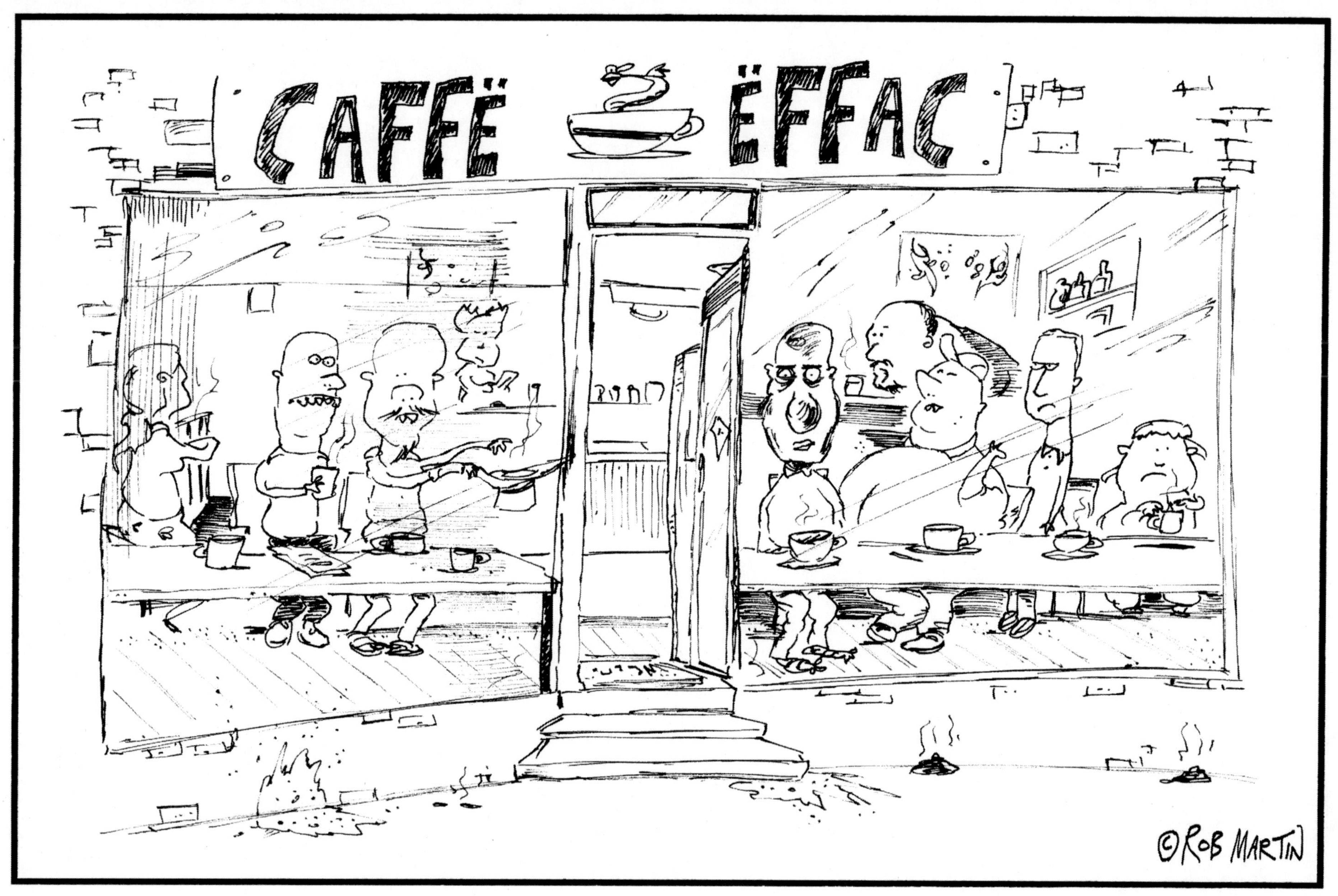

Coffee cultural unemployables.

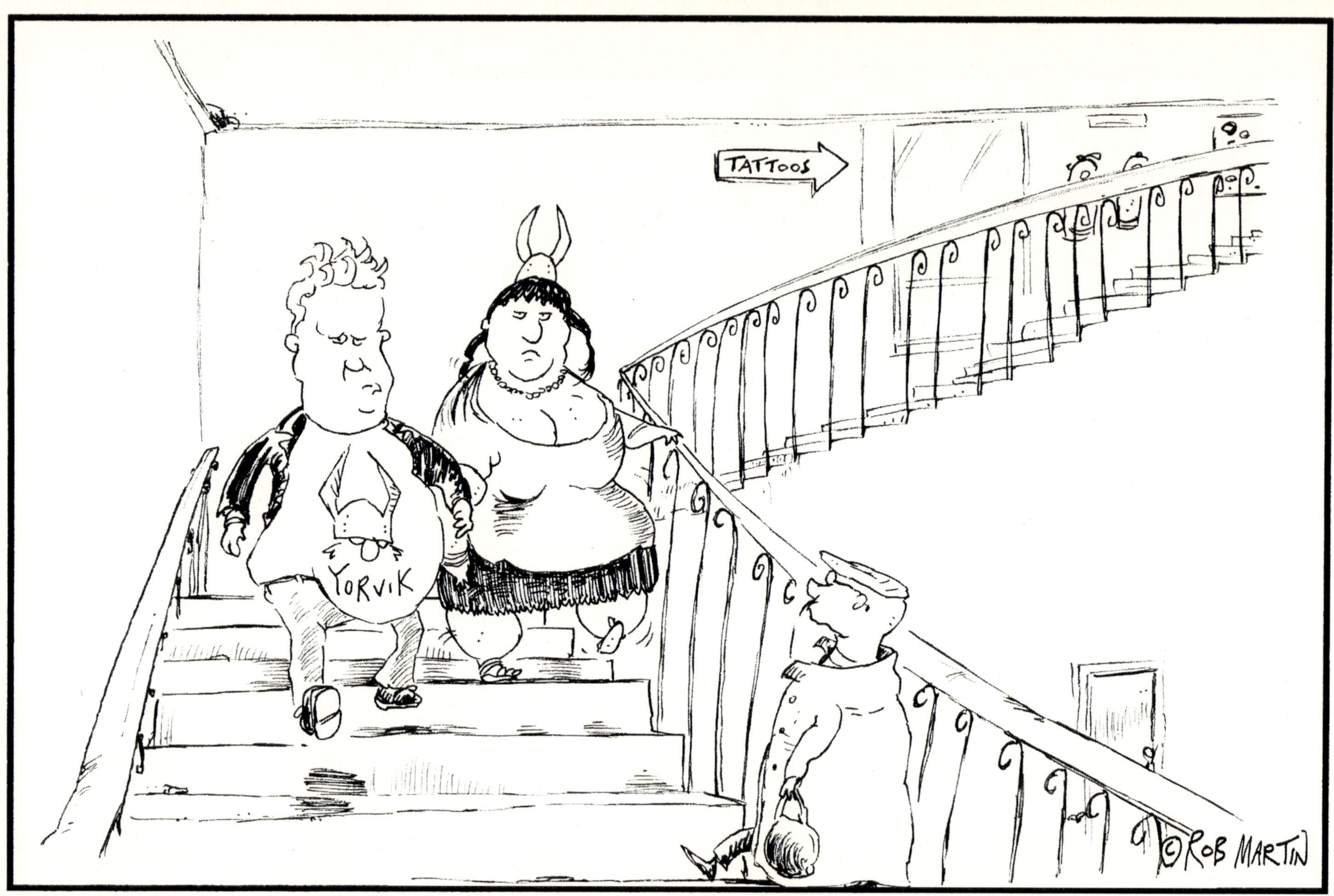
TATTOOS
YORVIK
©ROB MARTIN

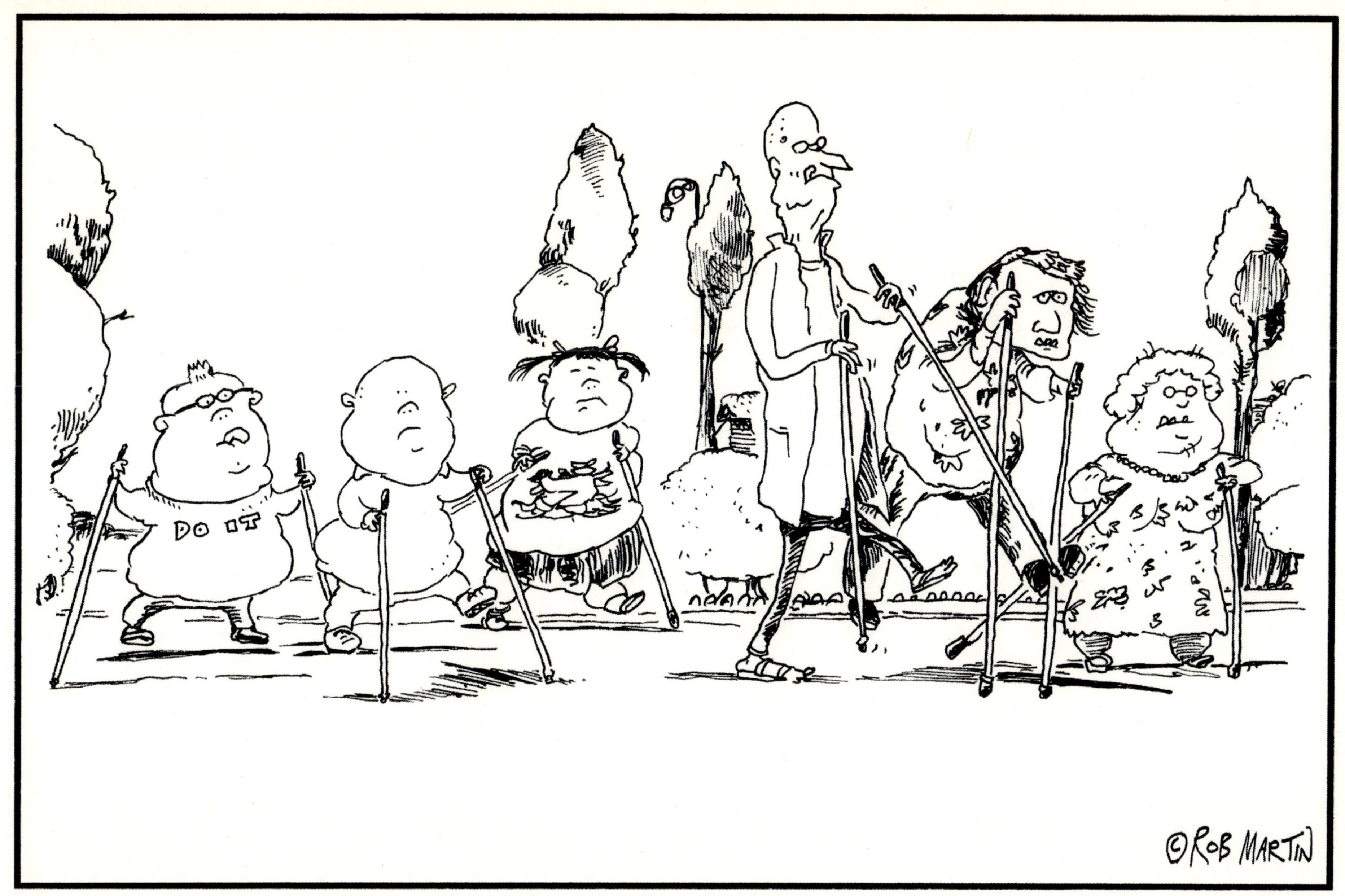

Nordic pole walking on Sunday afternoons.

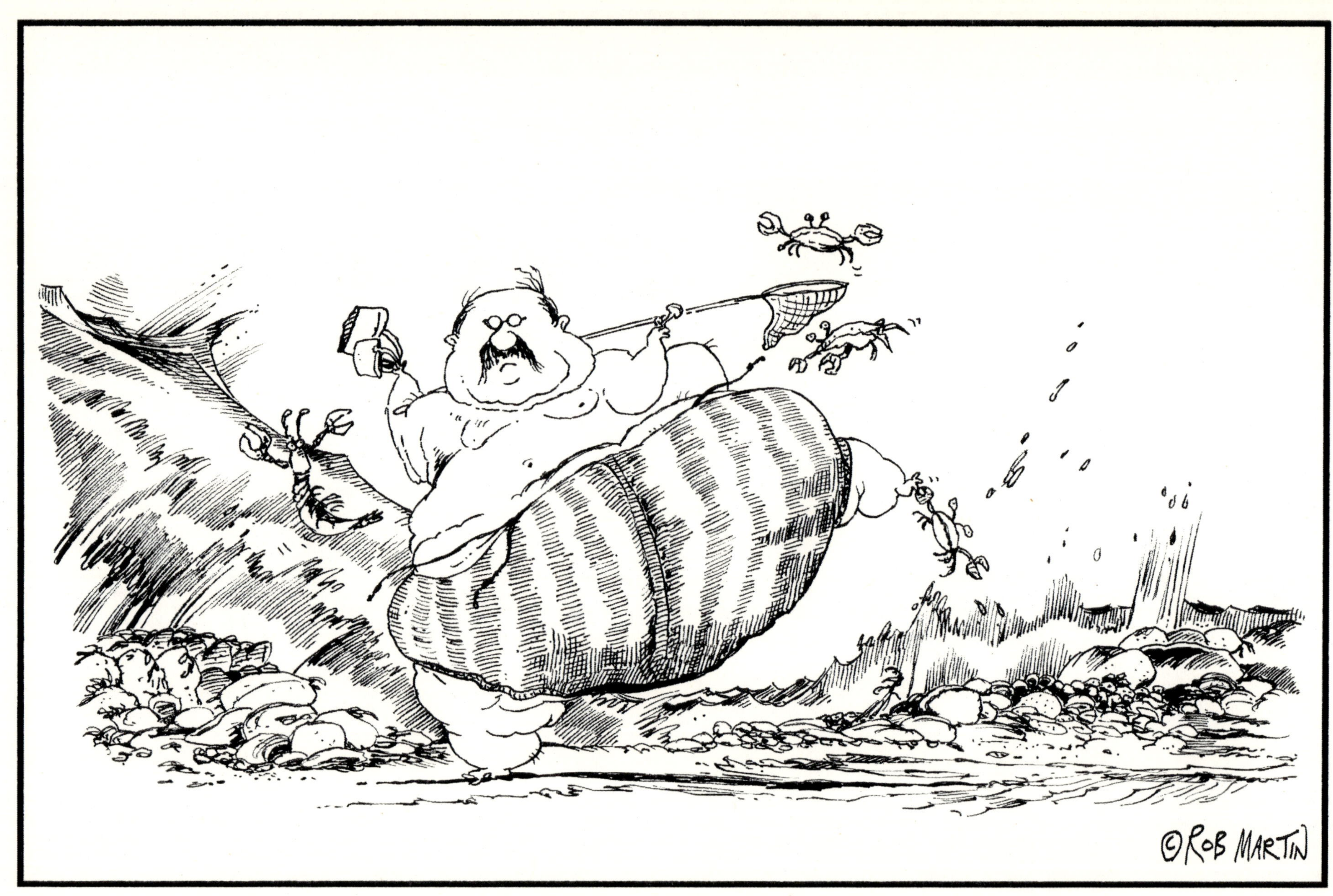

Mr. Handy in his wildly savage underpants catches crustaceans and decapods.

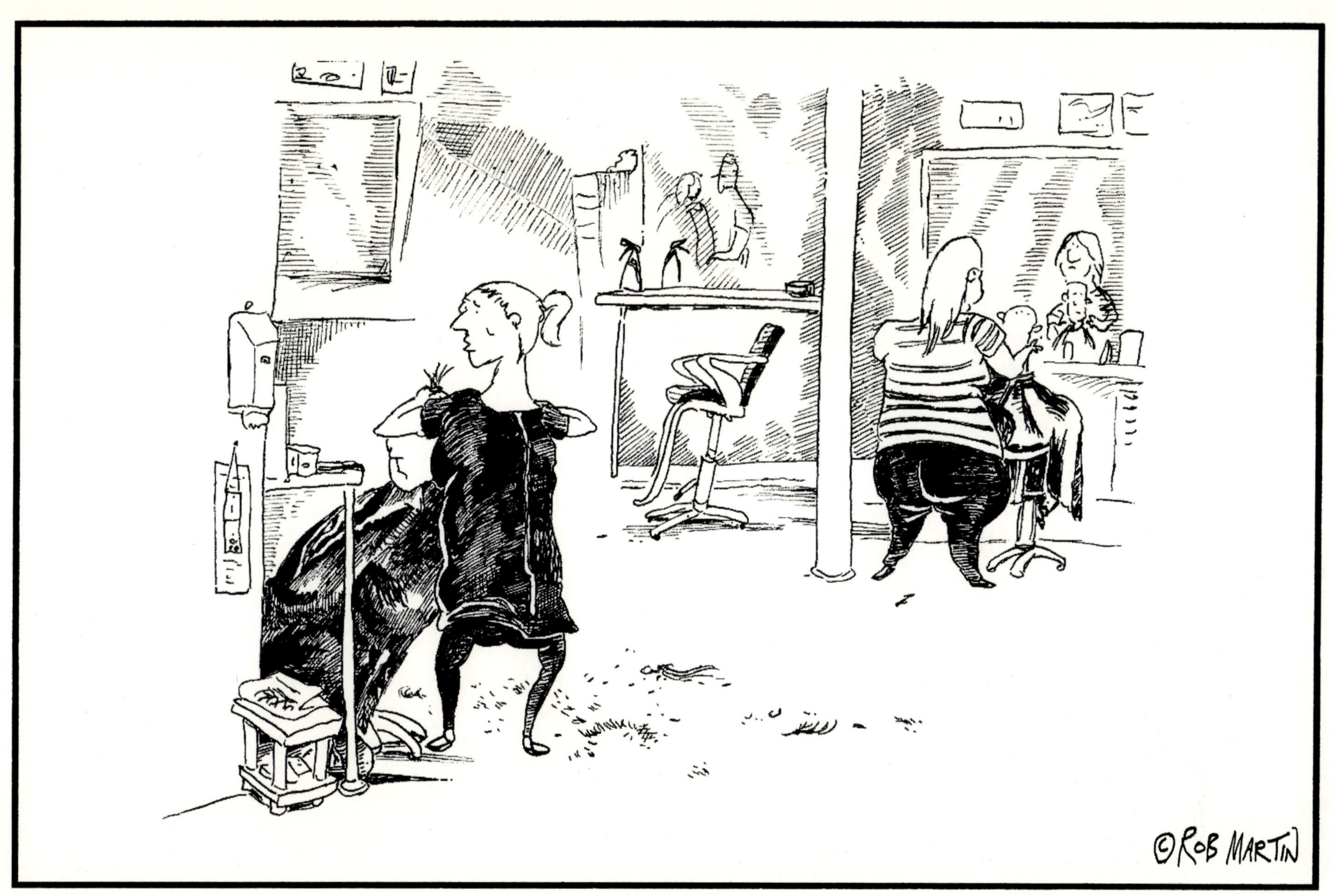

Anita the hair-dresser, reduces a ladies hair
to the shape of a scarecrow.

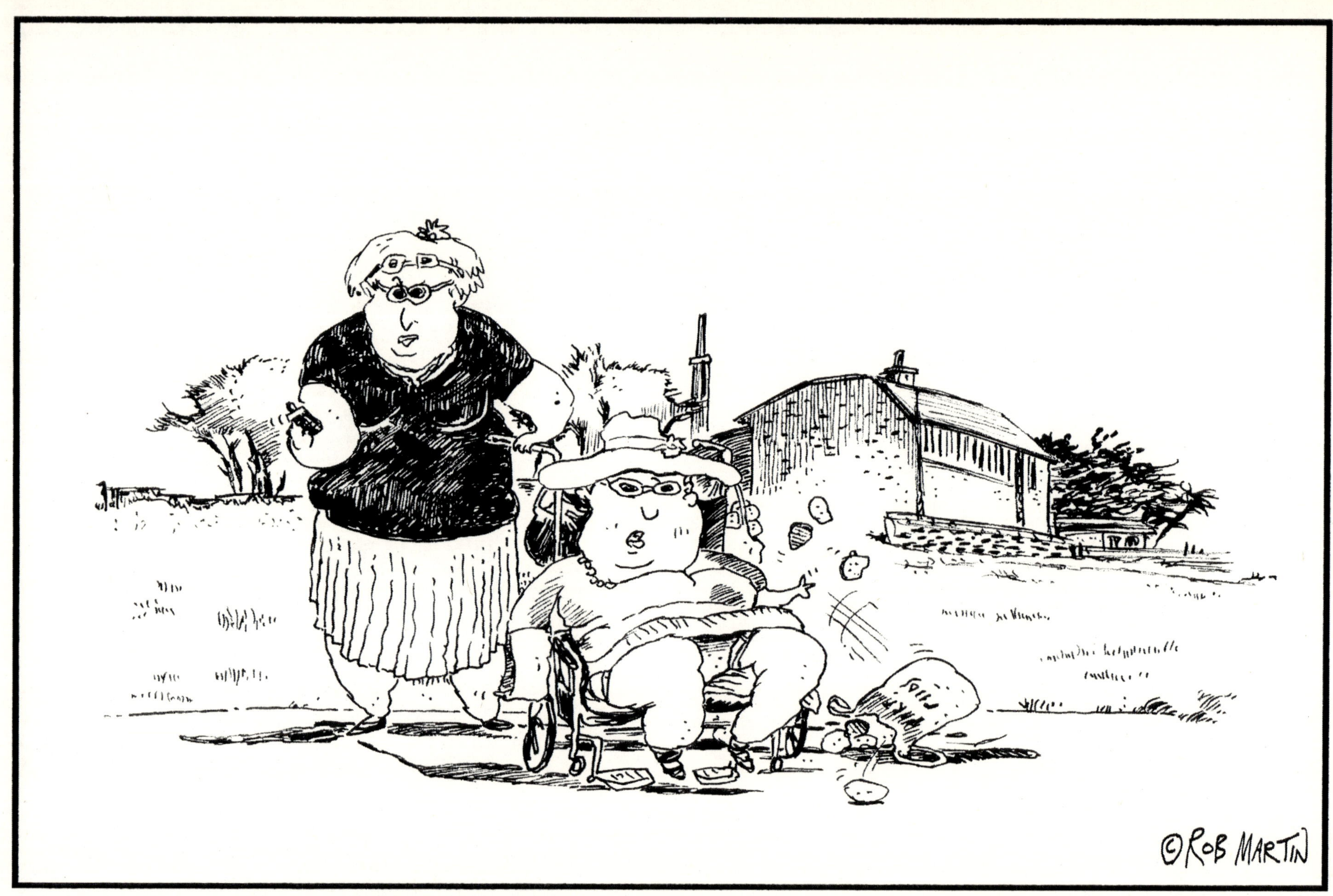

On a sunny day, a woman reads a text whilst her Mother throws the bag of potatoes again.

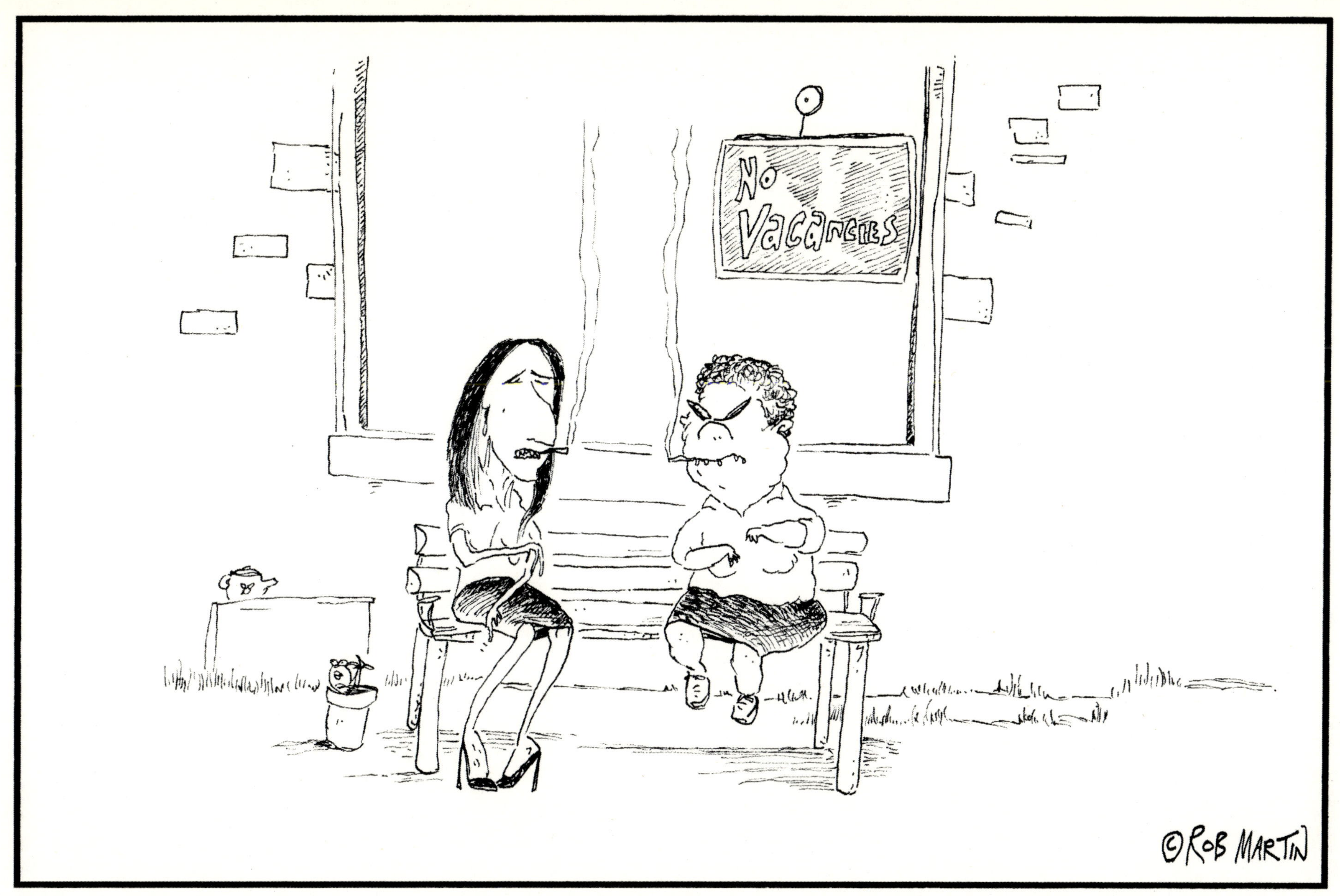

Rat face women stare at the road.

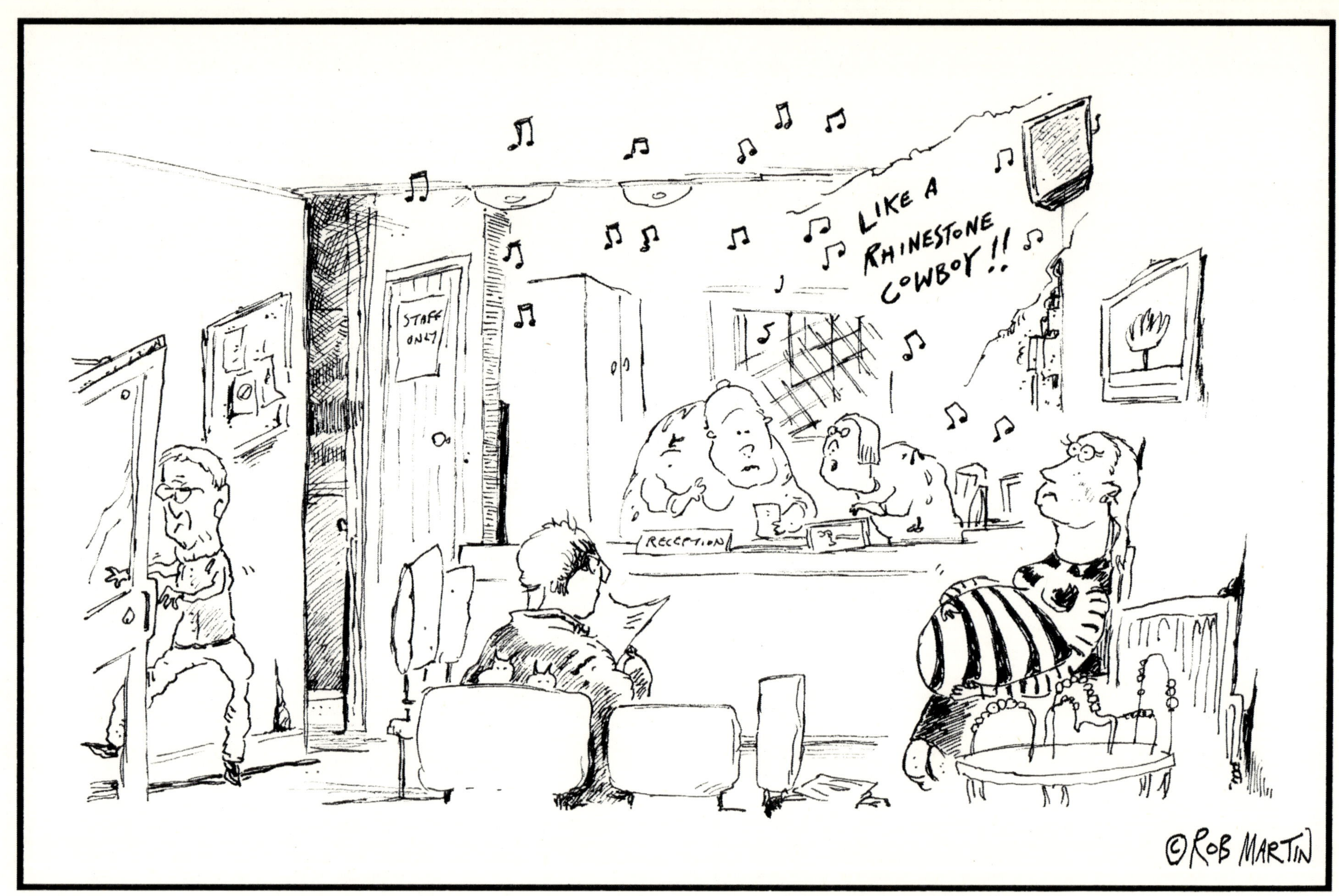

A pregnant woman waits in a Doctor's surgery as Country and Western plays on the speakers.

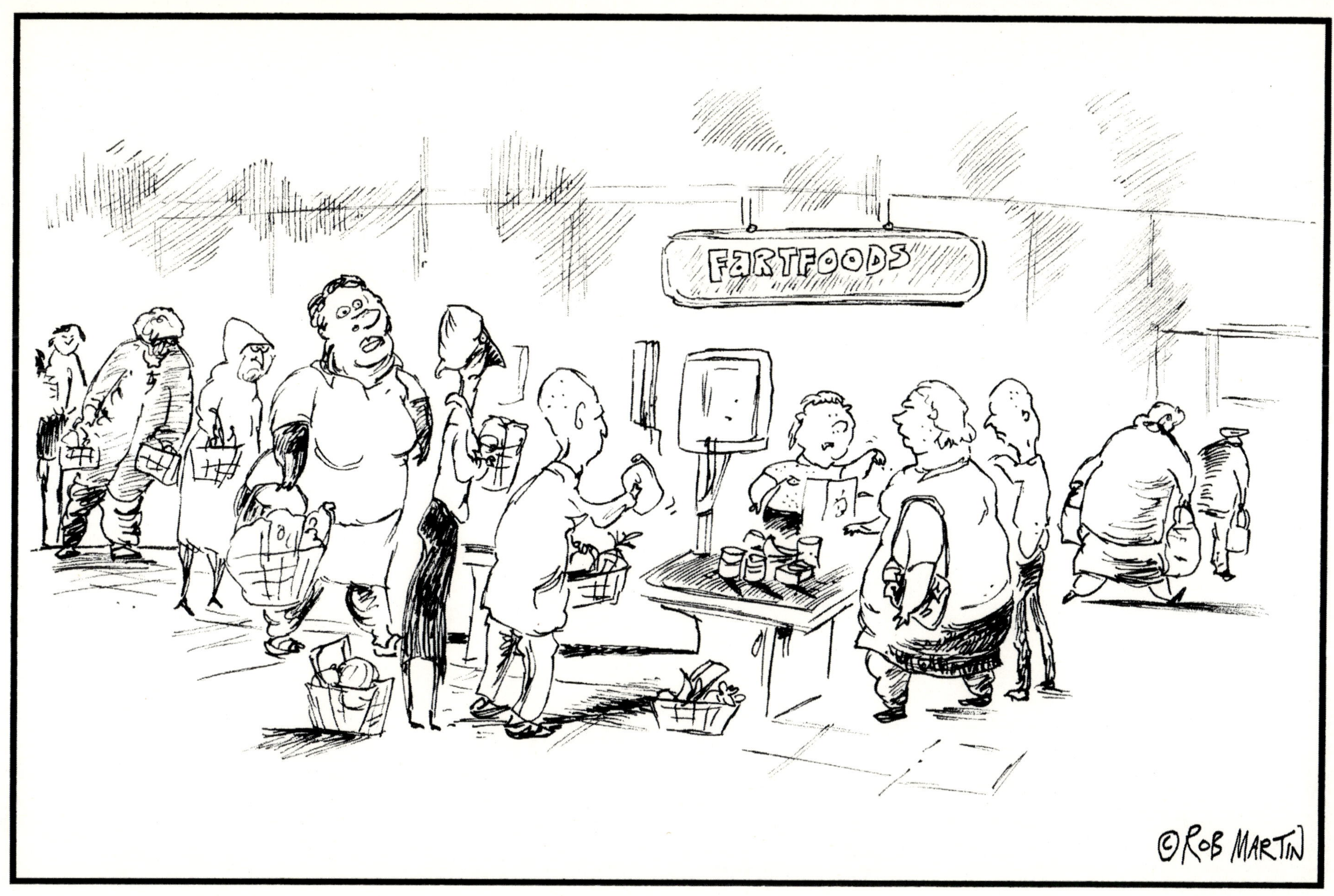

A lone check-out girl serves a none stop conga line of consumers.

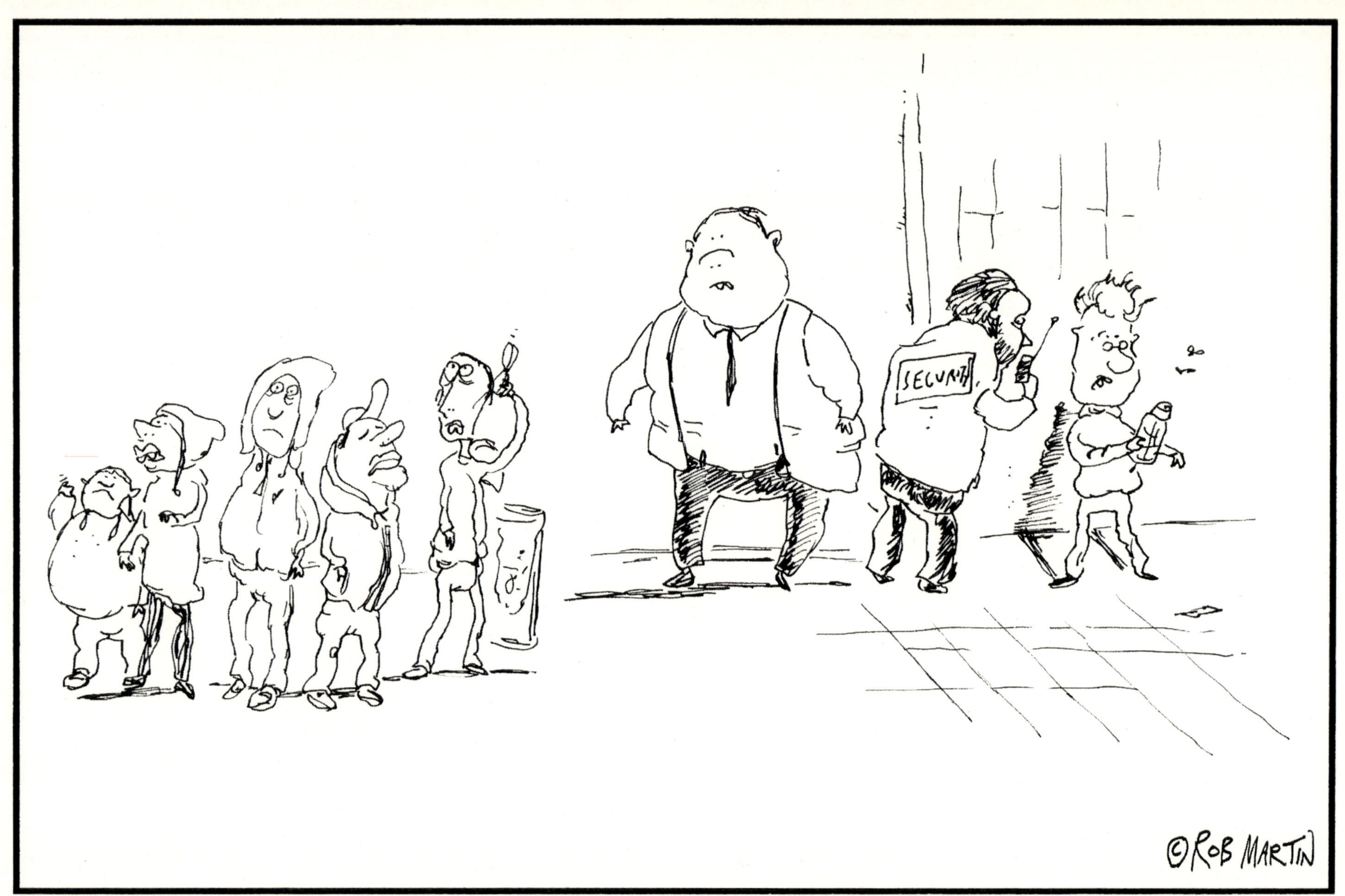

Bus station security call the Police to a drunk, whilst turning a blind eye to loiterers with intent.

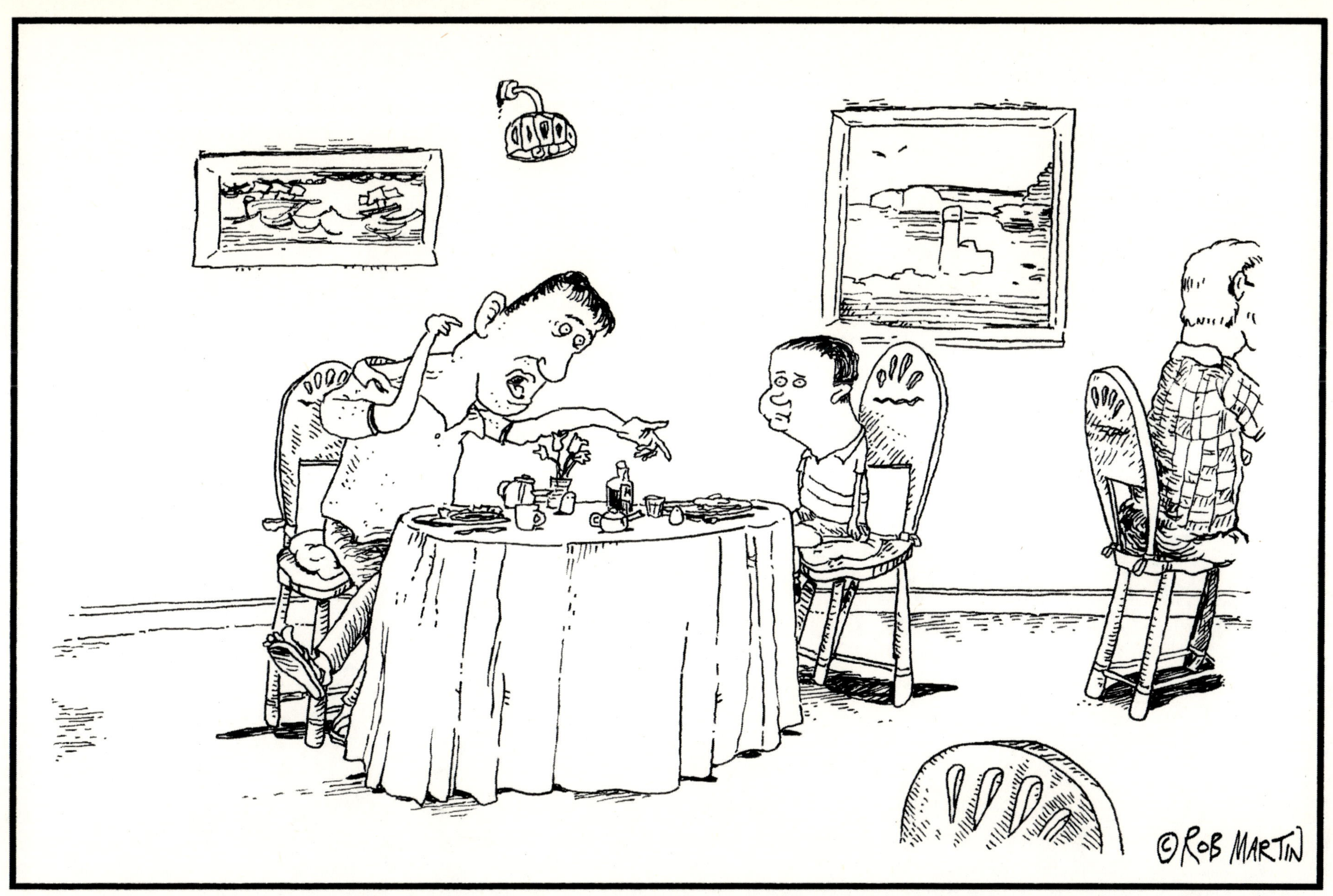

At breakfast in the Lighthouse Hotel. "Cutty with knifey", says a father in a baby voice, hoping his quiet son will attack the bacon.

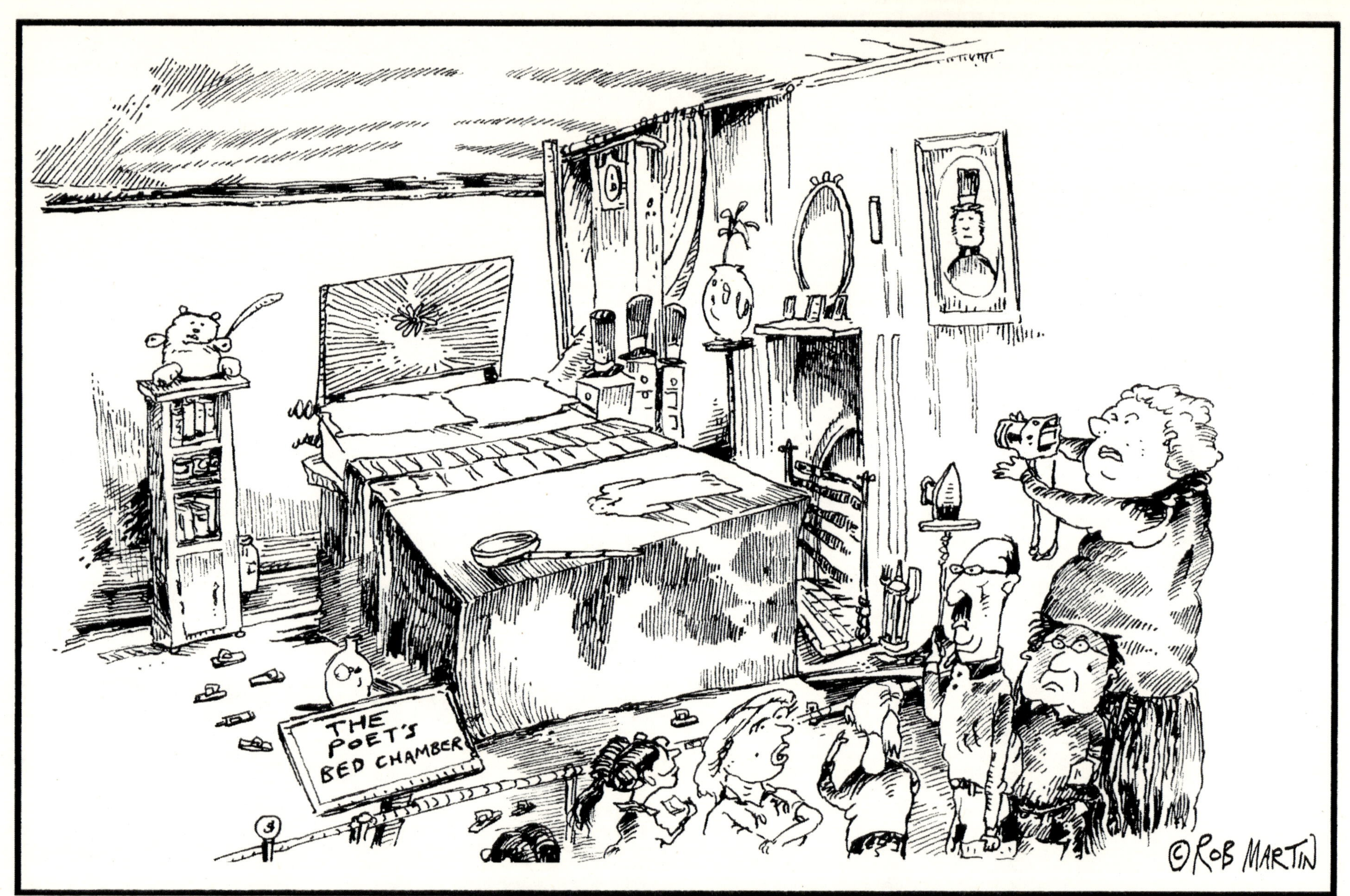

158 years after the great Poet
took his last breath. Tourists gather remembering
his famous poem 'Look at my dirty bed'.

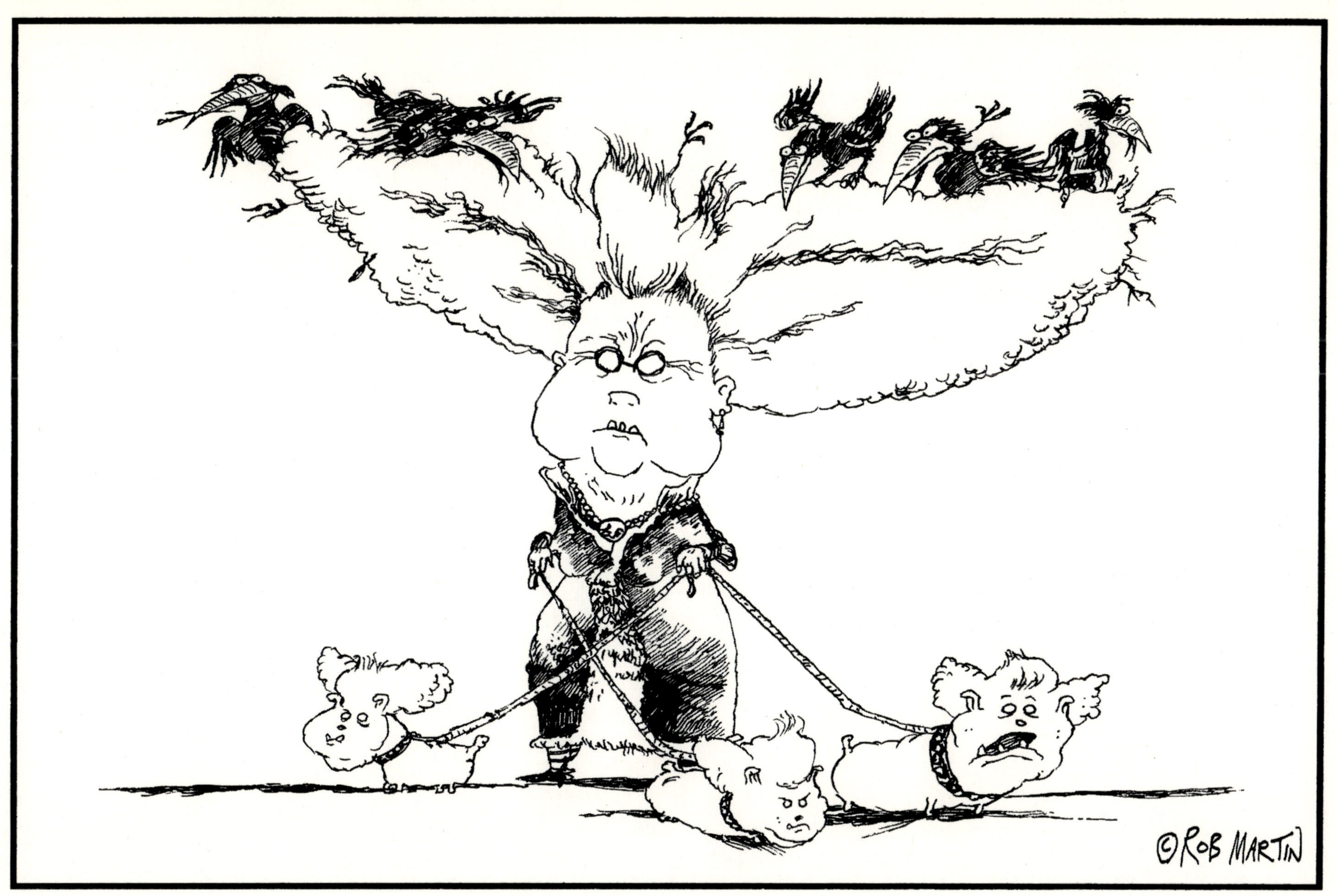

The old crone in her silence, succeeds in stopping her Shitladors
from dragging her through another hedge.

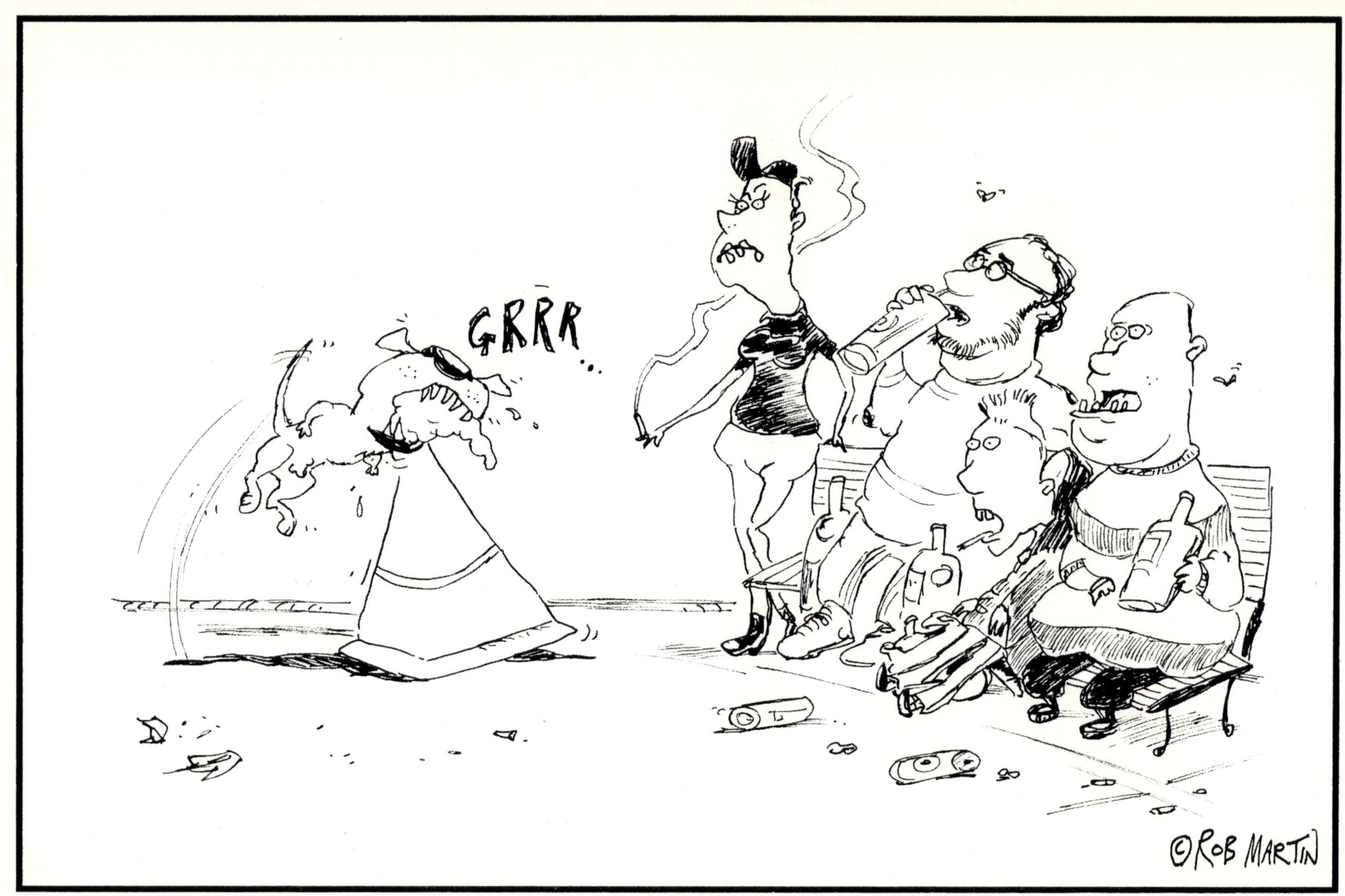

In the park, drunks watch a dog chew up a traffic bollard, thinking it's the best entertainment they've ever seen.

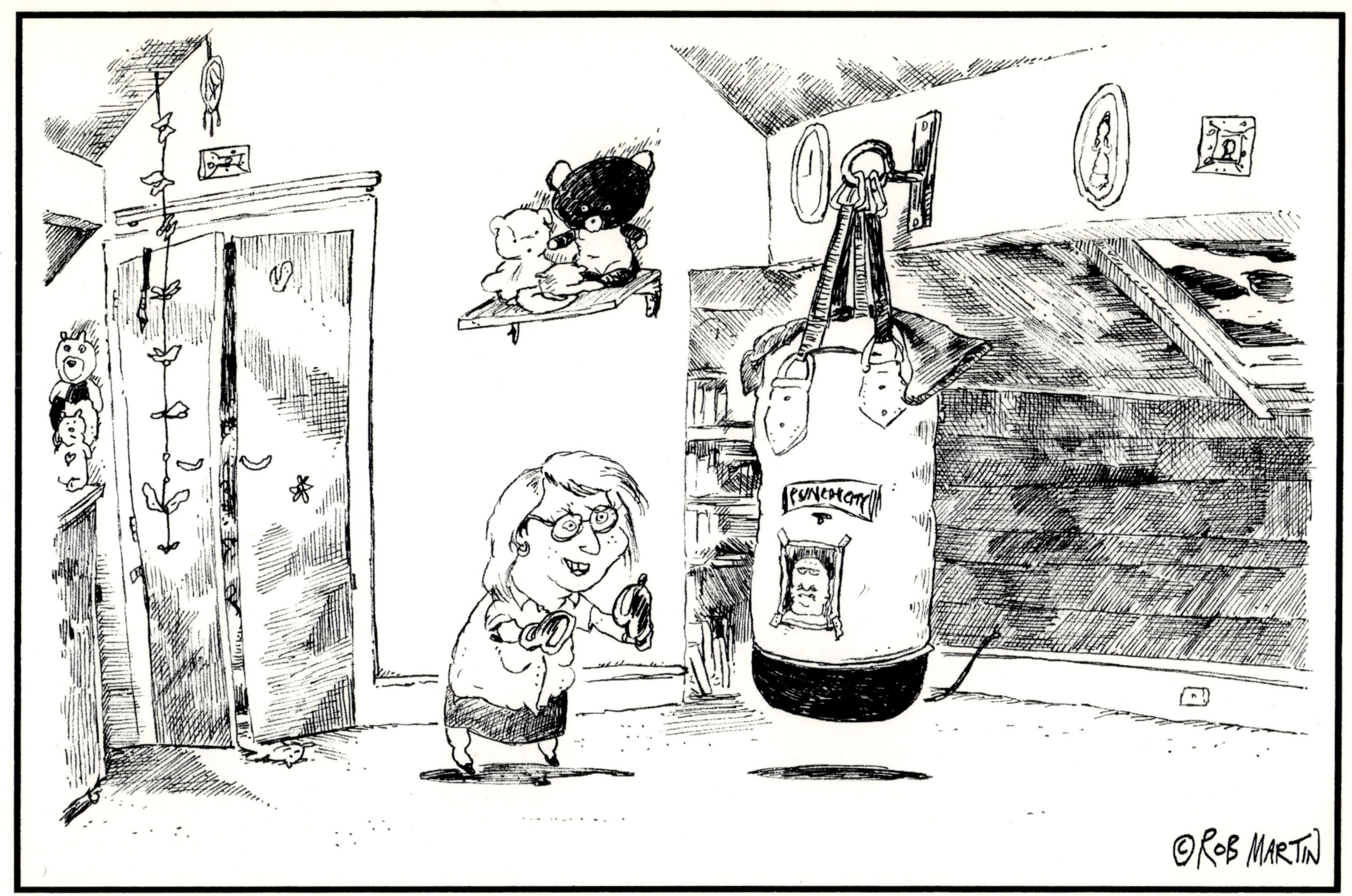

A recently divorced woman gets ready to hit a photo of her ex husband, on a newly purchased punchbag.

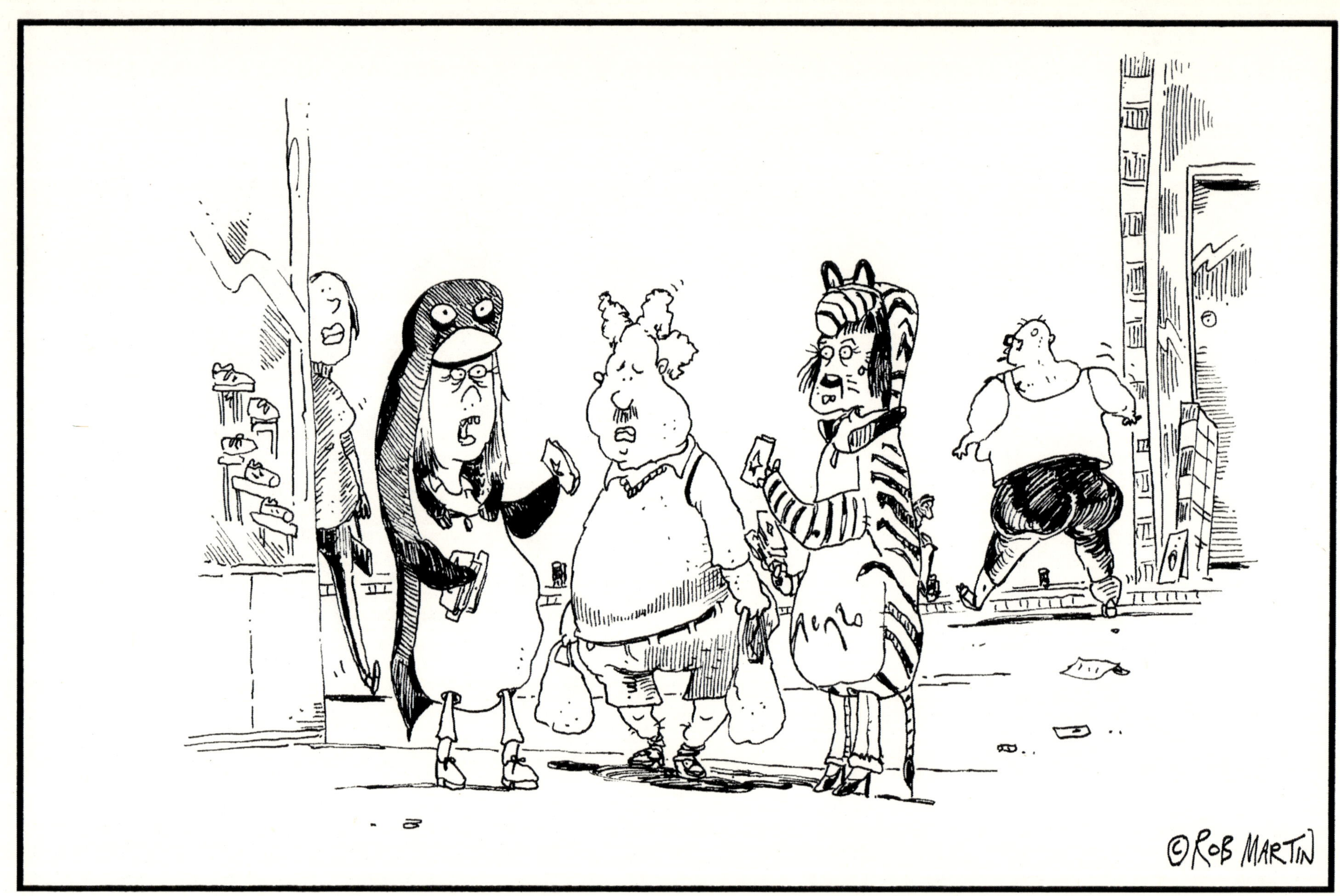

Selling very poor joke books and wearing tatty animal costumes, Tracy and Samantha stop Tobias, telling him, "It's very very funny!"

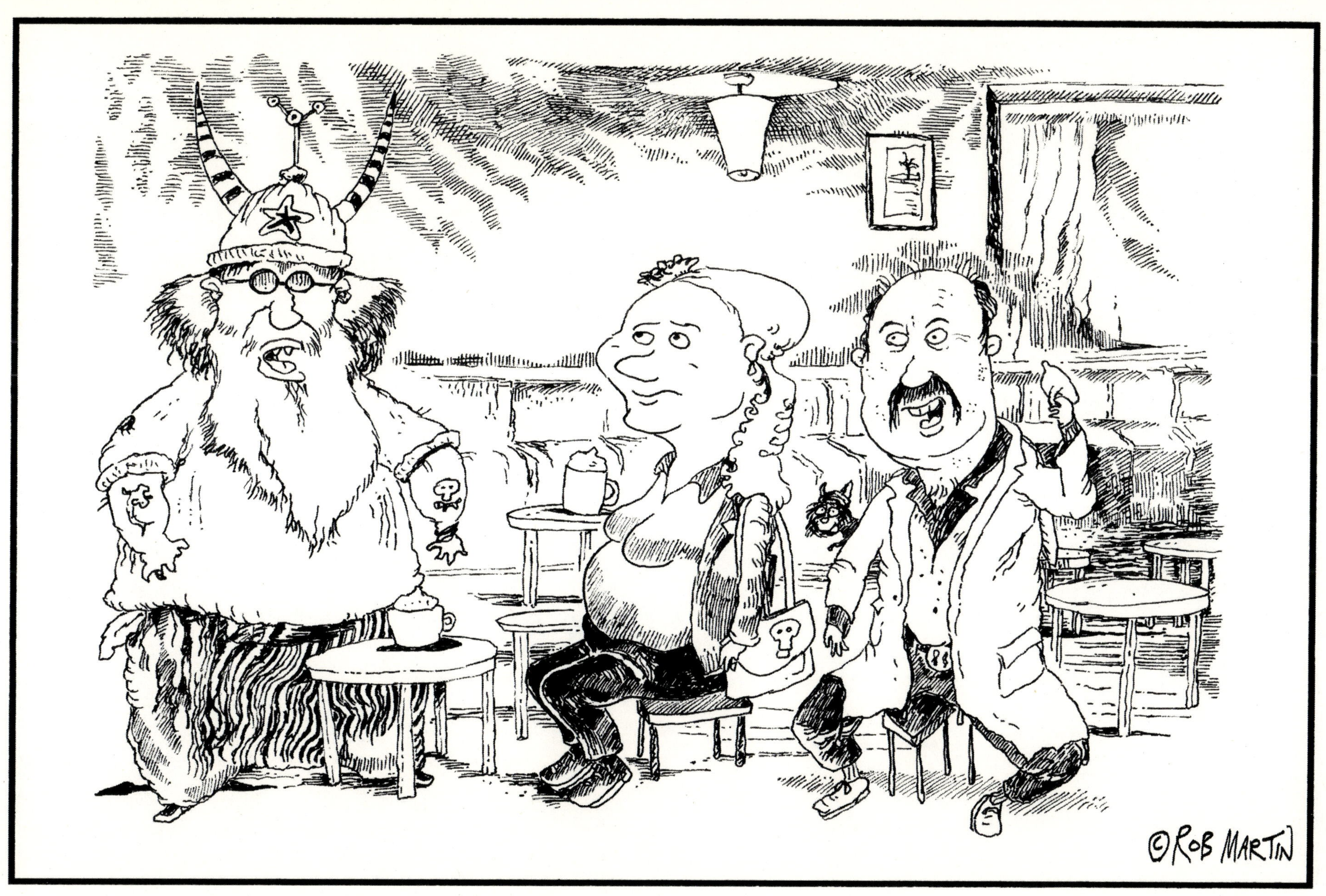

"I am the wild man. Well blow the cream from my Volcano!" Shouts Odin Smith. Referring to his regular hot chocolate.

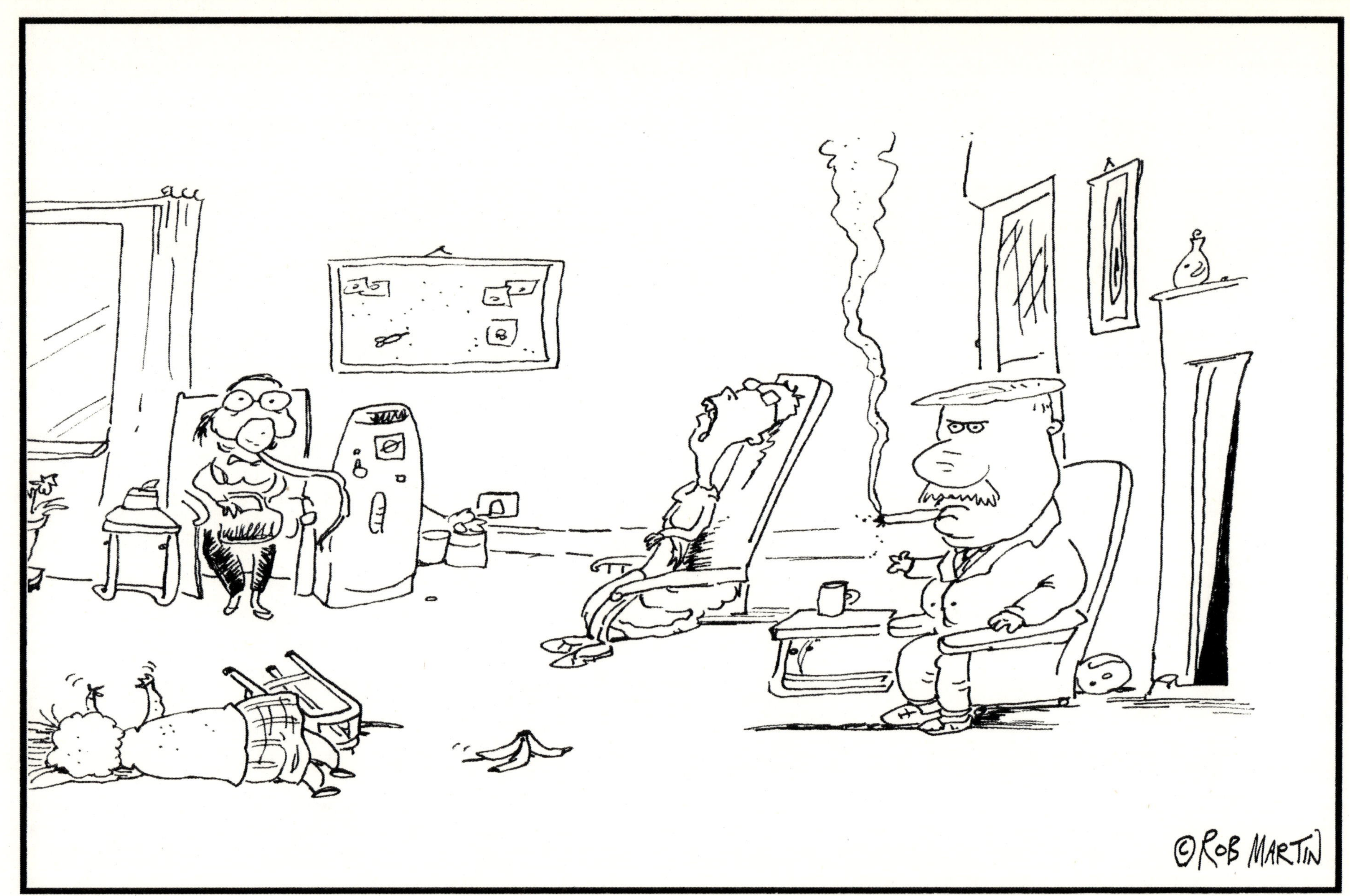

Wednesday afternoon in the care home.

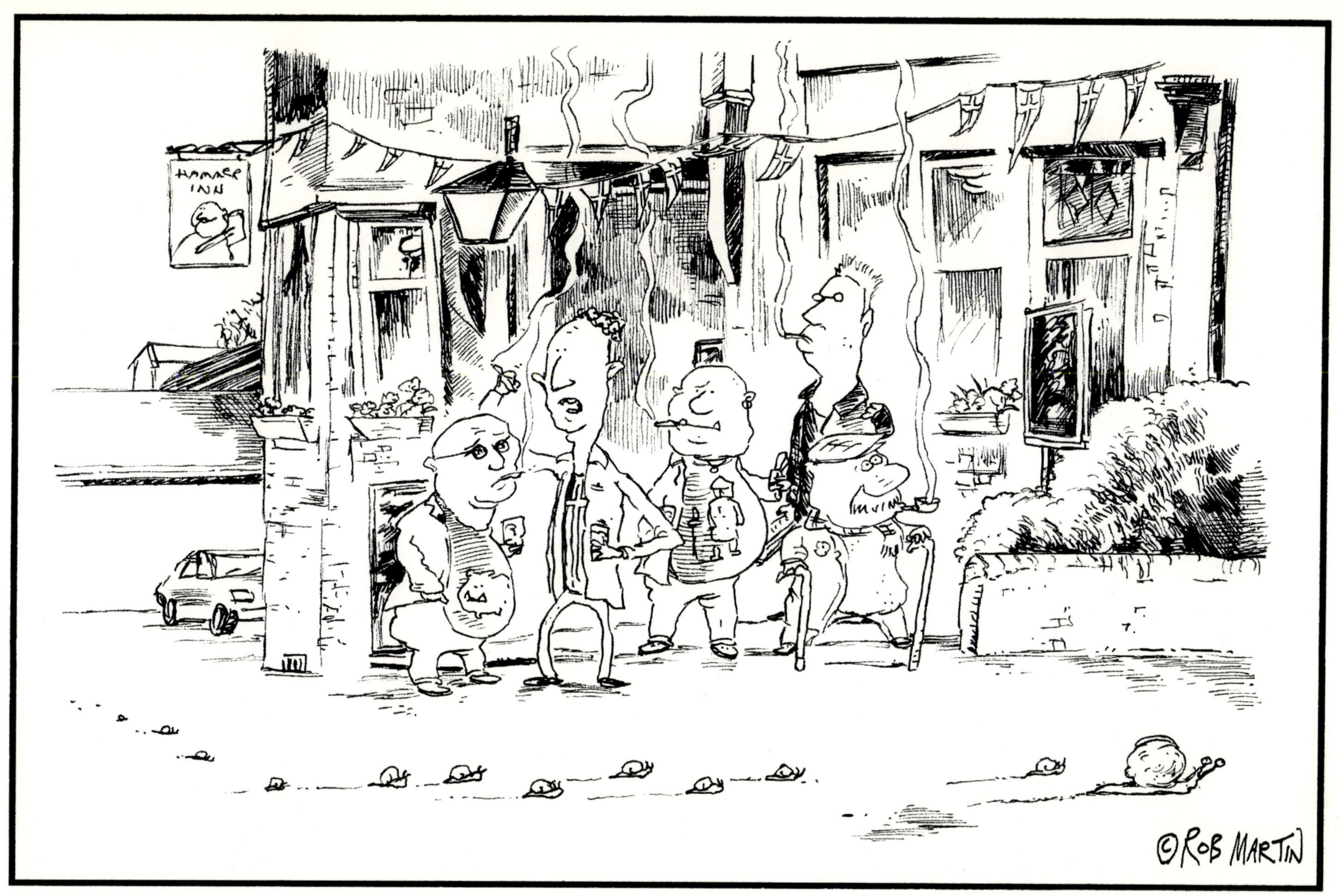

Smokers stood outside a pub, talk about outcasts of society.

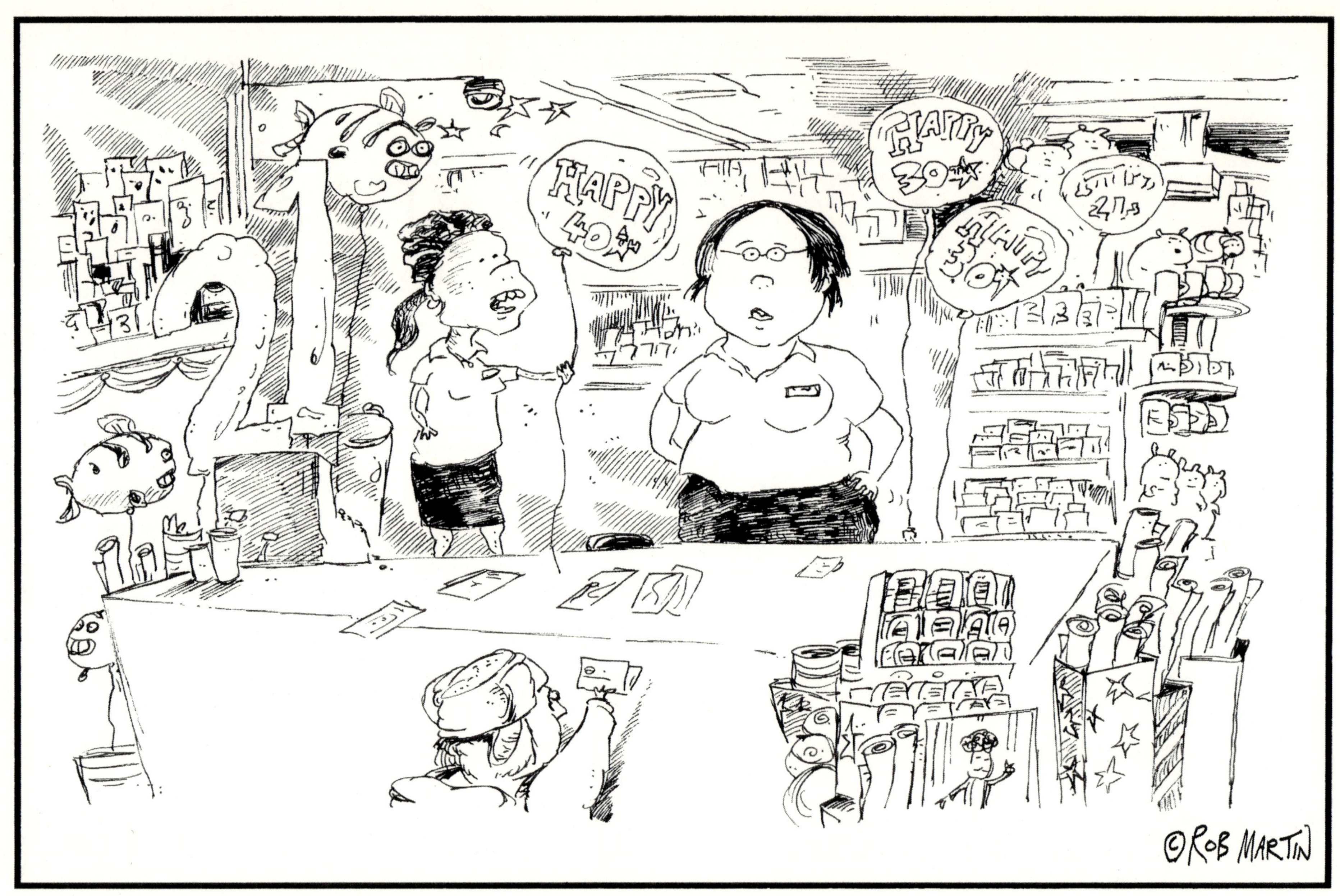

In a greeting card shop, the manager discovers her under crackers are stuck to her fat arse like a slimy pancake.

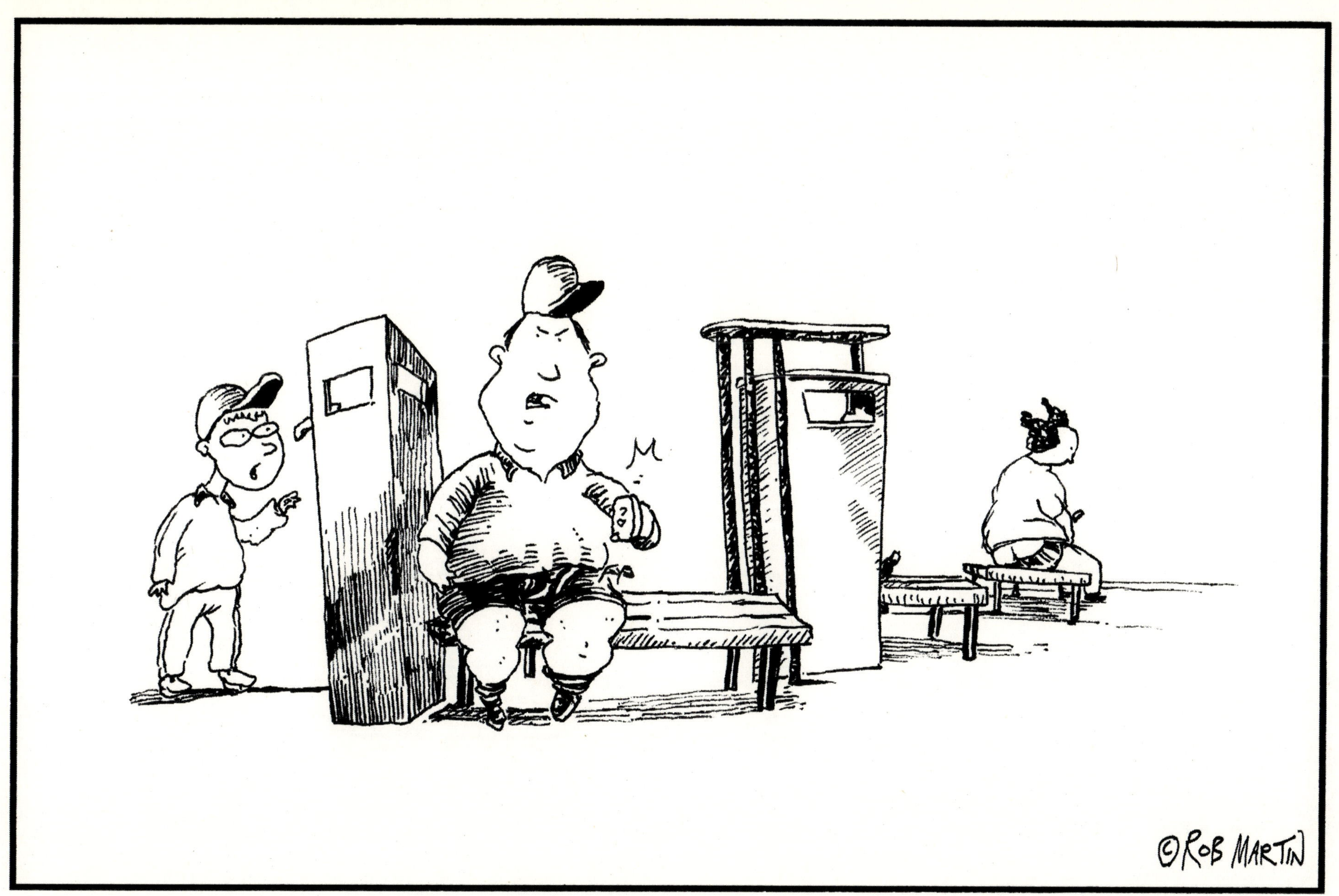

A man of low self esteem, wiggles his gold painted knuckle duster in the hope he can scare and intimidate someone.

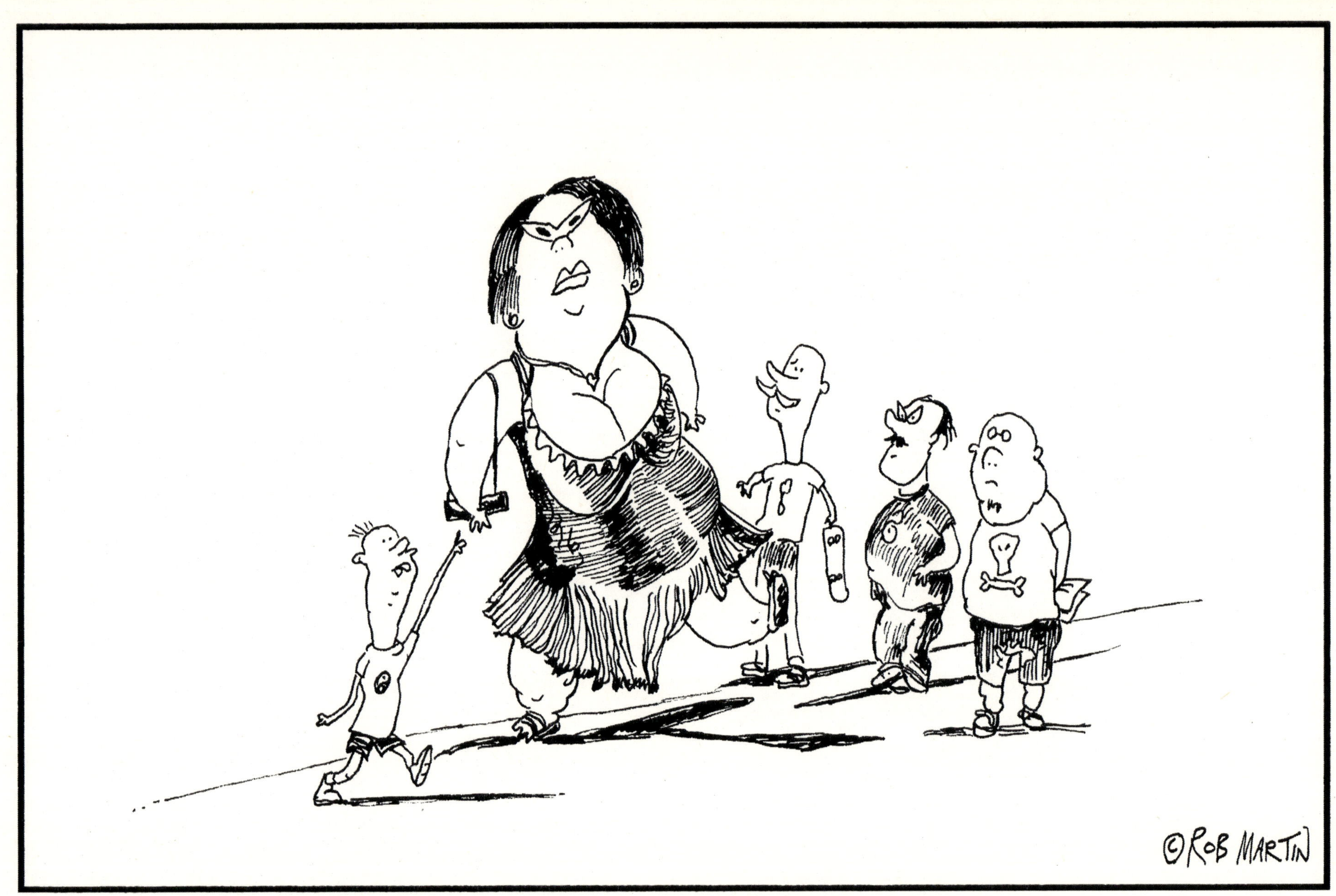

Hetty Jugs gets all her admirers together using 'Cakebook' messenger. They will now have to grovel to the death.

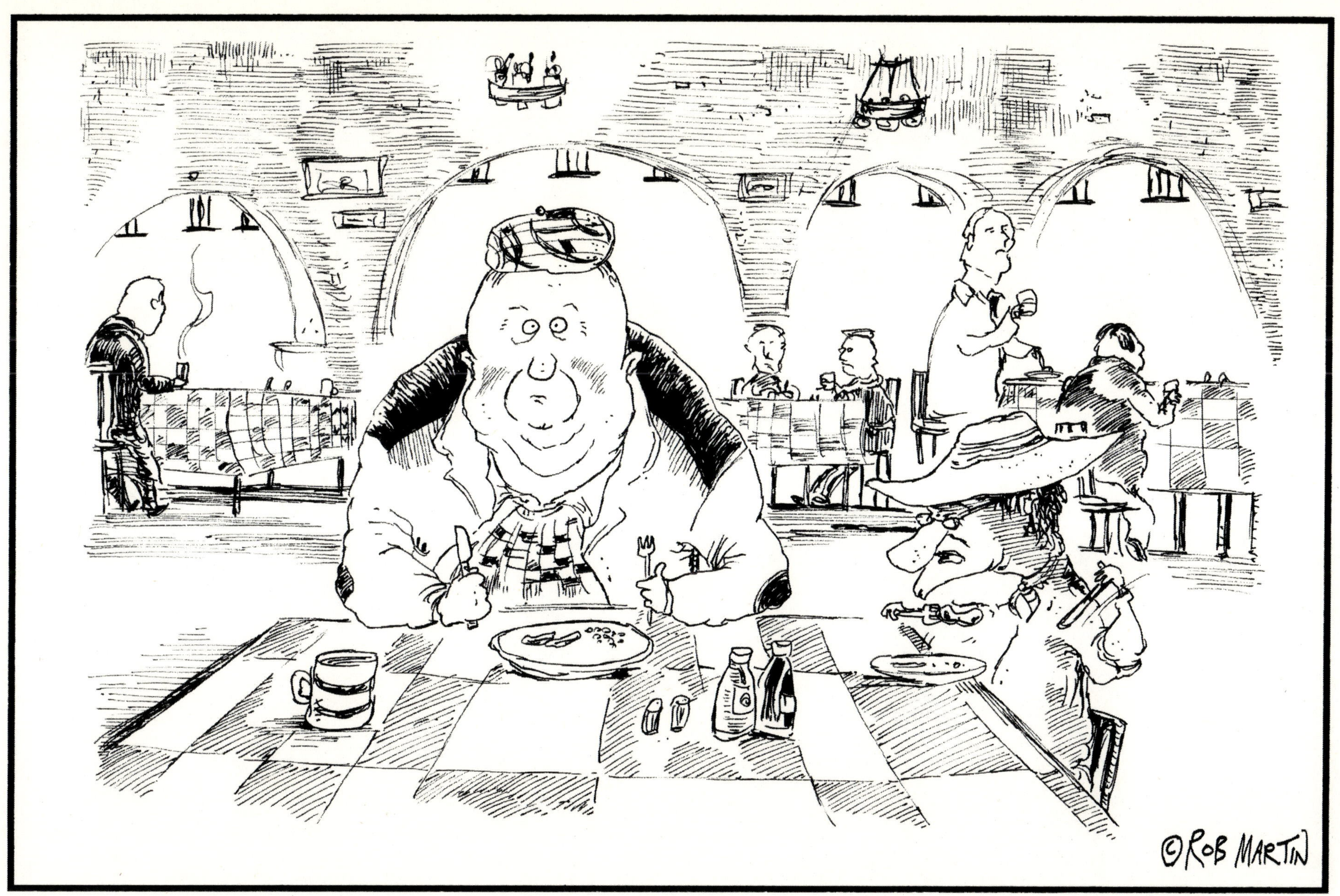

Gordon - the secret millionaire has his fourteenth free meal of the week. This time in the Methodist Mission.

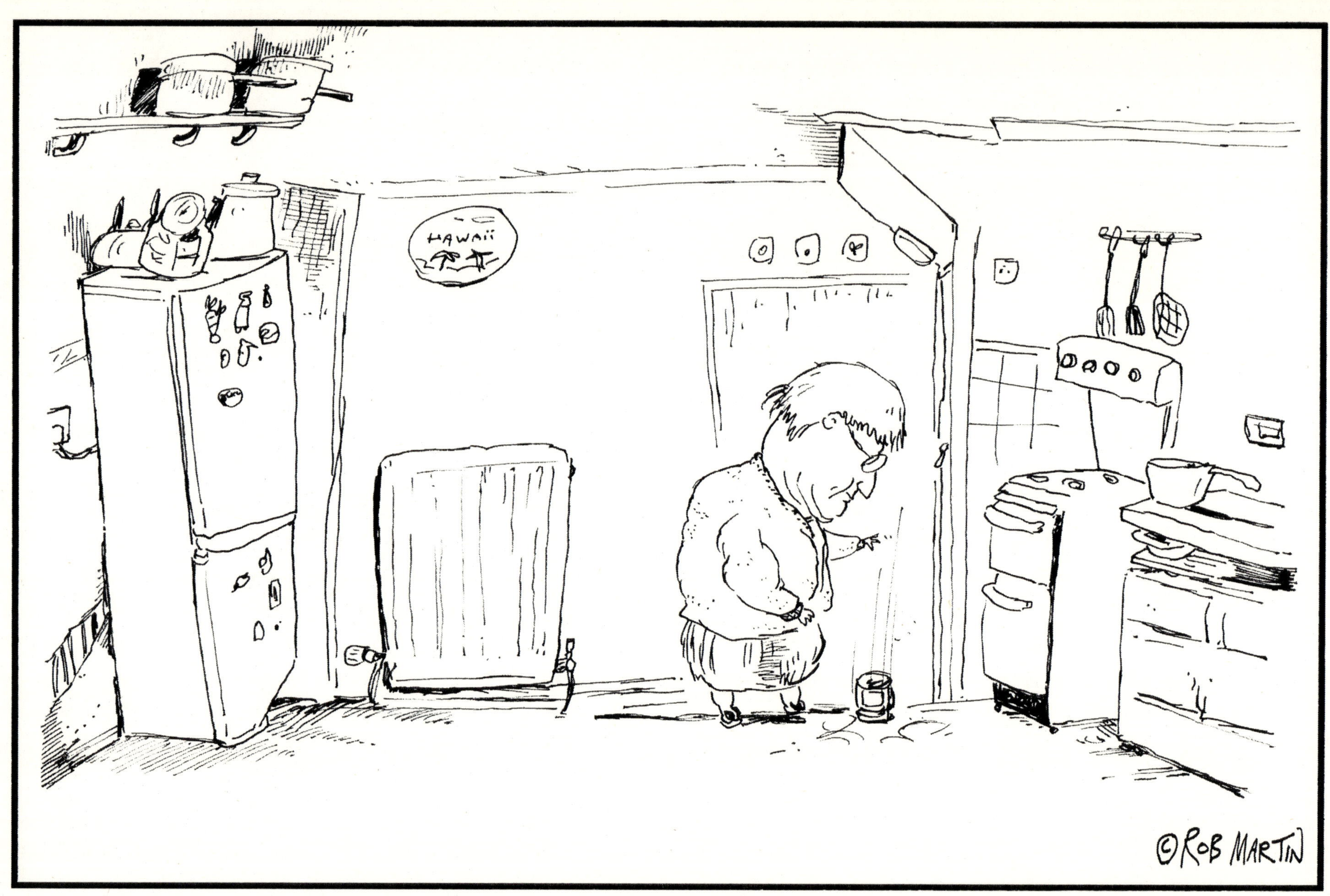

Trying to get the lid off a chutney jar - only gets more frustrating!

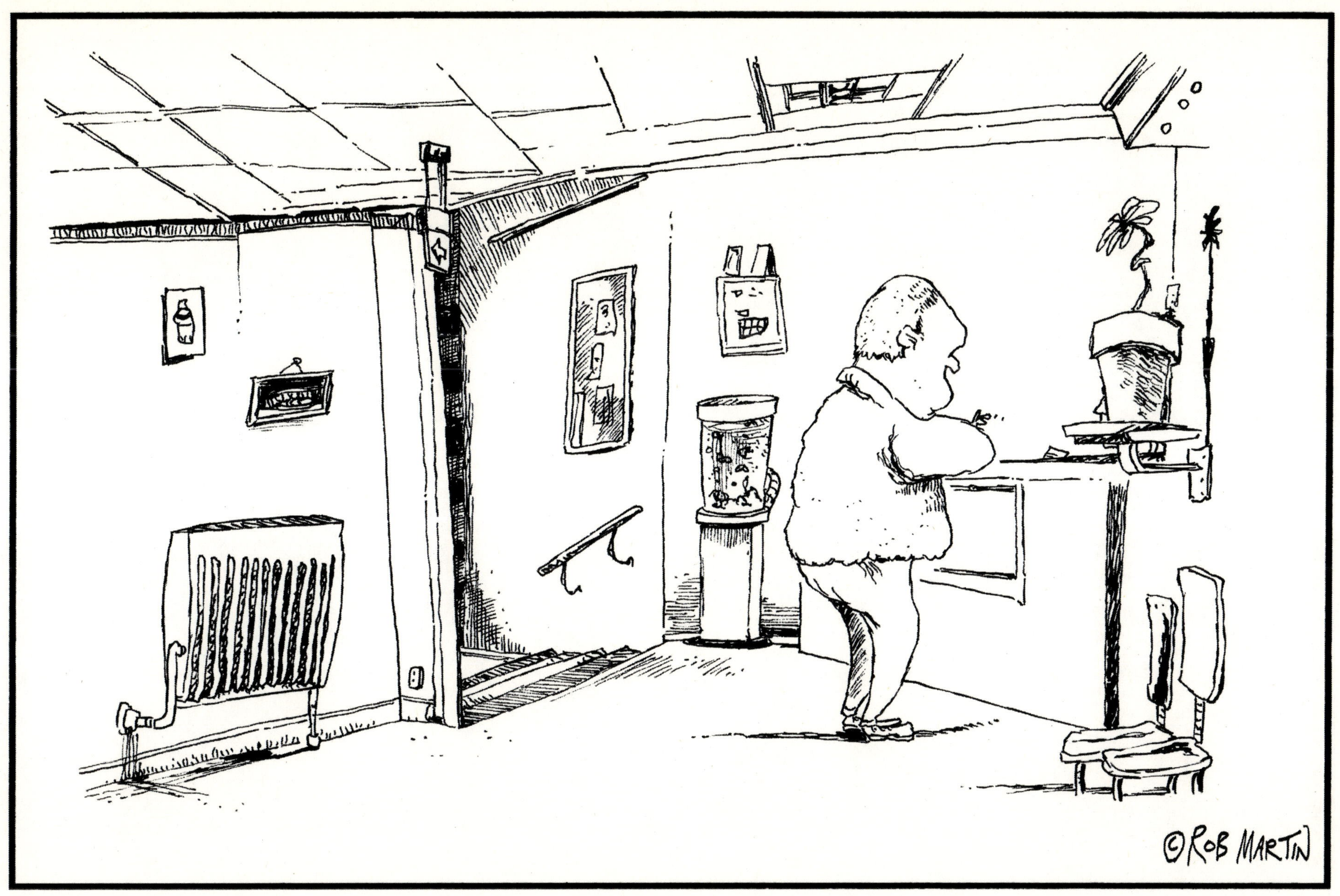

Mr. Salt waits at the Dentist reception. Mumbling with cracked dentures.

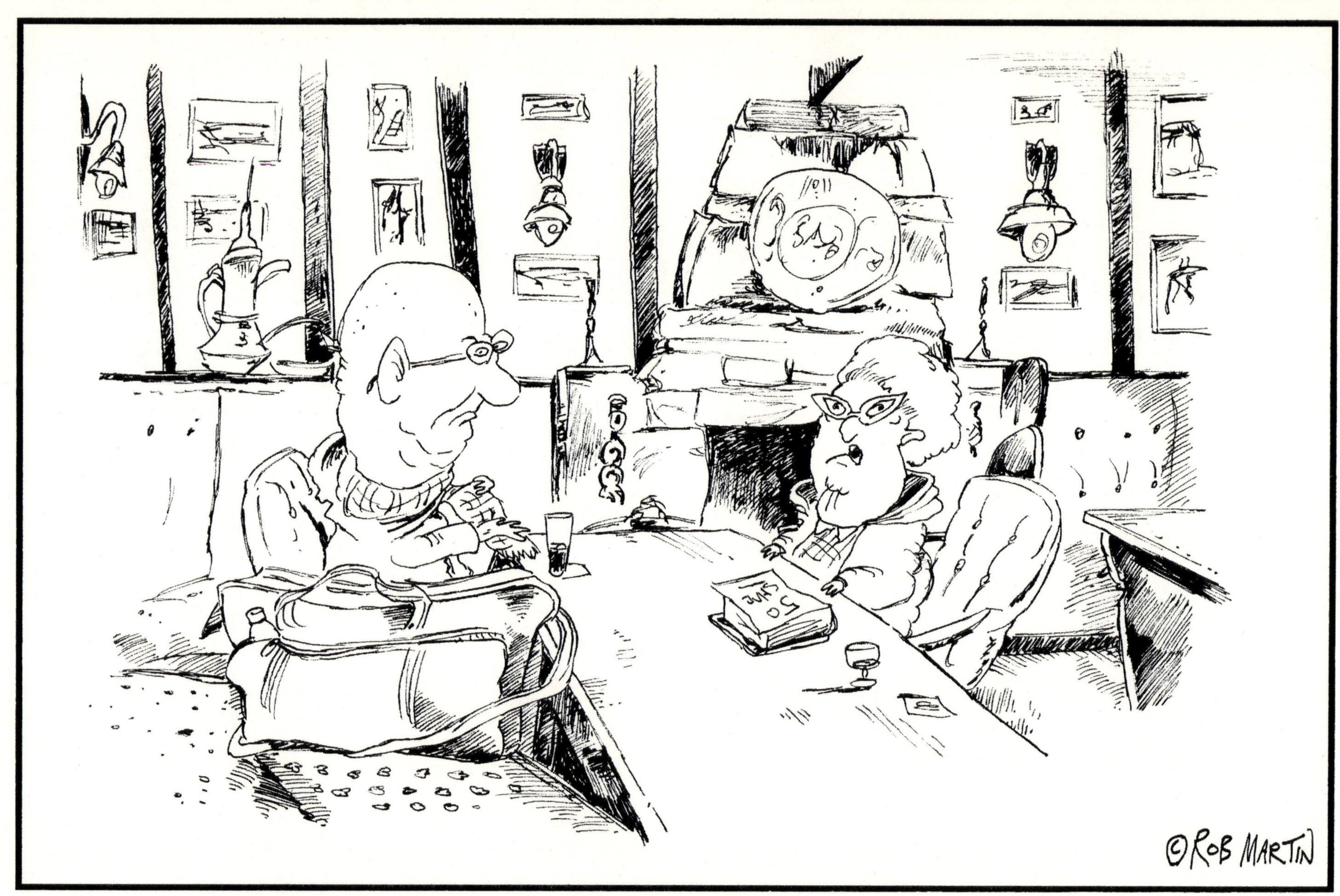

"Have you actually studied positive thinking, how to manifest amazing possibilities, like being able to fly up a chimney?"

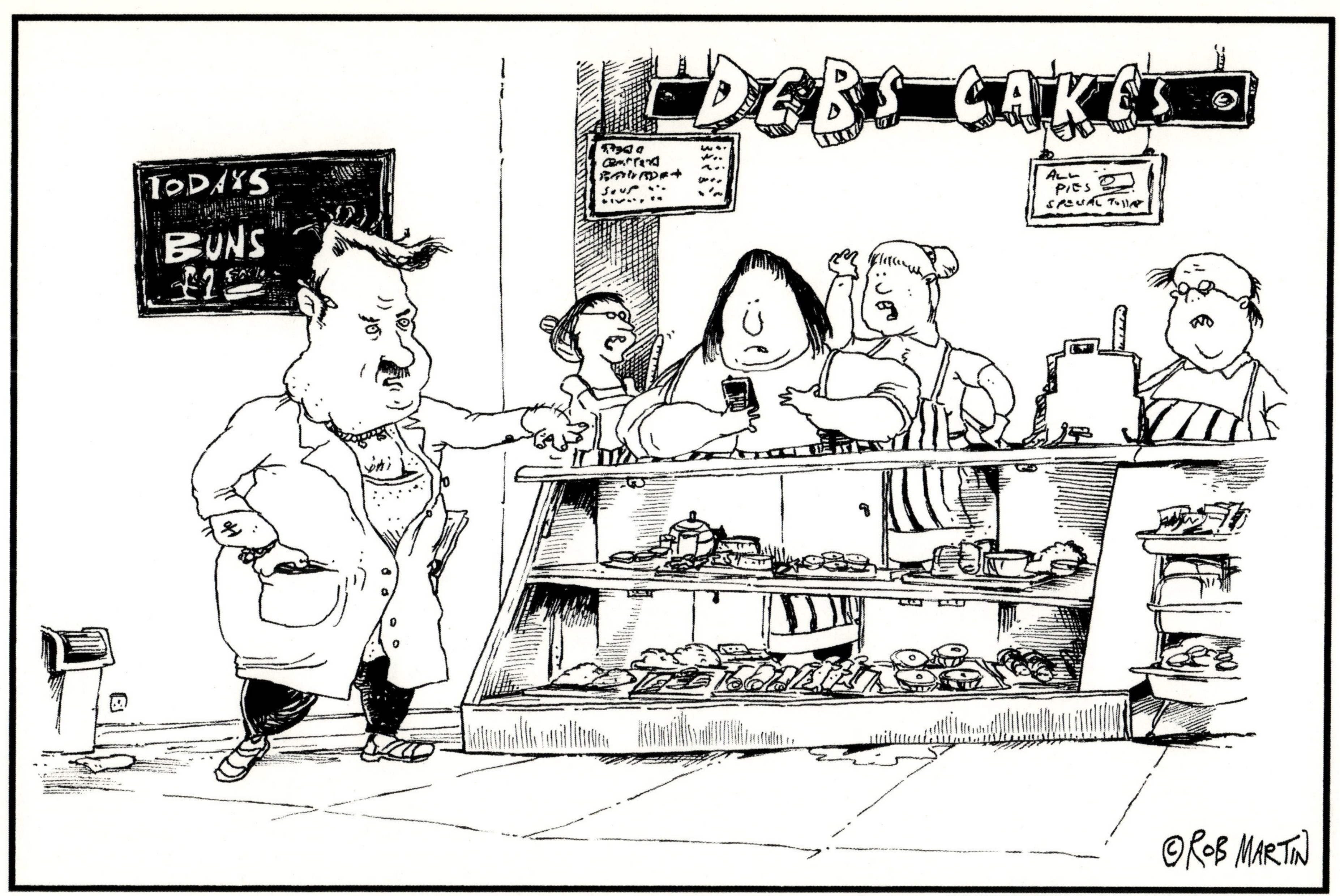

Bakery staff are shown a suspected Ghost photograph.
But Sandra can only make out a photo of a puddle.

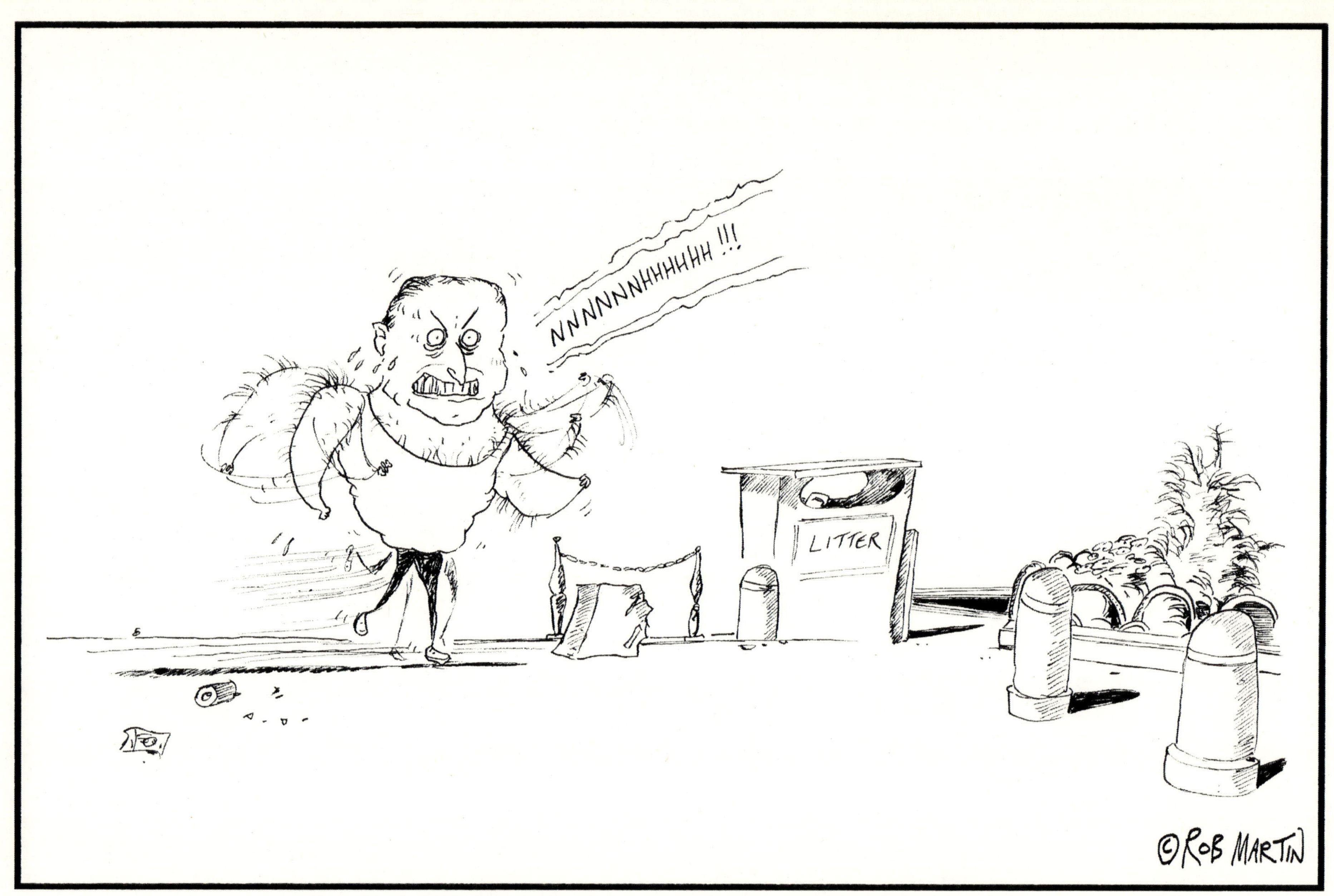

The hairy jogger goes for his afternoon run.

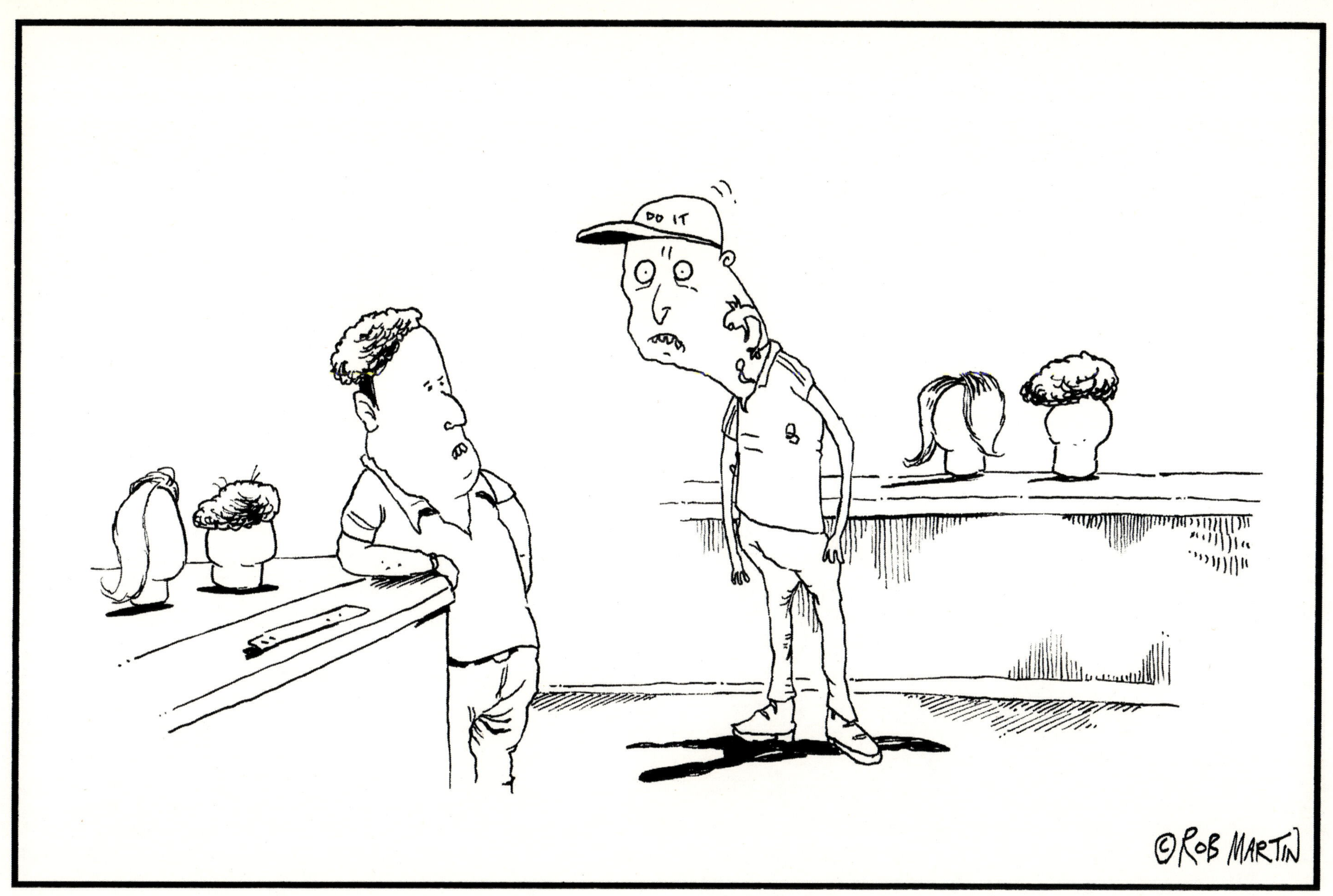

"Get a proper job!" Grunts the scaffolder to the wig maker.

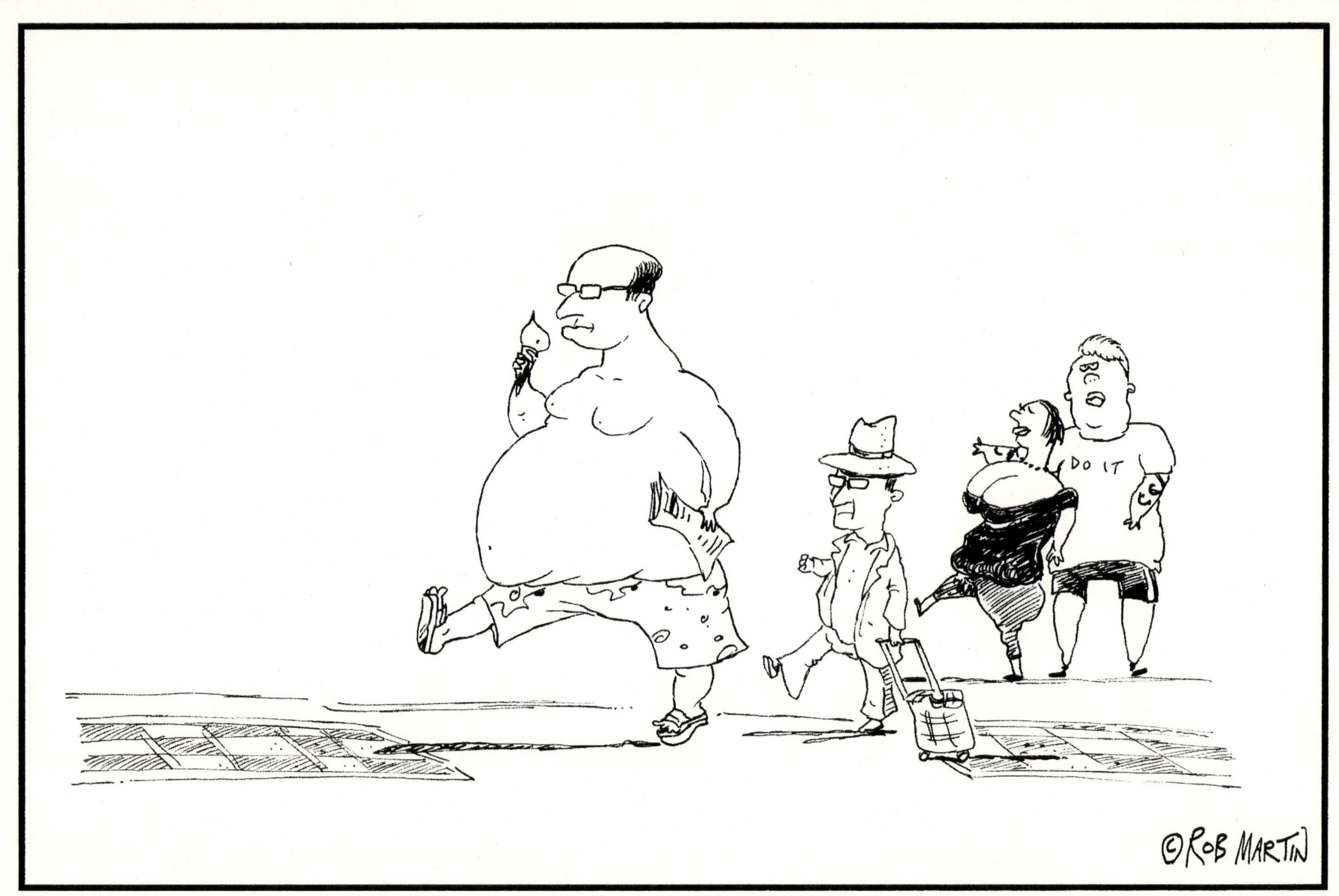

H.G. Bell wanders off for a scratch card.

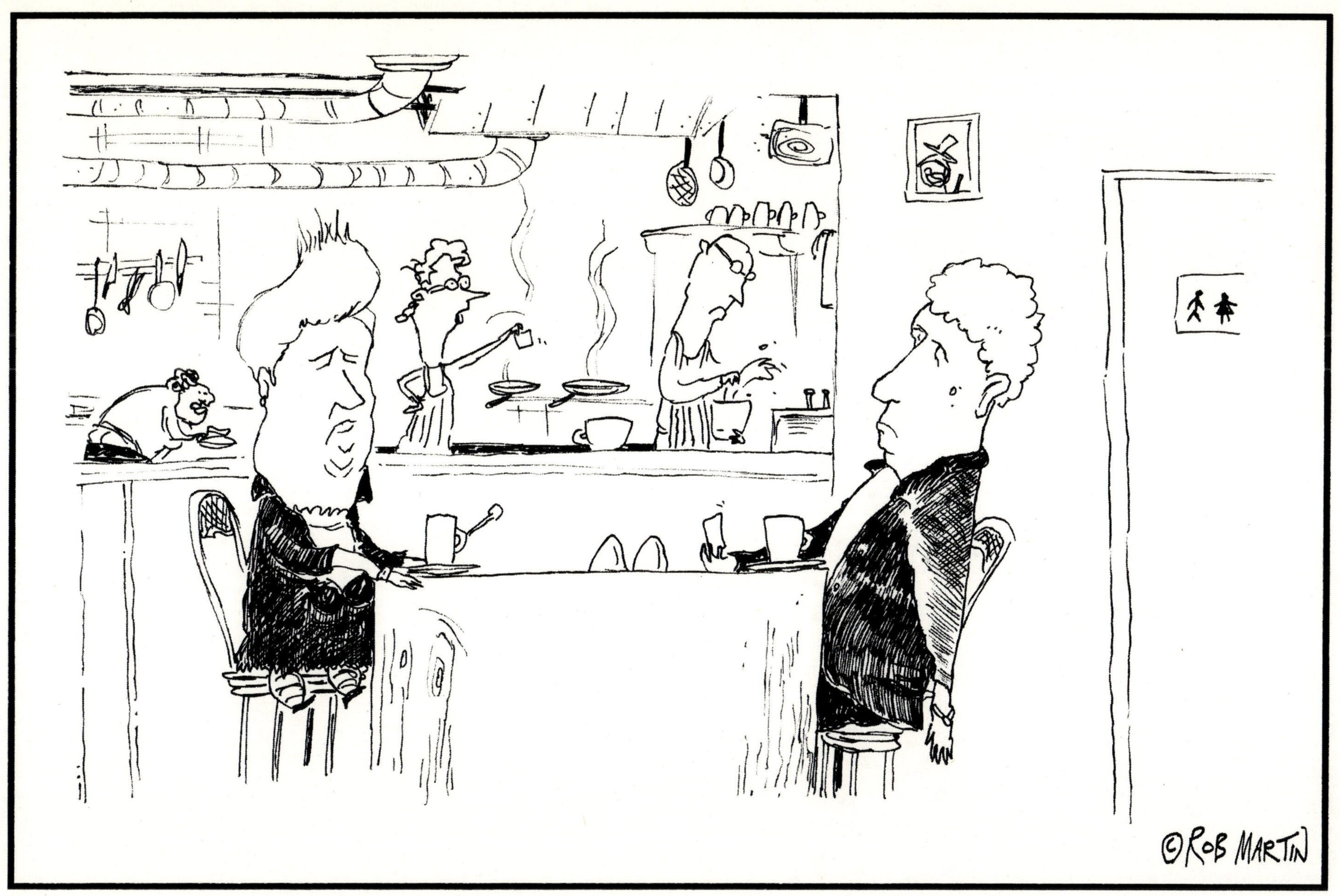

In the over rated cafe, the silent couple consider changing cheesecakes.

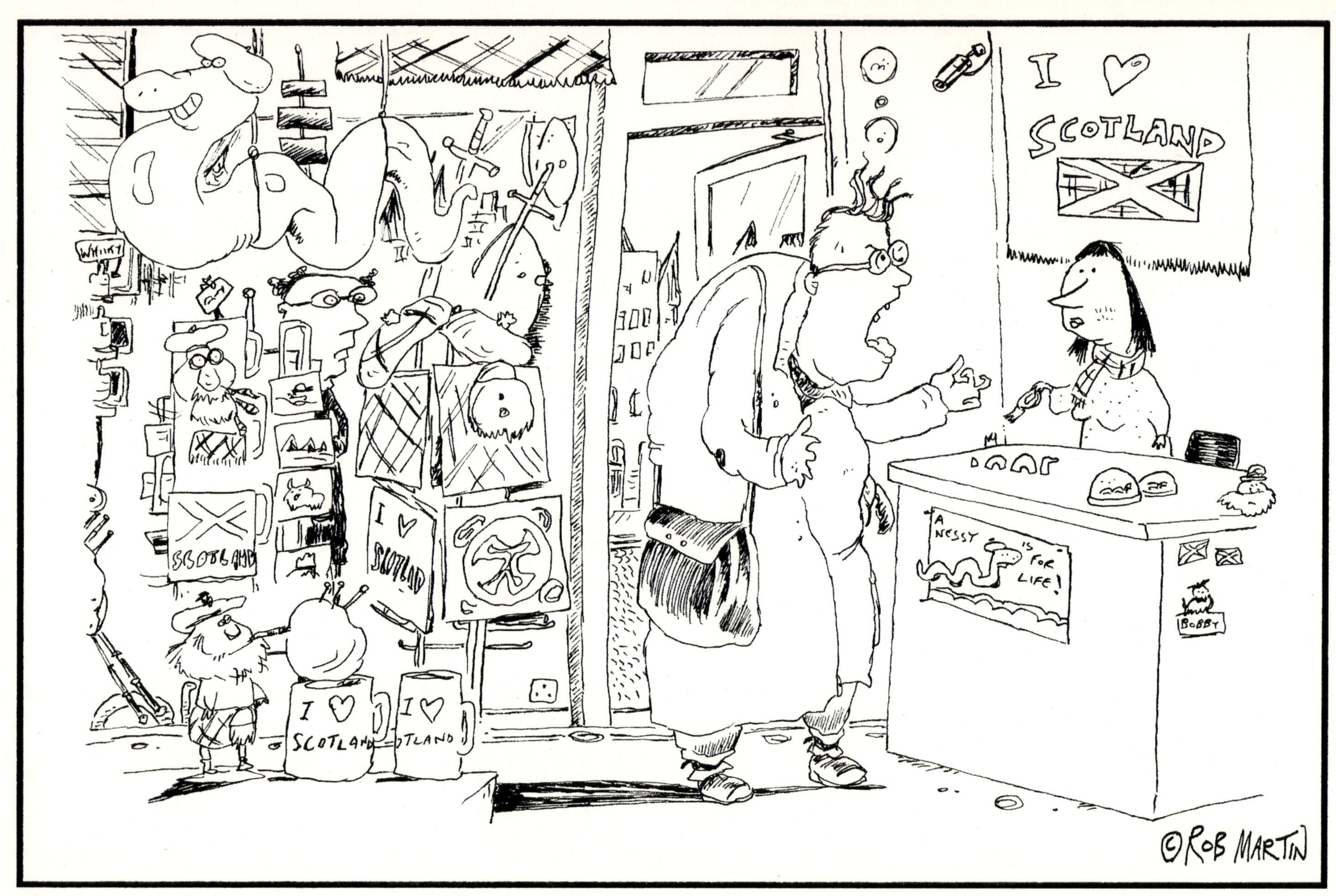

"Do you have a furry Haggis?"

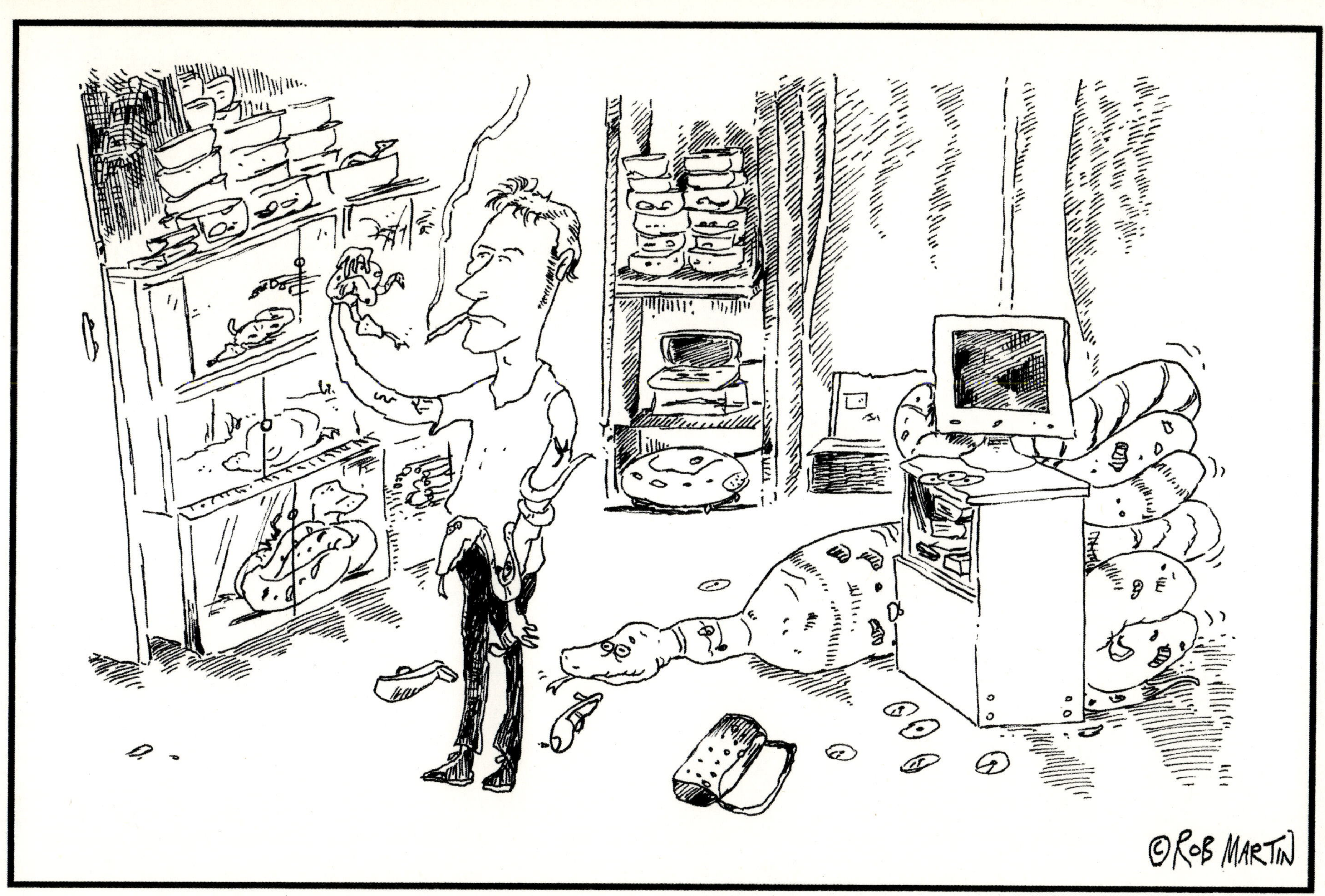

A man with a collection of 69 snakes, shows his girlfriend a newly hatched Python.

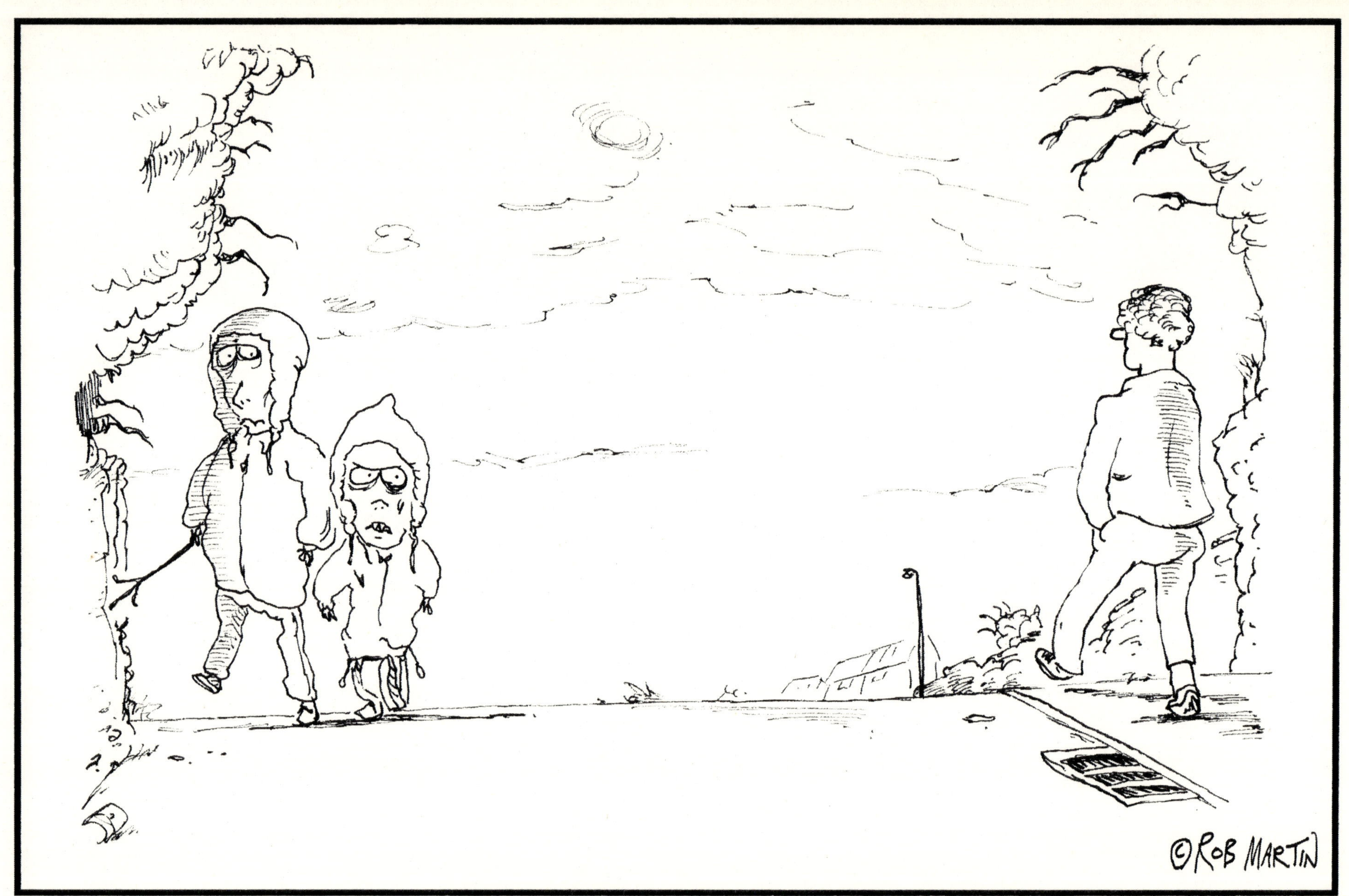

"Eer mate, got a pound?"
"Eer mate, you listenin'?"
"Oy you! Ig-o-rant! Want a fight specky?"

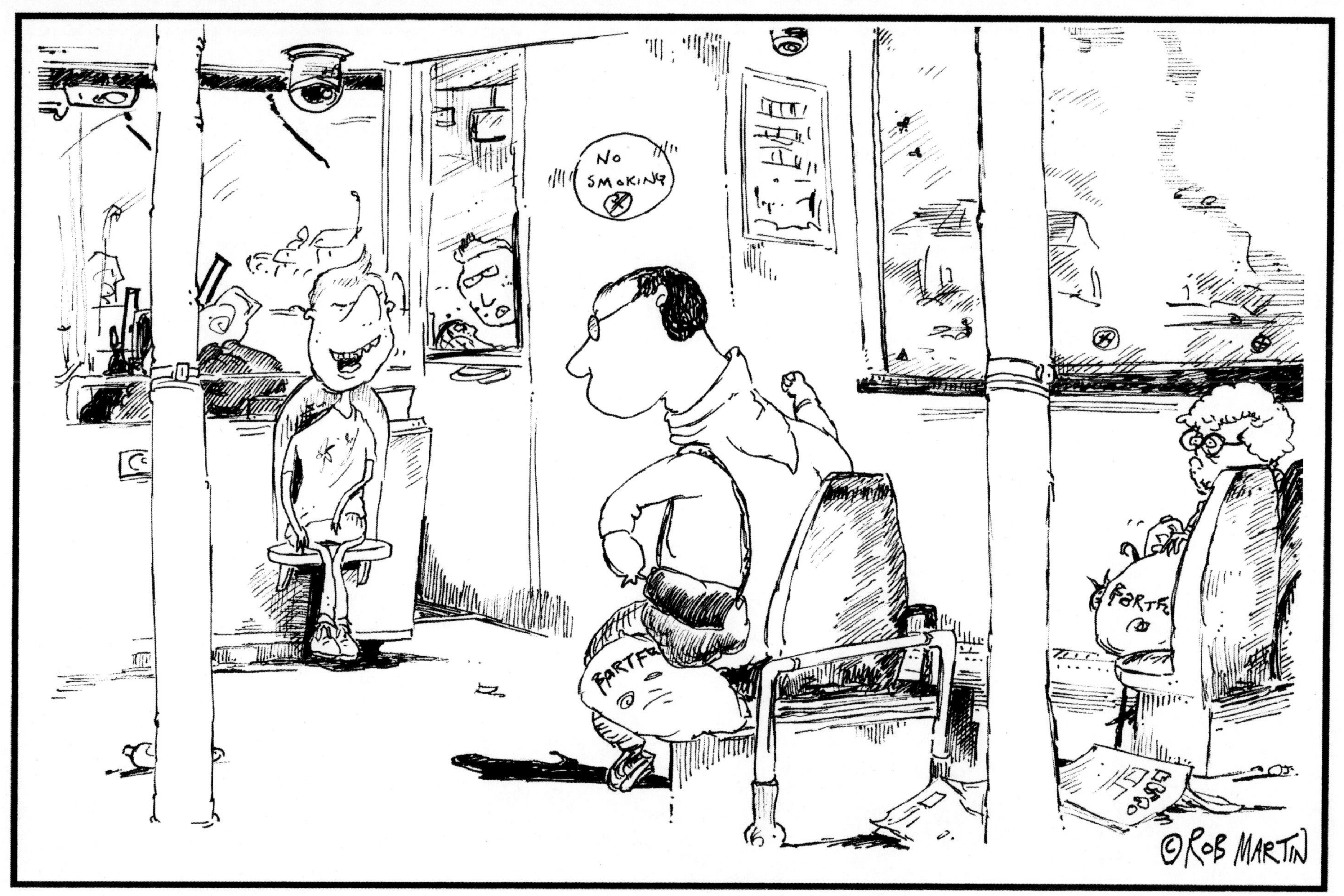

"What you looking at you weirdo?" Remarks the student sat in the wheelchair bay.

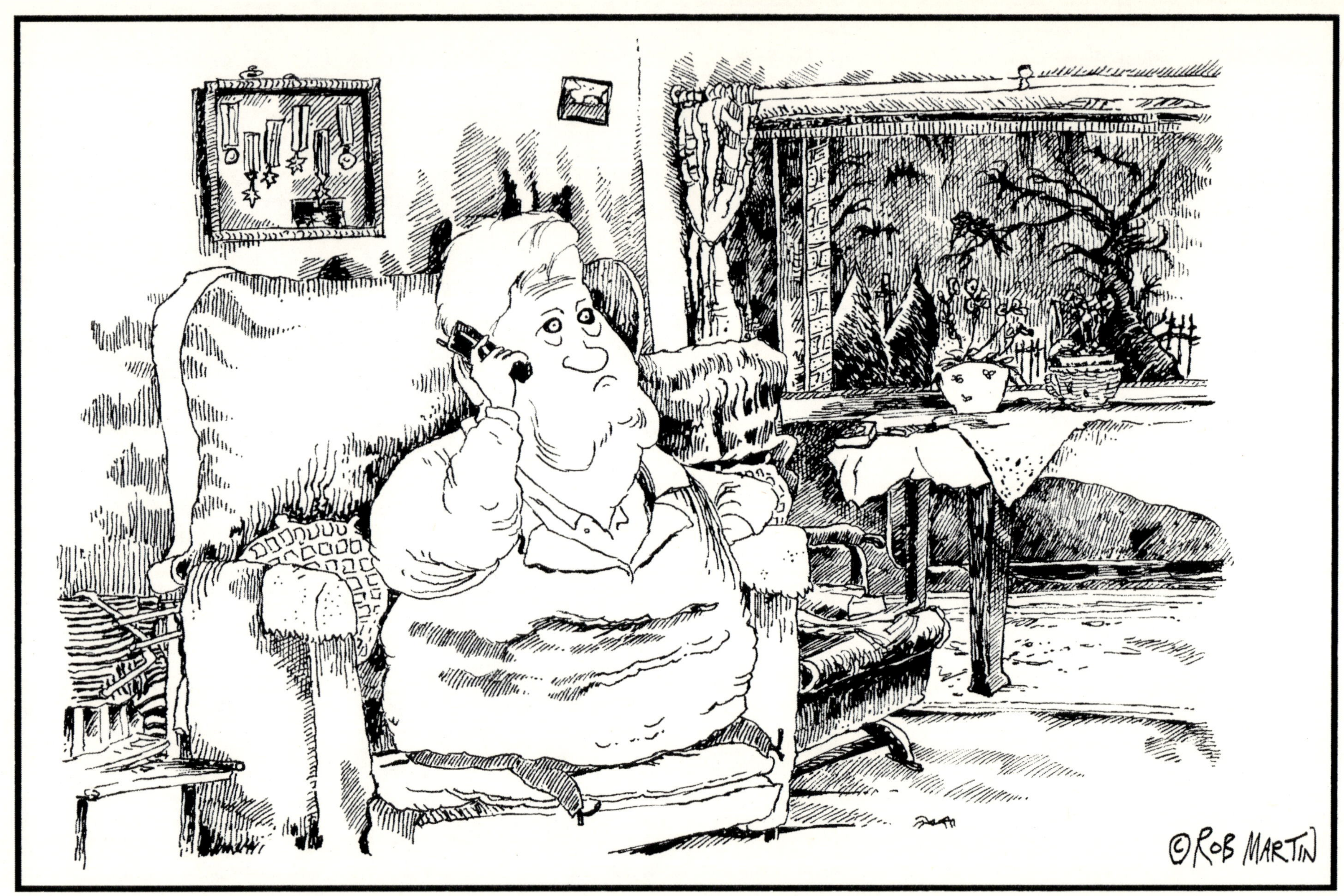

Brian Bell receives the 14th phone call of the day. This time from 'Sardine and Pilchard'. Specialists in injury caused by eating fish.

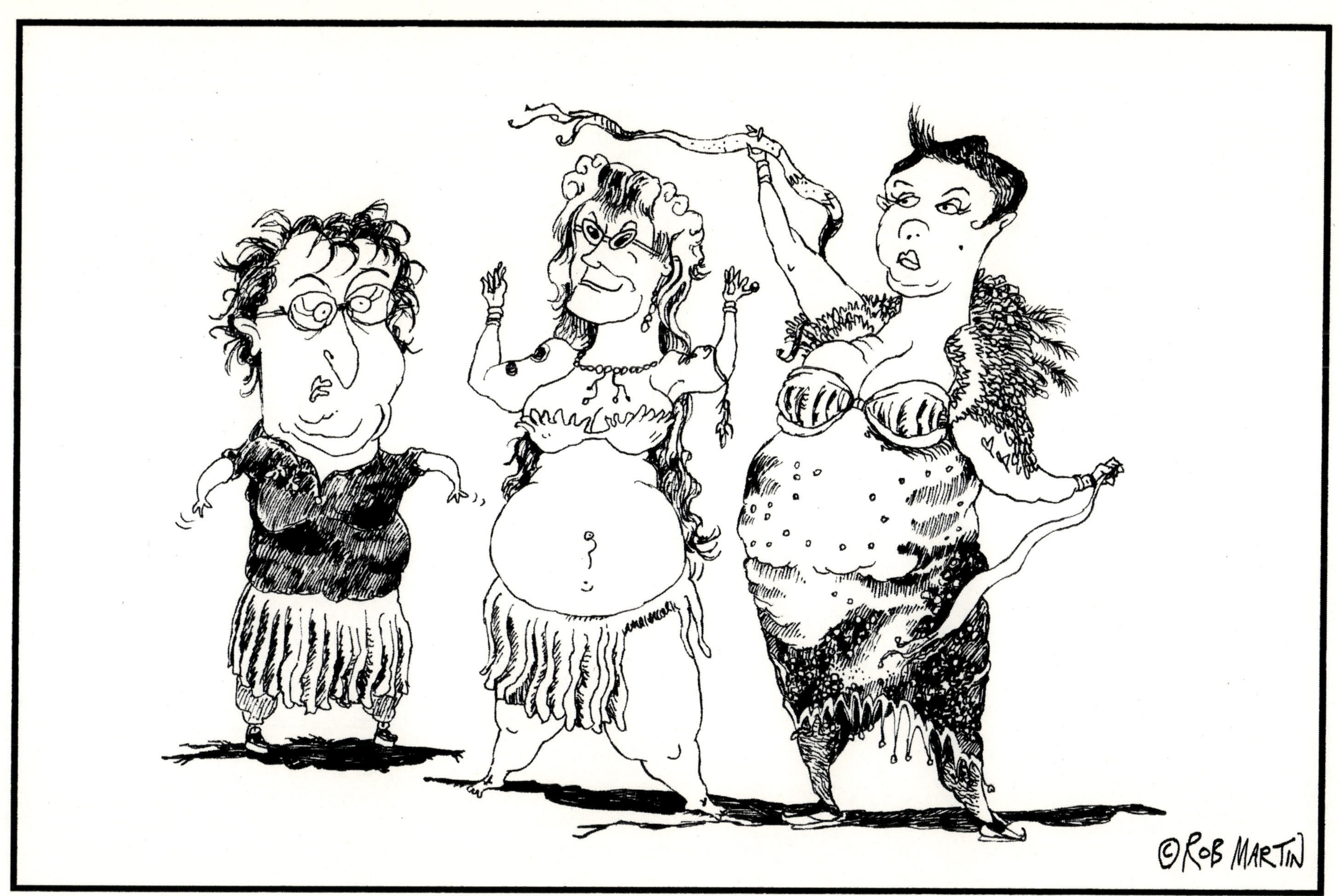

Margaret is unsure whether or not she
is going to be any good at tribal belly dancing.

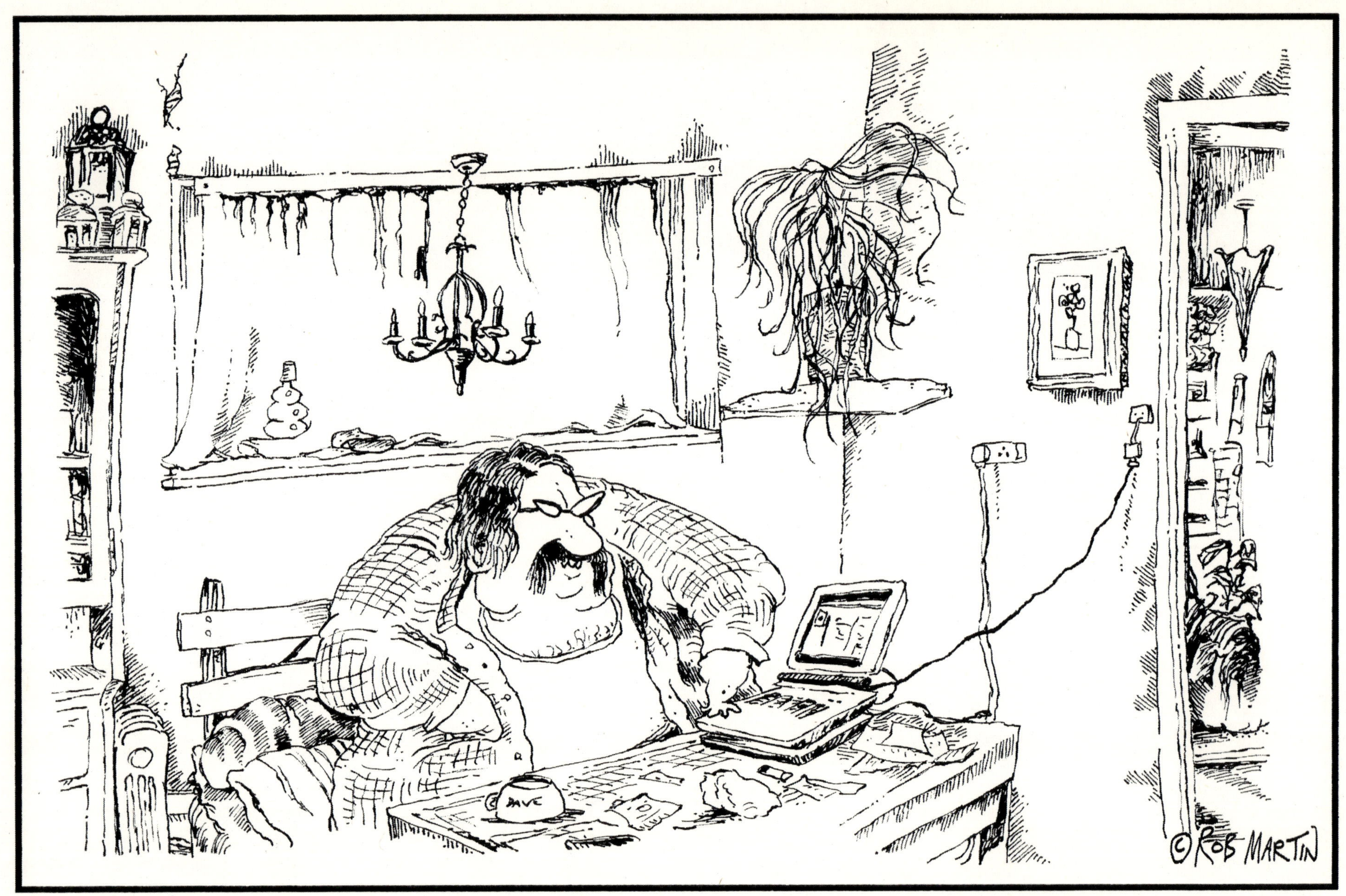

A man doesn't know what to do, when an ex girlfriend sends him photos of herself and a Goose.